STANLEY COMPLETE
BASEMENTS

Meredith® Books
Des Moines, Iowa

Stanley Complete Basements
Editor: Larry Johnston
Copy Chief: Terri Fredrickson
Publishing Operations Manager: Karen Schirm
Senior Editor, Asset and Information Manager: Phillip Morgan
Edit and Design Production Coordinator: Mary Lee Gavin
Editorial and Design Assistant: Renee E. McAtee
Book Production Managers: Pam Kvitne,
    Marjorie J. Schenkelberg, Rick von Holdt, Mark Weaver
Contributing Copy Editor: Michael Maine
Contributing Proofreaders: David Craft, Paula Reece,
    Patrick Smythe-Eagle
Contributing Indexer: Donald Glassman

**Additional Editorial Contributions from
  Abramowitz Creative Studios**
Publishing Director/Designer: Tim Abramowitz
Designers: Kelly Bailey, Joel Wires
Writer: Martin Miller
Photo Researcher: Amber Jones
Photography: Image Studios
    Account Executive: Lisa Egan
    Photographers: Bill Rein, John von Dorn
    Assistants: Bill Kapinski, Josh Nadke, Rob Resnick
    Technical Advisor: Rick Nadke
Additional Photography: Doug Hetherington
Illustration: Art Rep Services, Inc.
    Director: Chip Nadeau
    Illustrator: Dave Brandon

Meredith® Books
Executive Director, Editorial: Gregory H. Kayko
Executive Director, Design: Matt Strelecki
Managing Editor: Amy Tincher-Durik
Executive Editor/Group Manager: Benjamin W. Allen
Senior Associate Design Director: Tom Wegner
Marketing Product Manager: Brent Wiersma

Publisher and Editor in Chief: James D. Blume
Editorial Director: Linda Raglan Cunningham
Executive Director, Marketing: Steve Malone
Executive Director, New Business Development: Todd M. Davis
Executive Director, Sales: Ken Zagor
Director, Operations: George A. Susral
Director, Production: Douglas M. Johnston
Director, Marketing: Amy Nichols
Business Director: Jim Leonard

Vice President and General Manager: Douglas J. Guendel

Meredith Publishing Group
President: Jack Griffin
Executive Vice President: Bob Mate

Meredith Corporation
Chairman and Chief Executive Officer: William T. Kerr
President and Chief Operating Officer: Stephen M. Lacy

In Memoriam: E.T. Meredith III (1933–2003)

All of us at Meredith® Books are dedicated to providing you with the information and ideas you need to enhance your home and garden. We welcome your comments and suggestions about this book. Write to us at:
Meredith Corporation
Meredith Books
1716 Locust St.
Des Moines, IA 50309–3023

If you would like more information on other Stanley products, call 1-800-STANLEY or visit us at: www.stanleyworks.com
Stanley® and the notched rectangle around the Stanley name are registered trademarks of The Stanley Works and subsidiaries.

Note to the Readers: Due to differing conditions, tools, and individual skills, Meredith Corporation assumes no responsibility for any damages, injuries suffered, or losses incurred as a result of following the information published in this book. Before beginning any project, review the instructions carefully, and if any doubts or questions remain, consult local experts or authorities. Because codes and regulations vary greatly, you always should check with authorities to ensure that your project complies with all applicable local codes and regulations. Always read and observe all of the safety precautions provided by manufacturers of any tools, equipment, or supplies, and follow all accepted safety procedures.

A GUIDE FOR HOMEOWNERS AND REMODELERS

Whether you're a do-it-yourself novice or a veteran of several remodeling projects, you'll discover information in this book that can preserve and even increase the value of your home.

Whether you're turning unused basement space into a new bedroom, bathroom, kitchen, or kid's room—or all of those—you'll find help in this book for every step of your remodeling, starting with tips on designing the space. Even if you're trying to decide whether to do the work yourself or hire a contractor for all or part of the job, this book shows you what's involved in all aspects of the project so you can make the right decision. Whether your goals are modest or ambitious, this book will guide you through your basement remodeling.

How the book is organized
The book opens with a gallery of great-looking rooms to serve as a springboard for your imagination. You'll see how you can create remodeled spaces that aren't just functional, they're highly decorative.

Next, you'll find solid advice on choosing the right materials and selecting the correct tools to bring your project to life. Then, because all jobs start with preparation, the book shows what you need to do to get your work started.

The chapter on framing gets your project off on the right foot. It includes the basics of wall construction and incorporates helpful special topics such as building soffits.

You'll see how to plan your drywall job and master the material, making straight cuts as well as cutouts for electrical boxes and ceiling fixtures, and hanging, taping, mudding, and sanding.

From there you go through wiring and plumbing techniques, methods for installing bathroom and kitchen fixtures, finishing walls and floors, increasing storage space, and installing lights and electric heat.

The book's format
This book packs dozens of how-to photo sequences across the top of the pages. This format reduces even complicated topics into small steps that you'll quickly understand and put to work.

In addition to the how-to advice, the book also covers the whys behind each process.

The bottom of each spread packs valuable advice on options and techniques. Helpful Pro Tips reveal trade secrets to make your job go faster and give you better results.

Take time for great results
Even if you're a novice, you can achieve high-quality results right from the start by following the steps and advice in this book. They will guide you confidently to project

completion. Be sure you read and follow manufacturers' instructions for use of their products.

If you exercise some patience, you can achieve great results. Often the only thing that separates merely acceptable work from superior workmanship is the willingness to work more carefully and invest a little more time to finish the job correctly.

CONTENTS

CREATING NEW SPACES

Whether you need an extra bedroom or bathroom for guests or a growing family, more room to entertain, or a home office, hobby room, or workshop, creating new spaces in your home is an exciting adventure. And often the best place to start looking for more living space is in your basement.

Almost all basements are good candidates for remodeling: They contain large quantities of unused space, allowing you to design it for almost any use.

Along with their potential versatility, however, basements have a few restrictions, especially those in older homes. There might not be enough headroom or floor space to meet local building code requirements for occupied space. You may have to reroute wiring or plumbing. In many cases the space will actually be too big and too open for your proposed use so you'll have to divide it into smaller sections with partition walls.

Solving these problems is, in part, a matter of time and budget limitations. But even more, reaching a solution is a matter of attitude and approach: If you treat obstacles as design opportunities or challenges, you'll get the job done.

Modern trends in basement finishing are different from the sparse wood-paneled recreation room or subterranean bedroom and bathroom of the past. Plush bedrooms, comfortable and stylish baths, expansive family rooms, and cozy dens are now the rule.

Perhaps this move toward creating more luxurious and livable space is normal evolution, but the unique characteristics of the basement have certainly played a role. A basement, for instance, offers space that's separated from the more public spaces of the house but is still close by. Or the basement can become the home's public space, with insulated ceilings and soundproofing that allow you to enjoy all kinds of family activities without disrupting the use (or the order) of other areas of your home.

Remodeling your basement can adapt your home to meet the changing needs of your family.

CHAPTER PREVIEW

Gallery of room designs
page 8

Walls, floors, and ceilings
page 18

Lighting
page 20

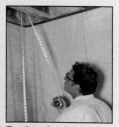

Evaluating your basement
page 22

Plan your basement project on paper to ensure it includes all the features you want. You can move walls and features more easily at this stage than after work begins.

Accessible installations
page 26

Drawing plans
page 28

GALLERY OF ROOM DESIGNS

Planning a bedroom

Your first consideration when planning a basement bedroom should be size—make the room large enough to house the bed, dresser, and other furnishings, and provide plenty of closet space. Although the minimum size required is only 80 square feet, allow about 125 square feet to comfortably fit a double bed.

Basements generally stay cool even in hot climates, so air-conditioning usually is not a factor, but consider it if you have a problem with condensation. If you don't have a walk-out basement you'll also need to install an egress window (see "Building codes for habitable rooms," below).

Here are some more ideas to consider when you plan a basement bedroom:

■ Install a light switch immediately inside the bedroom door and three-way switches at the top and bottom of the stairs.

■ Change awkward stair configurations for convenient entry and exit.

■ Install hardwired smoke alarms and a carbon-monoxide detector.

■ Soundproof the basement ceilings to keep family noise out of your private retreat.

■ Consider a full- or half-bath close to the bedroom (with a luxurious tub and two sinks for a master suite).

■ Include plenty of window area for light and ventilation. Window area equal to one-tenth of the room area is a design standard.

A built-in wall unit helps disguise the high window often found in basement rooms. The room must also have an egress window if it isn't in a walk-out basement.

STANLEY PRO TIP: **Building codes for habitable rooms**

A habitable room is one used for sleeping, living, cooking, or eating. Closets, hallways, baths, laundries, and utility rooms are not habitable.

■ **Room size:** Habitable rooms must have at least 70 square feet of floor area (50 square feet for kitchens) with one horizontal dimension of at least 7 feet.

■ **Ceiling height:** Habitable rooms must have ceiling heights of at least 7½ feet in 50 percent of their areas (7 feet in kitchens). The ceiling height can't be less than 5 feet anywhere in the

room. Beams and girders spaced at least 4 feet on center may hang a maximum of 6 inches below a ceiling.

■ **Exits:** Sleeping rooms must have at least one exterior door or an egress window that can be opened. Egress windowsills must be 44 inches or less above the finished floor. The window must have a minimum clear width of 20 inches, a minimum clear height of 22 inches, and a minimum clear opening of 5.7 square feet or 8 percent of the total floor space.

Built-in closets flank the head of the bed to make a compact and cozy sleeping nook with adequate storage space. Reading lights are recessed into the ceiling.

Planning a bathroom

The first consideration when planning a new bathroom is the location of the existing plumbing. You can reduce your construction costs by putting your new bathroom as close to the existing plumbing as possible.

The size of the bathroom should be next on your planning agenda. For a master bath, the space should be large enough for two adults and include both a shower and a tub, double sinks, and plenty of storage and vanity space.

Make the bathroom easily accessible from the bedroom. Direct access is best, but you can locate the bath down a hallway. Shield the bathroom doorway to prevent direct view in from family activity areas.

Set the vanity closer to the door than other fixtures. It's usually the last stop on the way out of the bath.

Enclose the toilet, tub, and shower in a separate compartment for increased privacy. Glass-block walls obscure the view without reducing the light. Insulate the walls to soundproof the bathroom; quiet enhances the feeling of privacy.

Patterns in the floor and wallcoverings affect the perception of space. Diagonal floor tiles can disguise an out-of-square room. Squares will call attention to it. Vertical stripes make a room feel taller. Horizontal lines can visually lengthen and shorten the room.

This master bath features luxurious surface finishes and a long vanity with double sinks in a relatively narrow space. Adding a basement bathroom may require design flexibility to accommodate existing plumbing.

MINIMUM CLEARANCES

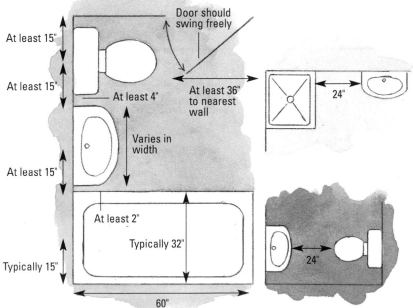

At least 15"

At least 15"

Door should swing freely

At least 4"

At least 36" to nearest wall

24"

Varies in width

At least 15"

At least 2"

Typically 32"

Typically 15"

24"

60"

A bathroom with a 5×8-foot interior space allows the minimum clearances that most municipal codes require for fixtures. While exploring layout options, maintain these clearances in your plan to ensure ease of use and installation.

STANLEY PRO TIP

Adding an apartment?

You might find an opportunity to turn basement space into added income. Adding an apartment is a little like adding a bedroom, but more restrictive. Local codes usually require at least 400 square feet of floor area with safe and adequate egress. Additional building codes or zoning ordinances may also specify a minimum lot size, existing number of bedrooms, parking space, covenant restrictions, and other requirements related to safety and neighborhood concerns. Before planning a rental apartment, check with your local officials.

Large windows brighten this family room. Put in shades or draperies for daytime TV viewing.

 PRO TIP

Planning for use

Once you move beyond the dreaming stage for your new basement space, make your plans more specific. You should base the design of the new room or rooms on the intended uses.

For example, if you're planning a bedroom and an office in separate rooms, each should incorporate design elements specific to its use. But combining a bedroom and office in the same room changes the requirements. You'll need a larger room with a design scheme that unifies the space while keeping the two functions separate and distinct.

Clarify your goals before you start building walls. This will save time and money and create a space you will enjoy long after the dust of remodeling has settled.

Planning family rooms

If your basement remodeling project includes the family room you've dreamed of, don't let the long wait limit your plans to past dreams. Plan for the future: Families and family rooms change.

A family room 20 years ago, for instance, probably included comfortable seating and a TV set, but little else. The family room of today serves a number of roles—it's not just a place to watch TV. It now houses a whole wall of media modules, counters, tables, and desks for hobby or office activity, even space for exercise equipment.

Follow these tips to make your family room practical, comfortable, and enjoyable:

■ Decorate it with brightly colored furniture and accents that reflect your personality.

■ Open the room to light with a south-facing window, but protect it from direct sunlight or glare with window coverings.

■ Arrange seating so it's comfortable—make conversation groupings at least 10 feet square, with no more than 8 feet between any two people. Place seating for television viewing no farther than 10 to 12 feet from the screen and at an angle of 45 degrees or less from it.

■ Provide tables and countertops for games, hobbies, and snacking.

■ Install a kitchenette for casual food preparation—an apartment-size sink, refrigerator, and counter will do the job.

■ Build in cabinetry that will display— or hide—your media equipment. Mix open shelving with drawer units and storage protected by doors.

■ Plan electrical wiring for the future. Wire the room with enough outlets, and install special circuits for any equipment that needs them. Run cable and computer wiring in walls when possible.

Built-in cabinetry and baskets on drawer slides make it easy to keep this playroom organized. Resilient tile is easy to clean—perfect where messes can happen.

Planning kids' rooms

Creating just the right space for children's activities calls for balancing the size of the space, access for supervision, and sound control—for both the noise the children make and outside sounds that can wake them.

If your children are young, you'll want convenient access so you can supervise them; a first-floor bonus room might be a better location than a basement room. Basements, however, can be ideal for older kids. The low ceilings, high windows, and structural supports associated with basement construction are of little concern to youngsters. The solid floors and walls will take a lot of abuse, and it's easy to control basement noise.

Keep these points in mind:

■ Make sure the floor area—their playground— is spacious and uncluttered and that you can alter it as the children grow.

■ Use a space-saving bunk or trundle bed and add storage for books, games, and all of the other things kids collect. Bins on casters make cleanup easy.

■ Build a table or child's work surface for drawing and painting.

■ Install flooring material that can take abuse. Resilients are a good choice, along with laminate and engineered wood products.

RECOMMENDED ROOM SIZES

Room	Minimum Area*	Minimum Size	Preferred Size
Bedroom	80 sq. ft.	8×10 ft.	11×14 ft.
Master bedroom	not specified	12×16 ft.	
Family room	110 sq. ft.	10½×10½ ft.	12×16 ft.
Living room	176 sq. ft.	11×16 ft.	12×18 ft.
Other habitable room	70 sq. ft.	7×10 ft.	
Bathroom	35 sq. ft.	5×7 ft.	5×9 ft.
Apartment	400 sq. ft.		

U.S. Department of Housing and Urban Development minimum net floor area within enclosed walls, excluding built-in fixtures, closets, and cabinets.

Children spend a lot of time on the floor, so use area rugs to make it comfortable for them. The rugs are easy to take up for cleaning too.

Planning an office

Whether you need an office for a home-based business or simply want a place to take care of the household business, your home office space should be separated from household traffic. The ideal office should offer convenient access, privacy, quiet, sufficient record storage, and enough room to work comfortably.

You'll need plenty of work areas—make them at least 29 inches deep and 30 inches from the floor. Build in space for file storage, computer equipment, and desk accessories. Additional space to reserve for future needs is valuable too. You may need only enough space for computing taxes and paying bills now, but those needs may change.

A home business can require a few additional elements. Include these elements in your office plans:
■ Create an atmosphere conducive to work and client meetings. Windows and interior fixtures should provide ample light and present a businesslike image.
■ Locate the office near an outside doorway or interior stairs so visitors and delivery persons can come and go easily.
■ Soundproof the stairwell and ceiling (or floor in an attic or bonus room) to keep other family activities from interfering with work.
■ With multiple work surfaces you can manage several projects at once. Arrange the work areas so you can convert them to conference space.

Light and bright, this basement office provides a pleasant place to work along with plenty of space for visitors or clients for a home-based business.

List your wishes

To simplify your planning, make it as complete as possible and maintain family harmony by gathering the family together for a basement brainstorming session.
■ Ask each family member what he or she wants in the new basement space. Combine everything on one wish list. Use your imagination but keep descriptions simple. Then prioritize the list.
■ Next draw up a list of what the family really needs and compare it with the wish list. Make decisions about what you can do without and what you can't afford and base your plans on the remaining items.

Working up a workshop

A home workshop is every do-it-yourselfer's dream. Although you might first think of putting it in the garage, a basement offers an advantage—you can heat it more easily.

Here's what you need for a great workshop:
■ Light-colored walls and bright, general room lighting.
■ Locked storage to keep children out of hazardous substances. Also provide adequate ventilation and locate a fire extinguisher in a convenient place.
■ A centralized vacuum dust-collection system with outlets for each power tool.

■ Electrical outlets in the ceiling for stationary equipment and along the edge of workbenches for power hand tools.
■ Workbenches and rolling storage on lockable casters.
■ Soft, removable, area floor coverings— rubber or vinyl mats that lift for easy cleaning.
■ Wall-mounted tool storage, as well as storage under workbenches.
■ Work zones with separate areas for benches, portable tools, and power tools.
■ A way to bring in lumber and supplies without traipsing through the whole house.

Planning a recreation room

Your basement can provide a haven for that unused treadmill, stationary bike, or stairclimber in the bedroom and maybe improve your health. That's because a well-planned, spacious exercise room is more likely to be used regularly than a machine pushed into a corner of a bedroom. With modern noise-suppression materials, you can create a place where family members can exercise without disturbing other family activities.

Here are some design factors for an exercise room:
■ A room measuring at least 8×12 feet with tough, durable flooring.
■ A resilient mat for floor activities.
■ Built-in seating with padding for comfort.
■ A nearby bathroom with a shower and, for real comfort, a whirlpool tub.
■ Large mirrors, a music system, and a TV for viewing fitness tapes. Placing the TV on a swivel-mounted wall or ceiling platform allows you to adjust it so you can see it from any part of the room.
■ Adequate ventilation.
■ Sound insulation.

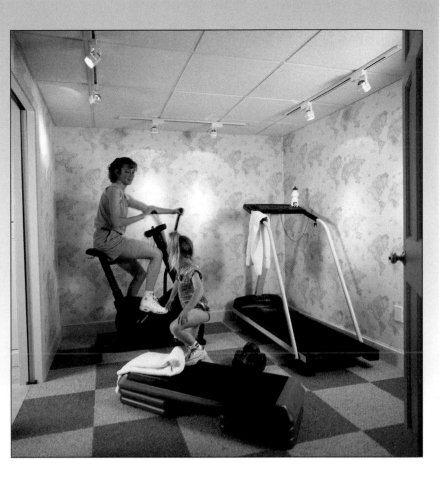

A basement gym saves health-club costs and allows family members to exercise anytime.

Planning hobby rooms

A basement offers the same advantage for hobby space as it does for other activities. Whether it's a studio for painting, a model-building center, a recital hall for your chamber music, a sewing room, or a meditation space, basements provide the out-of-the-way location that most homeowners prefer for a hobby room.

When planning a hobby room, include these features:
■ Easy-to-clean floors and work surfaces.
■ Counter space to spread out comfortably.
■ Well-placed ambient lighting with task lighting over work areas.
■ A sink, if your hobby requires cleanup.
■ Sufficient ventilation from windows or a forced-air system to exhaust any fumes produced by glue or paint.
■ Lockable storage to protect children from hobby materials and equipment and vice versa.

Keep your hobby supplies and equipment in a workroom to make your spare time more enjoyable. You can leave projects spread out without disrupting family life.

Planning a kitchen

Whether you need a full-size kitchen in your basement or just a small one will depend on your needs. If your basement will include an apartment or space for a live-in relative, you'll probably need a complete kitchen with all the appliances. The same goes if you plan to use the basement space for formal entertaining, complete with meals. Small parties and get-togethers with family or friends won't require as much space. A wet bar or kitchenette will do nicely.

Like a basement bathroom, your kitchen should be located as close to the plumbing as possible. From there, you can design your new space just as you would a first-floor kitchen. Include separate workstations for food storage, preparation, cooking, and cleaning. Plan each area so you don't have to travel far between them. Because a conventional oven is likely to be the least-used appliance, put it outside the main workspaces in the kitchen.

For two cooks, be sure to make the space large enough for cooking comfort. Put pantries close to food preparation areas and plan doors so they open away from the workstation for maximum convenience.

A second kitchen for entertaining can be part of a family room or recreation room. Plan it for the kind of cooking you will do there and easy cleanup.

A bar can be as simple as a counter for setting beverages on, or it can be a kitchenette that includes a sink, refrigerator, and even a microwave oven or small stove.

STANLEY PRO TIP: **Choose a style that suits you**

Discovering a style for any room that best expresses your personality can be a confusing process. Here are some steps that will help you:
■ Read home decorating magazines and books. Gather photos of rooms that appeal to you. Put your clippings in a folder.
■ When you visit other homes or show homes, notice the details of the rooms. Make mental notes of colors and other decorative aspects, both things you like and those you don't like. Inquire about the advantages and disadvantages of the materials used. When you get home, jot down your impressions and put your notes in the folder too.

■ Visit home furnishings stores, decorating showrooms, and home improvement outlets. Gather material samples, brochures, and paint chips that you can put into your folders.
■ When you're ready to plan your basement remodeling project, go through your collection of design ideas. As you study them, certain themes will emerge—you'll find colors, textures, and patterns that appeal to you. Make notes about these features and select the ones you think will look best in the room or rooms you will build.
■ Design the project around these themes to suit the new rooms and their uses.

A media center gathers all of your entertainment electronics into one place. This room offers seating for conversation or listening to music as well as watching movies or TV.

Planning a home theater

Technology has almost eliminated the single family TV set in the living room. A home theater is now within the reach of most family budgets. Because a home theater installation is likely a new space demand for a household, the best place to find space for one is usually in the basement.

Home-theater equipment requires a good deal of new wiring, so include wiring runs in your floor and framing plans. Beyond that, you may want to consult a professional home-theater designer, or at least get as much information about room design as you can from the equipment retailer. A complete category of interior design has grown around the home-theater business.

For starters, you should plan to locate seating back from the screen about 2 to 2½ times the width of the screen. At a minimum, you'll need a speaker on each side of the screen, on a plane with your ears when you are seated and about 3 feet from the sidewalls. You'll need two more speakers at the rear of the room, from 6 to 8 feet off the floor, and a fifth speaker for dialogue located above the screen. All the equipment should be housed in ventilated cabinets so it won't overheat.

Wine cellar

Once considered the province of the ultrarich, a wine cellar—or storage rooms—can now be found in many homes. The primary concern is to maintain the space at the right temperature. That calls for insulated walls between the cellar and other heated spaces.

In addition, include these in your wine cellar plans:
■ Window coverings to keep out direct sunlight.
■ A solid floor that won't vibrate.
■ Storage racks capable of holding bottles of standard sizes, as well as floor and shelf space for cases.

Stadium seating is just as appealing in your basement as in the cineplex. Special furniture is available for home theaters.

Planning a laundry room

Even though you probably have a washer and dryer in your home, you might not like their location. A basement renovation can provide an opportunity for upgrading your laundry facilities. After all, you don't want to put a well-appointed bedroom or a fancy recreation room in the basement and leave the washday appliances sitting out in plain sight.

After choosing a location that's close to the existing plumbing, here's what you should include in a complete laundry center:

■ Wall cabinets above appliances.
■ Base cabinets with countertops for folding and sorting clothes.
■ A large sink with paper-towel dispenser and storage for rags and cleanup tools.
■ A built-in ironing board.
■ A laundry chute from upper floors.

Make sure all surfaces are waterproof (laminate is a good choice) and that you've included plenty of space for sorting and folding clothes. Storage space for soap, dryer sheets, and stain removers should be big enough to accommodate two of each container so you don't have to set the spare supplies on the floor.

Decorate the space with bright colors and install plenty of light fixtures—both general and task lighting.

Plenty of well-organized storage, a large sink, and space to sort, fold, and iron clothes in this laundry room take some of the drudgery out of doing the washing and ironing. Bright, glare-free lighting makes the room more pleasant.

You'll need a sink in the laundry room, so use a kitchen sink and add an undercounter refrigerator to make it into a kitchenette. A sewing center is a natural add-on for a laundry room too.

Planning storage

Storage is often the last consideration when planning new space. A basement makeover is an opportunity to increase the storage capacity of your home and organize things at the same time. Here are some ideas:

■ Put dead space to work by building storage under stairs, above crawlspaces, and in ceilings. Most of these areas will have some architectural quirks and require custom solutions. If you have excess but attractive furniture stored in the basement, plan ways to use it in the new rooms.

■ Cover an entire wall with built-in shelving or enclosed cabinets with doors in a style that complements the overall design. Don't build in storage on sections of the wall where you will place furniture.

■ Put a lid on enclosed storage bins under windows. Use the lid for informal seating or for plants.

■ Jazz up your closet with ready-made rack dividers, shoe racks, and hanger bars set at different heights.

Even simple shelves under the stairs bring organization to the basement. Keep boxes and other stored items from sitting directly on the floor to prevent moisture damage.

Steps for stairway design

Getting to and from your new basement space is a major design decision when you're making your remodeling plans. Address this question early in your planning because you may need to alter the location of the stairs to make them safe and convenient.

Changing stairways almost always results in other decisions because stairs to habitable space must meet code requirements for primary stairs, which are different from codes for stairs to nonhabitable space. Here are typical requirements for primary stairs:

■ Riser height: 7½ inches maximum

■ Tread depth: 9 inches minimum

■ Width between handrails:
32 inches minimum

■ Headroom: 80 inches minimum

■ Handrail height: 30 to 34 inches above the tread

If your existing stairs aren't suitable for the job, you can build proper stairs in the same location, build new stairs in a different location, or construct a new exterior entry.

Where to put a new stairwell

Even if your present stairway meets code requirements, you may want to change its location for one of these reasons:

■ Headroom. Basement stairs in older homes are often built under another stairway so the headroom is compressed by the upper stringers. You may need to relocate the stairs.

■ Convenience. Locate the stairs to a multiple-room basement so family members don't have to pass through a bedroom or a bath to get to the stairs. Stairs leading to family rooms should originate close to the kitchen.

■ Noise. Noise travels both up and down staircases. Avoid connecting noisy and quiet areas with stairs, or soundproof the stairwell.

■ Structural support. Although a relocated stairway can be built parallel or perpendicular to the joists, a parallel installation requires less cutting, materials, and installation time.

Building stylish stairs

If your present stairs intrude into the space in your new room or their style doesn't suit you, consider other designs. Stairs take a lot more room than they first appear to. A simple straight stairway needs almost 40 square feet of floor area at its lower level. L-shape, U-shape, and other angular designs take up even more area. If your stairs are cramped for space, spiral stairs may solve the problem.

Spiral stairs are usually 4 to 6 feet in diameter, and moving furniture up or down them is difficult. Winders eliminate the need for a landing around a sharp turn. Their construction requires precision, so check with code officials before putting a winder in your plans.

Stair treatments

Stairways can act as the focal point for your interior design scheme. Here are some conventional treatments:

■ Cover the treads with hardwood or carpeting—or paint them before tacking down a carpet runner in the middle.

■ Replace the single overhead light fixture with wall sconces at the angle of the stairs.

■ Don't leave the walls bare—hang mirrors or a wall hanging in the stairway, or create display nooks for small sculptures or plants.

WALLS, FLOORS, AND CEILINGS

The way you finish your basement walls, floors, and ceilings will greatly affect your long-term enjoyment of the space. To choose the material that's right for each surface, consider how much wear and tear it will endure, how the pattern and color match the overall design of the room, and how much you can afford to spend on it.

Drywall
Drywall is the most widely used wall covering because it's inexpensive, easy to install, and serves well as a substrate for many wall coverings. It's fine for bathroom use except in tub and shower areas, where you should use greenboard, a moisture-resistant drywall. If you're installing ceramic tile, install cement backerboard on surfaces that will get wet.

Paint and wallpaper
Paint and wallpaper are inexpensive but effective ways to dress up the appearance of walls, ceilings, and trim. Flat or matte surfaces create a more subtle effect than gloss paints, but glossy surfaces are easier to clean. Wallpaper for a bathroom should be either a textured-vinyl product or vinyl coated. Even the more expensive uncoated brands tend to lift at the corners and edges.

Ceramic tile
Ceramic tile stands up better than any other material to the hard use required by a floor. Carefully chosen, tile will unify the design of the entire room.

When you're shopping for tile, take samples home so you can see how they look in the room and how they fit your overall design. Avoid too much reliance on single-color themes; a little variety can improve your design. Use accents sparingly so they won't overwhelm a space.

If you're planning to tile a bathroom, think of the tub, vanity, sink, walls, floor, and fixtures as an ensemble, and experiment with designs for the entire room. As you shop for bathroom tile, think small, at least at first. Tiles 4 inches or less fit more easily around sinks, tubs, and toilets, and require less cutting. Choose vitreous tile, either glazed or unglazed. Glazed tiles on the walls are much easier to clean than those with a matte finish.

No matter what floor you're planning to finish with tile, be wary of glazed tiles—they're slippery, especially when they're wet. Use tiles with a matte finish. Mosaic tiles are great for the floors because the abundance of grouted joints makes the floor more slip free.

Stone
You might not want stone tile on your bedroom floor, but it makes a beautiful, classic, and durable floor covering for bathrooms and kitchens. It's also a versatile material for walls. In addition to its high cost, however, stone tile has other drawbacks, depending on the kind of stone and where you use it.

Polished stone is not a good choice for floors—it's too slippery when wet and can cause dangerous falls. Tumbled stone surfaces like marble have a warm, soft texture but won't wear as well as some materials. Both polished and matte-finish stone work fine on bathroom walls.

Light-color wood flooring suits the clean, simple style of this family room, which has a home office enclosed in a closet.

Thick, soft carpet enhances the elegant style of this family room. Moldings on the wall and a high-style ceiling treatment add to the look.

Laminate flooring

Laminate flooring is made in many layers—a high-density fiberboard core covered with a bonding layer, a print layer (which is actually a photograph of the pattern you've chosen), and a hard, clear melamine wearcoat.

Laminate offers many colors and patterns, and its hard surface resists damage from dents and furniture. It is, however, prone to scratches and can't be refinished or easily repaired. Not all laminates are suited for kitchen or bathroom floors, so check the manufacturer's warranty. Snap-together planks, which are easy to install, require glued joints to seal against water damage.

Resilient flooring

Resilient sheet and tile flooring combines appearance, durability, and various colors and patterns with ease of installation. No flooring is completely dent proof, but resilients come close. Their surface is made to rebound when whatever is causing the pressure is removed. This is an excellent flooring choice for a children's room or family bath. It feels soft underfoot, resists stains, and is easy to keep clean.

Wood

Wood can add a feeling of quality, permanence, and elegance to any room, whether installed as a floor or wallcovering. Beadboard paneling can give any room a country or Victorian look, and some paneling evokes an elegant manor-house style. Tongue-and-groove panels and milled planks also make a good wainscoting.

Hardwood flooring, though stately, is not suitable for basement use because of its susceptibility to moisture damage. Engineered wood products, constructed much like plywood and laminates, feature a top layer of real wood. You can refinish engineered wood flooring, if necessary. Its cross-ply construction increases its resistance to moisture damage, and it can be installed in any basement room.

Carpet

Carpet muffles sound and is the most comfortable material underfoot. Sold in many colors, textures, and patterns, carpet will suit any room and any style.

Solid-surface panels

The same solid-surface materials found in countertops are also available in sheets for covering walls. They are too soft and damage-prone to be suitable for floors, but they make a good wallcovering, even in showers and tub surrounds. Most of these materials are hung on the wall with adhesives designed specifically for this purpose. Joining two sheets is usually accomplished by slipping them into tracks, which are also designed for this material.

Plaster

Thin-coat earthen plasters are rapidly moving into the realm of wallcoverings. You can use them to create textures and colors reminiscent of the work of Venetian craftsmen. They are remarkably easy to apply and are compatible with all existing wall surfaces. These plasters won't stand up to direct and constant water sprays, so don't use them on shower walls. They are fine for other bathroom walls, though some manufacturers recommend that they be sealed. Search the Internet for "earthen plasters."

Tile is a good choice for floors and walls in a bathroom. Wallpaper accents the tile on the lower part of this wall.

Trimwork

Trim and molding hide minor gaps and imperfections at joints and around doors and windows. They contribute to the style of a room too. Some popular moldings are:
- Picture-frame molding—with its straight lines and mitered corners—provides a simple complement to modern design schemes.
- Butted-head trim is easy to install and lends an Arts and Crafts air.
- Cabinet-head casings—a variation of the butted-head style—adds a small trim piece at the top of the casing.
- Corner blocks originated in the Victorian era, and their elaborate designs are well-suited to formal styles.

Wood cabinet-head window trim lends style to this basement home office.

LIGHTING

Basements are often dark, even after extensive remodeling. The best way to make a basement brighter is to install as many additional or larger windows as your budget allows.

Natural light should enter from more than one direction. If you're adding more than one window, place them on different walls. To minimize heat loss, install high-quality thermal windows. Windows should open to pleasant views, even if it means changing the layout of the room.

Lighting is critical to the appearance, safety, and convenience of your newly remodeled basement rooms. Once you complete the layout of the space, develop a lighting plan. Good lighting goes beyond placing a few recessed canister lights in the ceiling and a few sconces on the wall. It means lighting the room without creating shadows or glare. You will achieve the best results by combining two or three kinds of lighting and using different types of fixtures. There are three kinds of interior lighting:

General lighting
General lighting illuminates the entire room fairly evenly, usually from one or two ceiling fixtures, depending on the size of the room. For most rooms, you can light about 35 square feet with one fixture. More floor space will require additional fixtures. General lighting provides the base lighting to which you'll need to add task and accent lighting. Choose the location of new windows and indirect lighting fixtures (globe fixtures, recessed ceiling lights, wall sconces, or floor-mounted spotlights) so they provide warm, even light over large areas of the room.

Task lighting
Task lighting focuses on an area where you engage in activities specific to the space, such as applying makeup or shaving in a bathroom, sewing in a hobby room, or reading in the den.

Spotlights, track lights, wall-mounted fluorescent fixtures, portable lamps, or recessed ceiling fixtures can focus light on desks, countertops, or other activity areas.

Task lighting should illuminate without casting shadows. For example, wall sconces are perfect for bathroom mirrors. You may also want to light the shower and tub area, especially if your plan calls for half-walls to separate them from the rest of the space.

Check your building codes before installing tub and shower lighting. Most codes specify vapor-proof downlights. Place them so they light the area without shining in your eyes when you're relaxing in the tub. Install the switch at least 6 feet from the tub or shower.

Accent lighting
Accent lighting is a little like theatrical spot lighting, only on a smaller scale. Its purpose is to call attention to an architectural detail, a work of art, or other object whose function is strictly aesthetic. You can aim recessed ceiling spotlights or wall sconces at plants, pictures, sculptures, objets d'art, or features of the room to enhance their effect. Soft light that washes over the surface of the object is better than harsh, glaring light.

A row of windows brings daylight into this basement family room. Nighttime lighting comes from table lamps and ceiling fixtures.

Recessed ceiling lights provide overall lighting in this room. A table lamp and a pendent fixture contribute task light for reading and shooting pool.

Fixtures

No single fixture can do all of your lighting jobs, even in a small room. Good lighting calls for a variety of fixtures.

Canister lights are installed in the ceiling and provide downlight. They are an excellent source of general and task lighting and can be aimed as accent lights. To get even, uninterrupted coverage, set them so their light patterns overlap. You can get this information from the canister packaging or from the lighting dealer.

Pendent lights hang from the ceiling and can provide general, task, or accent lighting. Pendent lights attract attention, especially in small spaces; if you want an inconspicuous light source, choose a different fixture.

Surface-mounted lights, such as sconces for wall mounting, are available in many styles for both incandescent and fluorescent bulbs. Track lighting, another type of surface-mounted lighting, can be installed on a wall or ceiling. Track fixtures allow you to aim lamps at different areas for accent or task lighting. They are easier to install on a ceiling than canister lights because you don't have to cut into the ceiling.

Bulbs

Different light bulbs produce different kinds of light.

Incandescent bulbs, the most common type, have been around since electric lighting was invented. They cast light in different color ranges depending on their wattage and the kind of internal frosting or coating. Incandescents are now longer lasting and more energy efficient than they were just a few years ago.

Fluorescent lights use a gas in the bulb that emits light when excited by filaments at both ends. They are more energy efficient and longer lasting than incandescents. The earliest fluorescent lamps produced only a cool blue-white light. New ones offer a wider spectrum of colors. Subcompact models made to screw into standard incandescent sockets can reduce energy consumption and heat generation.

Halogen bulbs are incandescent bulbs that emit a powerful, bright white light. They can make excellent accent lights, but they produce a tremendous amount of heat. Make sure you install them in a fixture designed for halogen bulbs.

Bathrooms must have good light for the vanity and mirror. Wall sconces and recessed ceiling lights do the job in this bathroom.

Track lighting casts accent light on the painting. A floor lamp and table lamp make reading light.

Using windows well

Window area can be at a premium in a basement. Natural light dramatically increases the comfort of a room, so you'll want as much of it as possible. Here are a few ways to increase your window area:

■ Downslope the windows. Any wall that's mostly above grade provides a good location for a large window. Install as large a unit as you can with the bottom as close to ground level as possible. Install sliding glass doors or French doors where possible.

■ Cluster small windows. If the walls aren't big enough for large windows, cluster small windows to let in the light.

■ Build a large window well. You can install a picture window in a below-grade wall by excavating an area and building a large-scale window well. Make an entrance by adding steps and installing a sliding glass door instead of a window. Decorate the well with plantings or terrace the retaining wall to create a garden spot outside the window or door.

EVALUATING YOUR BASEMENT

Once you determine the purpose of your new room, you start to form a mental picture of how it will look, how large it will be, and perhaps how you will furnish it. By this time you may even have made some preliminary sketches. Take a close look at your basement before you rush ahead; you may find problems you hadn't anticipated.

Conditions in your basement may require work you hadn't thought of at first—expanding floor space, raising the ceiling height, changing stairways, removing old walls, erecting new ones, and rerouting electrical and plumbing lines.

One of the first problems you may encounter is that the space is too large or too small for the way you want to use it. Perhaps the ceiling is too low to meet local codes. There might not be enough floor area for your workshop or your proposed office space may be cavernous, when all you want is a place to take care of the family bills. Ductwork in the basement might clash with your teenager's sense of style for his or her new bedroom. Solutions exist for most of the obstacles you'll encounter, but first you need to know what those obstacles are.

Increasing headroom

Basements frequently lack headroom. Even if the floor joists overhead are high enough, pipes and ductwork are often installed below them. When you survey your basement, see if low-hanging pipes and ducts can be rerouted. (Remember that drain lines must have $\frac{1}{8}$ to $\frac{1}{4}$ inch of fall per linear foot of run.) Your new ceiling material will hide lines that run between the joists.

Lowering the basement floor will increase headroom too. But this is a difficult and costly solution—you have to break up the slab, remove it, excavate the soil, and pour new concrete. Seek the advice of a licensed engineer and experienced contractors before you decide on this method to increase basement headroom.

Bathroom specifications

Local building codes may not require specific minimum floor space for a bathroom, but they are usually quite specific about the spacing between fixtures. Measure the space set aside for the bathroom carefully to make sure everything will fit with the standard clearances.

Measure the headroom in all parts of the basement to make sure you have enough clearance to meet local code requirements. Allow for the finished ceiling when measuring.

STANLEY PRO TIP: **Check for rot**

Building materials that get wet and don't receive enough air to dry them are especially prone to rot. Rotted wood will not properly support the wall.

If you suspect rot in an existing wall, remove the wallcovering down to the studs and look for wood with dark blemishes, especially where the stud meets the bottom plate. Poke the wood with a screwdriver; if the screwdriver penetrates the wood without much pressure or if the wood feels soft, it's rotting. You should fix the water problem and replace the lumber with pressure-treated stock.

TYPICAL DIMENSIONAL DRAWING

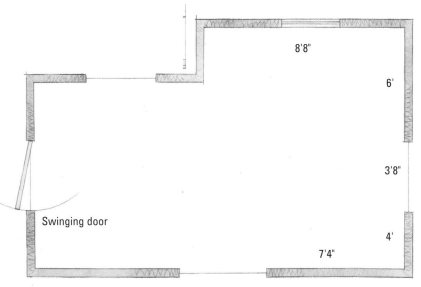

8'8"

6'

3'8"

4'

7'4"

Swinging door

To make sure the rooms you want will fit and meet floor-space requirements, make a scaled drawing of the basement. This drawing will become the foundation for the rest of your plans (see page 28).

For example, most codes require that any fixture must be more than 15 inches from the centerline of a toilet, and there must be at least 24 inches of space in front of the toilet. (It's OK for a door to swing into this space.) Sinks and vanity sink tops range from 20 to 30 inches in width. A standard bathtub is 60 inches by 32 inches. The framing for the tub—not the finished wall—must be the specified size; it will be difficult to make a tight seal along the wall if the framing is more than ¼ inch too long. Framing must be square too.

Pipe size might affect the location and thickness of new walls you intend to frame. Or existing walls may not be thick enough for pipes, which will require extra work. Most codes call for 3- or 4-inch PVC pipe for the main drain and the short length leading from the toilet to the drain, and 2-inch PVC for the other drain lines and the vents. Some plumbers prefer to run larger vent pipes.

In some cases these specifications are different from those required for accessibility under the Americans with Disabilities Act (ADA) (page 26). ADA standards represent minimums for accessibility.

Add space outside
If you must have additional space in the basement and your budget will absorb the expense, you can add a room by excavating outside the existing foundation walls and constructing new walls and a floor. The existing walls will then become new partition walls after you add doorways.

You'll have to roof this new space, of course, but excavation may prove easier than lowering the slab floor because you'll be digging in clear space and won't have to remove the slab from within.

Removing walls
An existing wall that stands in the way of your new room may be just a minor obstacle or it may support the house. Before you decide on a plan that requires a wall to be removed, determine whether the wall is bearing or nonbearing (see page 56). You can remove most nonbearing walls with little difficulty. But removing a bearing wall calls for temporary support walls and a new beam. Some can't be removed at all. If you must remove a bearing wall, consult a licensed professional engineer.

Check your existing wiring for risky wires and cables. Anchor all exposed cable with staples or straps to minimize the risk of accidentally snagging it. Never hang anything on exposed electrical cable.

Checking the floor

Work in 6-foot sections with a carpenter's level to check the floor for low spots, high spots, or any other imperfections that could affect the installation of the finished flooring materials.

Moisture in the basement

Moisture is one of the major enemies of building materials. Before you get too far along with your plans, inspect your home for evidence of moisture. Fix problems before you start remodeling.

Basement moisture can be caused by condensation, leaks, and hydrostatic pressure, which forces moisture up through the floor.

■ **Condensation:** Condensation shows up on walls and cold water pipes in warm weather. To prevent these surfaces from collecting water from the moist summer air, insulate pipes and walls and cover wall insulation with a vapor barrier. Adding windows to increase ventilation will help. So will a dehumidifier, but don't rely solely on it.

■ **Leaks:** If your basement leaks, first make sure gutters and downspouts are installed and in good repair. Many problems can also be solved by grading the soil around the house away from the foundation. If these remedies don't work, you may have to invest in an exterior or interior drainage system.

■ **Hydrostatic pressure:** White deposits (alkali) on the slab means you might have a moisture problem. To check for moisture, tape 2×2-foot clear plastic squares to the floor every 2 feet. Lift them after a couple of days. Droplets under the plastic mean moisture is wicking up from the soil and you may need to consult with an engineer for solutions.

Persistent leaking, puddles, or flooding are major problems that need immediate attention. Waterproofing the interior walls and sealing the cracks with hydraulic cement will sometimes cure these problems. Better yet, waterproof the exterior walls and install a sump pump and drain lines that run to a dry well.

EVALUATING YOUR BASEMENT (continued)

Erecting new walls

Building a new partition wall is the easiest way to reconfigure space to meet your needs. Stud walls go up easily and require only basic building skills. Concrete block walls in basement rooms are more difficult, but unless your plans include excavation or building codes require them, you probably won't need to use block for a partition wall.

Evaluate your wiring

Although you may be tempted to extend existing electrical circuits into your remodeled space, you should install at least one new general-purpose circuit to avoid electrical overloads. Here are some additional guidelines for adequate wiring:
■ You'll need at least one outlet on each wall that's more than 2 feet long; place outlets no more than 6 feet from each other.
■ Locate switches close to room entrances.
■ Install separate outlets and circuits for fixed appliances.

■ Provide ample lighting for stairways and install two-way switches at both ends.
■ Protect basements, bathrooms, kitchens, and laundry rooms with a ground fault circuit interrupter (GFCI) outlet. It shuts off power to the circuit immediately when it senses current imbalance.

Where to put the plumbing?

The best place to install new plumbing is as close to the existing plumbing as possible. You may have to build a separate wet wall—one with plumbing running inside it—if your kitchen, bathroom, or laundry room isn't on a wall that has existing plumbing. If you're tapping into drains, make sure the drains are large enough; drains for washing machines and sinks are almost never large enough for a new system. However, a toilet probably drains into a pipe of adequate size.

If you have to install a new branch drain, you'll have to dig up the slab floor and install new fittings, but it will be worth the effort if it's the only way you can install a new basement bathroom (pages 94–95).

Heating and cooling

Whether forced air, hot water, or steam, heating, ventilating, and air-conditioning (HVAC) systems can usually handle the extra load of remodeled space. Just tap into existing ducts and run additional ducts between the joists. New ductwork that crosses the joists will have to go below them, so watch the headroom. You can enclose ductwork that hangs below the ceiling. If your existing units won't handle the additional load, upgrade or install an additional heating or cooling source—electric baseboard or gas heaters, a wood-burning stove, or a room air-conditioner. Because cooling is also affected by ventilation, locate windows in the basement to provide cross-ventilation and install a ceiling fan if necessary.

Locating supply lines

Before you can draw an accurate plumbing plan for your new space, you'll have to know the location of the existing supply lines. Near the water heater, supply lines branch into cold and hot pipes—an excellent place to start tracing your supply system.

Most water heaters stamp "hot" and "cold" on the top of the metal housing. Some lines reduce in dimension along their run. Here a pipe steps down in size from ¾ inch to ½ inch. Note such reductions on your plan.

STANLEY. PRO TIP

Work with the building department

Working with your building department ensures safe and reliable plumbing. Here are some tips for getting off to a good start:
■ Find out if your building department requires a licensed plumber or electrician to do your work.
■ An inspector may be willing to offer advice, but don't ask for it. Instead, propose a plan and present it for feedback.
■ Draw up professional-quality plans with a complete list of materials. Make an appointment with the inspector to go over your plans. Take notes, and don't be afraid to ask questions.
■ Schedule inspections and be prepared for them. Don't make an appointment until the work is ready for inspection.
■ Above all, do not cover up any rough plumbing or electrical work until the inspector has approved it. Doing so runs the risk of having to tear out brand-new walls to revise the plumbing.

Evaluate existing circuits and calculate safe loads. To find the total capacity of a circuit, multiply amps times volts (usually 120). Most local codes require that all the loads on a circuit total no more than 80 percent of total circuit capacity. This 80-percent figure is the circuit's safe capacity.

15-amp circuit
total capacity: 1800 watts
safe capacity: 1440 watts (12 amps)

20-amp circuit
total capacity: 2400 watts
safe capacity: 1920 watts (16 amps)

30-amp circuit
total capacity: 3600 watts
safe capacity: 2880 watts (24 amps)

Building codes

Remodeling and finishing a basement involves several areas of construction—plumbing, wiring, and structural work. In almost every locality, these activities will be subject to building codes. Codes are established to ensure the safety and quality of materials and workmanship. Any major—sometimes even minor—work will require you to submit plans for approval, secure a building permit, and arrange for inspections. Do-it-yourself work done without the benefit of inspections could be faulty and dangerous.

At the beginning of the project planning, visit or call your building department and collect any printed information about local codes that may apply to your remodeling project. Draw a detailed plan that includes a list of all materials and have the plans approved before starting the work. Make sure that the quality of work you perform will satisfy the inspector.

Common electrical codes

Here are some common general requirements for home electrical systems:
■ **Boxes:** Plastic electrical boxes are common, but metal ones may be required.
■ **Receptacles, fixtures, and appliances:** All new receptacles and appliances must be grounded. Fixtures and appliances should be approved by Underwriters Laboratories (UL).
■ **Cable:** Nonmetallic (NM) cable is the easiest to run and is accepted by most building departments. Wherever cable will be exposed rather than hidden behind drywall or plaster, armored cable or conduit may be required.
■ **Circuits:** Most 120-volt household circuits are 15 amps; lights must be on 15-amp circuits. In kitchens and utility areas, 20-amp circuits may be required.
■ **Wire size:** Use 14-gauge wire for 15-amp circuits and 12-gauge wire for 20-amp circuits.

Common plumbing codes

These are common code requirements for most remodeling projects:
■ Fixtures must meet spacing requirements.
■ Drains, vents, and supply lines must be sized appropriate to their application.
■ In most cases drainpipes must slope at least ¼ inch per running foot. Codes may require that vent pipes slope at ⅛ inch per foot.
■ The installation of plumbing must not weaken the structure of a house. The inspector may require that you reinforce joists that have been cut to accommodate various pipes.

Other requirements call for the use of caulking around pipes and placement of protective plates over pipes.

If you're simply replacing an existing fixture, there's usually no need to contact the building department. But when you run new lines, be sure to work with a building inspector.

ACCESSIBLE INSTALLATIONS

Kitchens and bathrooms have often presented obstacles to the elderly or people with disabilities. But a growing list of plumbing products engineered for easier use plus some simple design changes now can be combined to create accessible kitchens and baths in any home. Often these changes benefit everyone in a household, as well as relatives and guests.

Available resources

The Americans with Disabilities Act (ADA) of 1991 establishes accessibility standards for commercial and public facilities. Some of these regulations pertain directly to plumbing fixtures and the design of bathrooms and kitchens.

The ADA standards are not requirements for private residences, but they are a valuable planning resource. Visit the ADA website at www.usdoj.gov/crt/ada/.

Your local building department should be able to help you design kitchens and baths that are universally accessible. Some plumbing manufacturers offer a full line of accessible products. Other firms offer ADA-approved sinks and other fixtures, including those with pedal-operated controls.

Customize your plan

Don't just follow the rules; make sure your layout and fixtures will be useful for everyone in your family now and in the future. Whenever possible test a product or layout to make sure it can be used easily by a person in a wheelchair or walker.

Purchase ADA-approved grab bars and position them with these two purposes in mind: A grab bar should enable a person to easily enter and exit an area, and there should be a grab bar at a convenient location so a person can reach it in case of a slip or fall. Be sure to anchor grab bars with screws driven into studs.

Planning an accessible kitchen

This sink has a specially designed enclosure that covers the plumbing. It is usually not possible to install a garbage disposer inside this type of unit. Enclosures are usually made of vinyl. A one-touch faucet with a pull-out sprayer is often preferred. An ADA-approved unit will ensure easy access.

ACCESSIBLE SINK SPECIFICATIONS

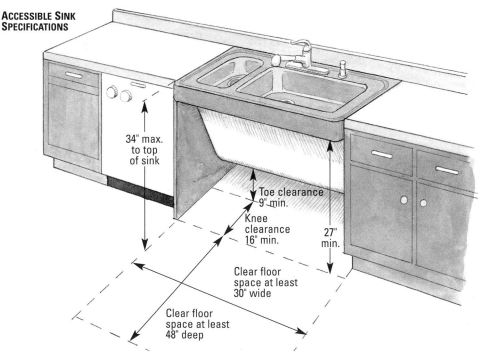

34" max. to top of sink

Toe clearance 9" min.

Knee clearance 16" min.

27" min.

Clear floor space at least 30" wide

Clear floor space at least 48" deep

Provide a 48×30-inch clear area in front of the sink. Test with a wheelchair to make sure the entry and turnaround areas are large enough, and make sure a person can wheel up to the sink, operate the faucet handles, and reach the sink's drain plug.

The top of the sink should be no higher than 34 inches—2 inches lower than a standard countertop—and you can put it as low as 28 inches to meet specific needs.

The area under the sink should be free of obstructions, such as electrical cables or a garbage disposer.

Provide a counter space for food preparation, with a countertop at the correct height and no cabinet below.

Planning an accessible bathroom

A bathroom sink should have the same accessibility as a kitchen sink (page 26).

There should be room to wheel into the bathroom and to move easily from one fixture to another. ADA-recommended clearances vary depending on the shape of the bathroom and the position of fixtures; some typical dimensions are shown at right.

Allow a space at least 56×60 inches around a toilet, with at least 42 inches to one side from the center of the toilet.

Provide a stable, ADA-approved seat in a bathtub. Usually it's best to have a detachable handheld shower unit so the person can wash while sitting.

A shower usually provides easier access than a tub. The stall should be at least 36×60 inches and have a solid seat. A curtain is generally easier to operate than a shower door.

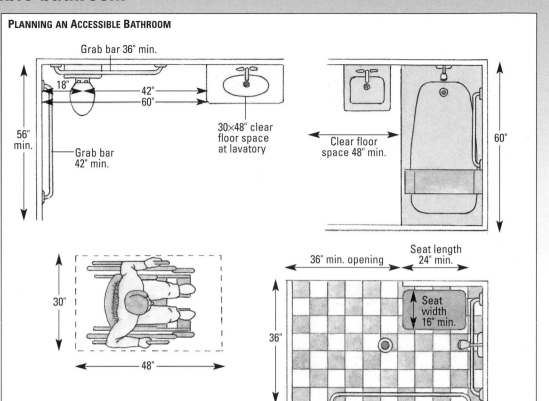

PLANNING AN ACCESSIBLE BATHROOM

The sink above has large, easy-to-use handles and roll-under space beneath. The tub and shower unit at right has solid, well-placed grab bars, a stable and slip-resistant seat, and a handheld shower unit.

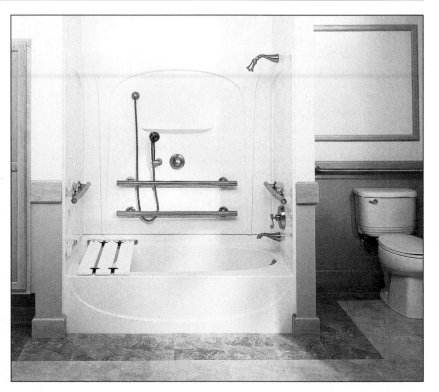

DRAWING PLANS

Accurately drawn plans will help you spot problems before you start framing walls and running plumbing lines. They will also show the building inspector you've thought through your project. The tools are simple: a ruled straightedge, a compass, color pencils, an eraser, and a 30-60-90-degree triangle. Use graph paper to establish a scale—¼ inch to 1 foot is convenient. Then start with a rough sketch of the room and a scaled floor plan.

Making a scaled floor plan

First, make a rough sketch of the room, identifying appliances, closets, nooks and crannies, cabinets, and other built-in features (even if you plan to remove them). Then start in a corner and measure the length of a wall from each change of direction to the next. Measure the location and opening size of existing windows and doors and note them on your sketch.

Transfer the sketch and all of its details to graph paper. You now have an accurate rendering of the existing space. Now you are ready to draw a plan—several, actually—of the proposed room layout.

The new floor plan

Tape a piece of tracing paper over your scaled drawing and trace the existing elements that will stay in the new room or rooms. Leave out (or draw with dotted lines) elements you will remove—a wall, for example. Draw in new framing details—doors, windows, walls—and label them. When you're done, your drawing should look something like the floor plan shown at right. If something doesn't look like you had imagined it, modify the plan until you are satisfied with it. This is the time to experiment with changes. If you do your experimenting on tracing paper, you'll avoid erasing the drawing and starting over.

Although the floor plan reflects what your new room will look like, it's not detailed enough for construction. For that, you'll need additional drawings for framing, electrical, plumbing, and HVAC plans.

Drawing a plumbing plan

You may think that a rough sketch is all you need for the plumbing. After all, you can

1 Start by drawing a floor plan of the existing space on graph paper. A scale of ¼ inch to 1 foot usually allows plenty of detail without being so big that you need a large piece of paper. Show all the walls, doorways, and windows.

2 Once you have completed your floor plan, make tracing paper overlays to test out possible room layouts. Avoid erasing—if you make a mistake or if you don't like the way something looks, just make another overlay.

BASEMENT FLOOR PLAN

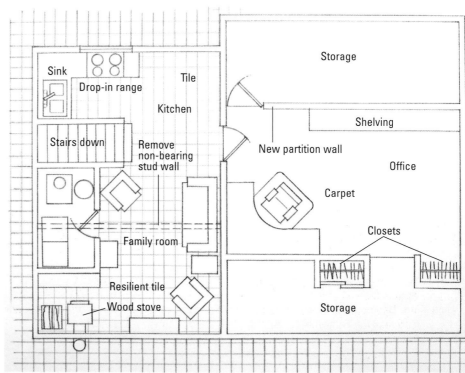

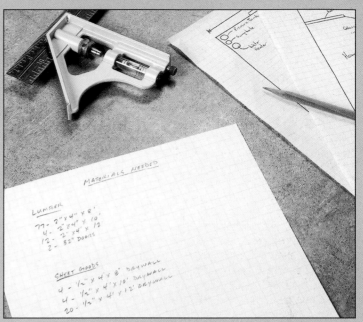

3 When you are happy with your new floor plan, draw elevations (views of the face) of all the walls. Create an overlay for the elevation drawing, showing stud spacing, door or window openings, wiring and plumbing paths, electrical outlets and switches, as well as all dimensions. Note potential problems or special circumstances in the margins.

4 Use your framing plan (as well as the remaining lighting, plumbing, and wiring plans) to make a complete materials list. You will probably also need these drawings when you apply for a building permit.

Drawing plumbing plans

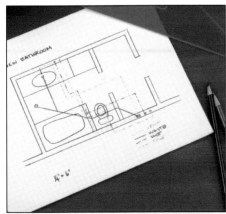

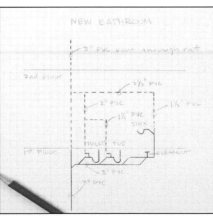

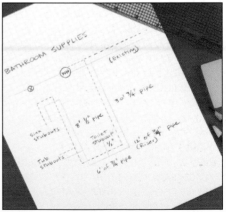

1 Once you have completed your floor plan, make tracing paper overlays of all the spaces that will require plumbing. Draw in the paths of the piping, with solid lines for drainpipes and broken lines for supply lines. Use notes to show vertical runs. Draw lines with different colors to make the function of each pipe clear.

2 Draw a drain-waste-vent (DWV) elevation to illustrate the path of the stack, vents, and revents along with the length of drainpipe runs and traps. The primary purpose of a DWV elevation is to show how the fixtures will be vented. It doesn't have to be drawn over an architectural drawing.

3 Draw a supply elevation to show the approximate length of supply pipes. The main purpose is to determine the minimum size of the pipes. Order more supply pipe than your estimate shows. You can only determine the exact lengths of the pipes as you install them.

DRAWING PLANS *(continued)*

figure out the details as you work, right? Even professional plumbers have to make on-the-job plan changes after they start work. The framing they find may differ from what they expected, or they may discover that their plan was incomplete. To keep surprises to a minimum, pros map a job in painstaking detail. Having a clear plan will also make the initial meeting with the building department go more smoothly.

Use standard plumbing symbols (which you can get from your building department) to produce your plumbing plan. Map the existing plumbing first, and use color codes to indicate the function of each pipe. Draw all the fixtures to precise scale and make sure they are not too close together. Then put in the drain lines, followed by the supplies and risers. Indicate the exact type of every fitting so the inspector can approve them. Note pipe sizes, including valves.

Drawing a wiring plan
First make a rough drawing of the existing circuits. Use the correct symbols and colored pencils to indicate each circuit. Then draw in the fixtures and the switches in convenient locations. Make sure all the circuits are correctly loaded and that all aspects of your wiring plan meet the specifications of your local electrical codes.

Create a clear materials list
Use your drawings to list the materials you need. Divide your project into three sections—framing, plumbing, and wiring. In each section you'll make a list of the specific items you need—lumber, trim, drywall, supply pipe, drainpipe, fittings, cable, electrical boxes, and fixtures.

Take your materials lists and plans to your materials dealer. The dealer will be able to provide an estimate of material costs. Cost of the materials you actually use will vary from the estimate.

How much will it cost?
This is the first thing most homeowners want to know when planning a project. Project cost depends on the size, complexity, and the quality of materials used.

With detailed plans, suppliers or contractors can provide accurate cost

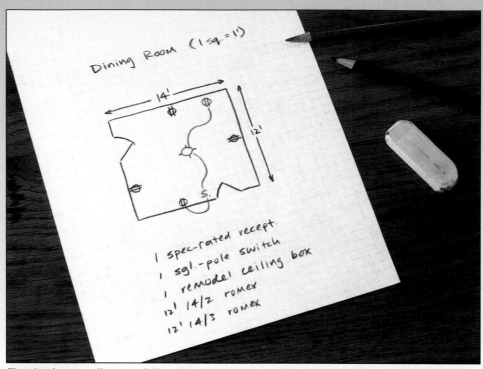

The plan for extending an existing electrical circuit—in this example, adding a receptacle and a switched light fixture—is easy to draw. Don't take the task lightly: Use the correct symbols and make the drawing clear and neat.

estimates. If the estimates are higher than expected, detailed plans will help you decide where you can save money without destroying the usefulness of the space or your future enjoyment of it. Settle on your design before you start work; undoing or redoing work you've already completed increases costs substantially.

How much can you afford?
This is the second—and more important—question. You probably won't find the answer by simply glancing at your checkbook. Remodeling a basement is usually an expensive undertaking; for many homeowners it will require a loan.

You may not know how much you can borrow until you actually apply for a loan. Gather financial data ahead of time. Make a list of current debts and payment amounts, figure your net worth, and list any anticipated new expenses (and income) that you will have during the life of the loan. Doing this ahead of time will speed your application.

STANLEY PRO TIP

Planning checklist

Organize your work following this outline.
■ Create a scaled drawing that includes all dimensions and design peculiarities.
■ Draw detailed plans.
■ Estimate your total costs and comparison-shop for the best deals.
■ Prepare a schedule that includes contract benchmarks and inspections. Allow adequate time at all stages.

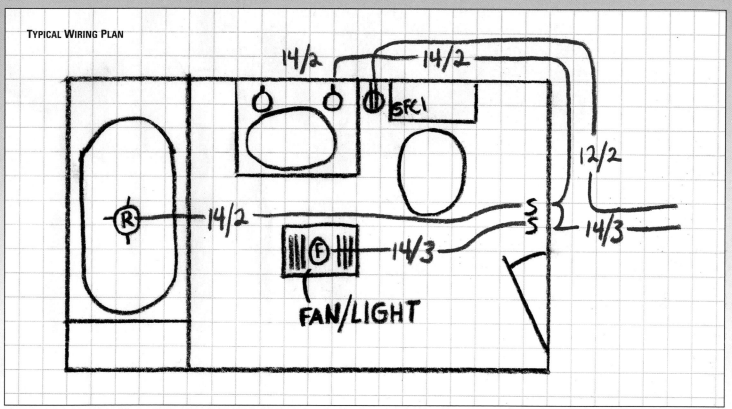

A complete wiring plan will show the locations of all fixtures, the wires that feed them, the load they will carry, and the name and type of each item. Color coding illustrates feed, return, and ground wires.

Dealing with disruption

One aspect of remodeling can't be planned on graph paper—the inevitable disruption and mess it generates. Basement remodeling projects often cause less annoyance than others because they're out of the way of daily activities in many homes. But things will happen: The water might be turned off when someone's in the shower, or rain could pour in through an unfinished window opening, or night might fall before you finish wiring and can turn the power back on. You can't prepare for these occurrences; you can only cope with them.

Here are a few steps you can take to minimize the stress of remodeling:

■ Clear out unwanted items and reorganize what you're keeping.
■ Rent a roll-off trash container to collect debris for a large job.
■ Order materials early; have all the preparations completed by the delivery date.
■ Make sure you have the right tools before you start work. Stopping work to go out to buy or rent a tool slows progress.
■ Choose the right season. Spring and summer are better times to cut through outside walls.
■ Above all, leave yourself plenty of time. Do things in a logical order.

Design pros can save money

Even if your budget is tight, hiring a design professional could be worth the expense. A designer can incorporate ideas you've seen in other homes, conceptualize design schemes, draw plans, and advise you about changes that will make your project more efficient and less expensive. Here are some sources for professional design help:

■ Architects, who are trained in building design and engineering. They are qualified to advise you on structural requirements.
■ Interior designers, who are trained to plan and style interior space.
■ Design/build firms, which often have staff architects or designers and can carry out your project from design through construction.

CHOOSING TOOLS & MATERIALS

Remodeling a basement involves a wide range of construction activities—carpentry, plumbing, wiring, hanging drywall, and perhaps tile and trim work. Each activity requires its own set of tools as well as a set of common tools. You might already have many of the common ones in your toolbox, but you will need to fill in any vacancies.

In all cases, buy the best tools you can afford. Quality tools will outperform inferior alternatives and will pay for themselves in the long run. Examine top-of-the-line tools and you'll quickly see the difference between them and the cheap ones. Hand tools should be flawlessly finished; handles should be tight and hefty. Well-made power tools will feature precise assembly, smooth operation, and user-friendly handles and adjustments.

Treat the cost of tools as an investment, not an expense. Even if you buy new tools, your project cost will probably be lower than if you contracted the work. Besides, you're certain to use your new tools for future projects, so you can spread their cost over a number of jobs.

The same idea holds true for material purchases. Although the quality of many building materials is fairly consistent from one supplier to the other, the cost of lumber and hardware can vary among retailers. Price is an important factor in every buying decision, but it's not the only one to look at. Consider return policies and delivery options before ordering. Some retailers consider a sale to be final when you leave the parking lot; others will accept returns of unused or defective materials. Some offer delivery, which may even be free for a large order. Fitting your order into the delivery schedule might take several days, however.

Large retail dealers might offer rental of a small flatbed truck to haul your materials. Call ahead to find out whether you need a reservation and to get other details of the rental agreement.

CHAPTER PREVIEW

Carpentry tools
page 34

Tiling tools
page 37

Drywall finishing tools
page 37

Plumbing tools
page 38

Wiring tools
page 41

Choosing lumber
page 42

Drywall and trim
page 44

Pipes and fittings
page 46

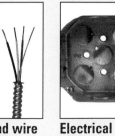

Cable and wire
page 48

Electrical boxes
page 49

Fasteners and clamps
page 50

Wire nuts
page 51

Receptacles
page 52

Switches
page 53

CARPENTRY TOOLS

Carpentry tools are the ones you're most likely to have in your workshop already. But even if you have a large collection already on hand, make sure they're high-quality items and in good condition.

You'll use a **carpenter's level** to level and plumb long sections of framing and pipe and a **torpedo level** for short sections. A good **16-ounce framing hammer** is essential; it's heavy enough to drive framing nails, yet light enough for trim work. Add a 22-ounce framing hammer for heavy work.

A **tape measure** provides a compact ruler for all measuring tasks. You should have one at least 25 feet long with a wide blade.

Use a ⅜-inch **variable speed electric drill** to bore holes. Buy several **spade bits** for drilling holes for water supply lines. When you need extra reach, attach spade bits to a **bit extender**. A **quick-change sleeve** speeds switching **twist bits** for small holes. Make finder holes with a **long bit**. For cutting holes larger than 1 inch, buy a **hole saw**. Renting or buying a **hammer drill** will speed tough-

to-bore holes in concrete. A **cordless 18-volt drill** is portable and keeps the workplace free of extension cords. For installing screws, buy a **magnetic sleeve** and several **screwdriver bits.**

A **stand-up flashlight** will light up cramped, dark quarters. You'll find a **nail set** handy for setting the heads of finishing nails below the surface of moldings and extending your reach into hard-to-hammer places.

A **plumb bob** provides a vertical reference. A **chalk line** marks long, straight lines.

Torpedo level

Carpenter's level

Framing hammer

Magnetic sleeve and screwdriver bits

Bit extender

Long bit

Tape measure

Cordless drill/driver

Hole saw

Electric drill

Twist bits with quick-change shanks

Stand-up flashlight

Spade bits

Quick-change sleeve

Hammer drill

Nail set

Plumb bob

Chalk line

A **stud finder** will locate studs in existing basement frame walls. Buy an electronic one that locates a stud by measuring wall density, not by pointing to nails.

For cutting miters in trim, you'll need either a **miter box and backsaw** or a power mitersaw. Equipped with a fine-cutting blade, it will cut PVC pipe too. A **coping saw** is indispensable for cutting moldings at inside corners. A pair of heavy-duty **metal snips** comes in handy for many tasks, including the installation of metal studs.

Demolition tools

To remove a small section of concrete, a **small sledge** and **cold chisel** may be all you need. To chisel out a large area, rent an **electric jackhammer** and **jackhammer chisel**. A **12-pound sledgehammer** is also useful for large sections and for nudging frame walls into position. A **reciprocating saw** comes in handy for cutting through framing. Its long blades reach into awkward spots and can even slice through nails and screws. Several types of blades are

available, including metal-cutting blades. Buy blades in packages of five or so; they can become dull, break, or bend.

For pulling nails, nothing beats a **cat's paw**. A **flat pry bar** will enable you to disassemble most nailed-together framing members. Occasionally you may need a longer **ripping bar** for heavy-duty work.

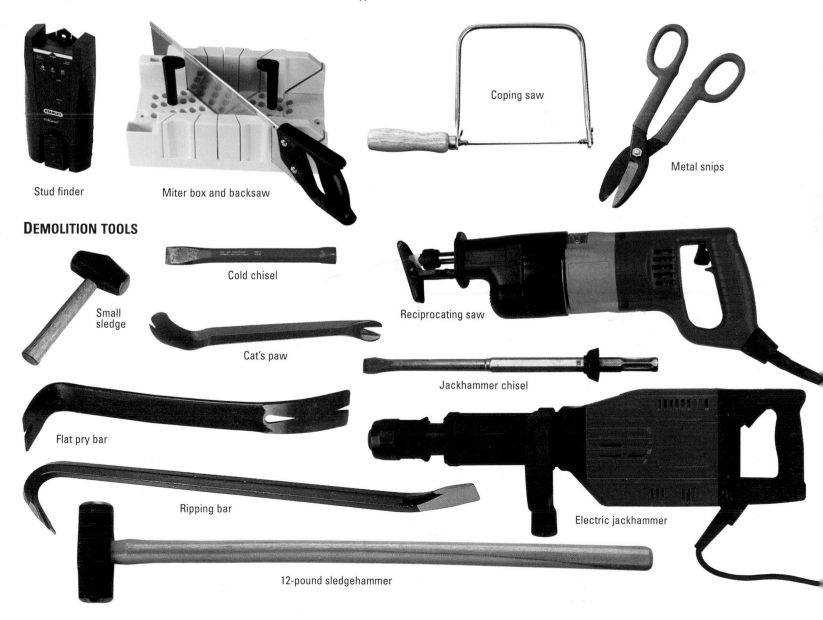

Stud finder

Miter box and backsaw

Coping saw

Metal snips

DEMOLITION TOOLS

Cold chisel

Small sledge

Reciprocating saw

Cat's paw

Jackhammer chisel

Flat pry bar

Ripping bar

Electric jackhammer

12-pound sledgehammer

CARPENTRY TOOLS (continued)

A **combination square** allows you to mark boards for crosscutting. A **layout square** does many of the same tasks and can serve as a guide when crosscutting with a circular saw or jigsaw. Use a **framing square** to mark larger layouts. A **T-bevel** transfers angles from one place to another.

You'll need to cut holes in drywall or paneling to fit electrical outlets, switches,

and fixtures. A **drywall saw** is good for a few holes; use a **spiral saw** for a neater, faster job. A full-size **hacksaw** is useful for cutting steel and copper pipes and for removing rusted fittings and old sections of pipe. Have a **close-work hacksaw** for working in tight areas. Most use full-size hacksaw blades as well as shorter metal-cutting blades. A **utility knife** does

everything from sharpening pencils to cutting drywall. Keep plenty of blades on hand and change them often so you always have a sharp edge.

Use a **circular saw** for cutting framing lumber and, with a metal-cutting blade, for cutting cast-iron pipe. For quick work, a **toolbox handsaw** packs a lot of cutting capability into a compact size. For cutting access panels and holes for sinks, use a **jigsaw**.

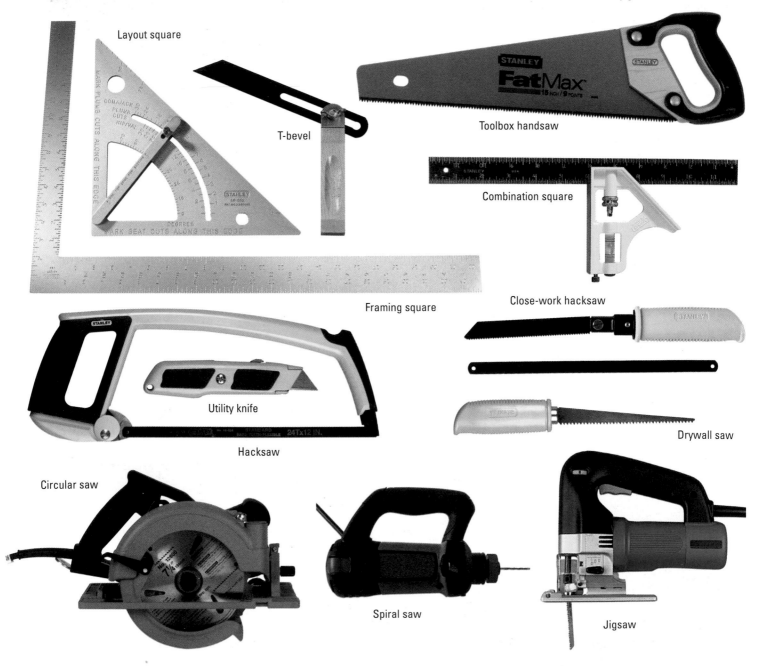

Layout square

T-bevel

Toolbox handsaw

Combination square

Framing square

Close-work hacksaw

Utility knife

Drywall saw

Hacksaw

Circular saw

Spiral saw

Jigsaw

TILING TOOLS

Installing ceramic tile calls for a few special tools. To mix thinset mortar, use a **heavy-duty drill** and a **mixing paddle**. Different jobs require different **trowels**, and filling the joints properly calls for a **grout float**. You'll need a **sponge** to clean the grout off the surface of the tiles. Cutting tiles is easy with a **snap cutter**; a **wet saw** makes quick work when you have lots of cuts to make. You can rent either one. Use **tile nippers** to chip away small pieces of tile when cutting circular or unusual patterns. A **masonry stone** removes rough or sharp edges. A **margin trowel** will get mortar into tight spaces and is a handy tool for scooping mortar from a **bucket**.

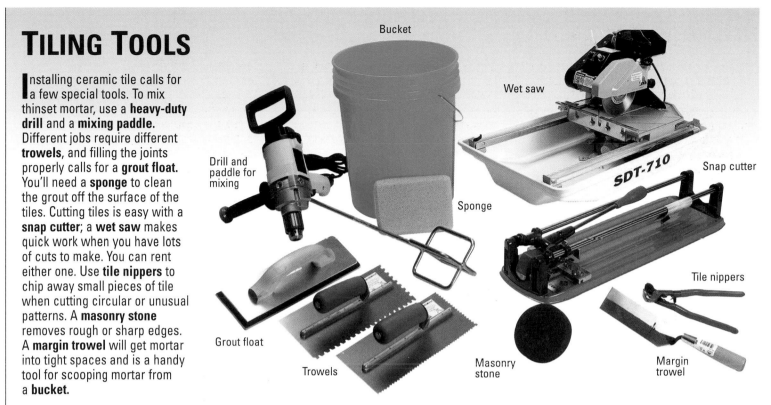

Bucket

Wet saw

Drill and paddle for mixing

Sponge

SDT-710

Snap cutter

Tile nippers

Grout float

Trowels

Masonry stone

Margin trowel

DRYWALL FINISHING TOOLS

Finishing drywall also requires specialized tools. For laying out and guiding cuts on a drywall sheet, nothing beats a **drywall square**. For light trimming such as planing an edge flush at a corner, use a **Surform plane**. Tools used for spreading joint compound over drywall joints are called **taping** or **drywall knives**. These come in a variety of widths. For most purposes a 6-inch, a 10-inch, and a 12-inch knife will handle the task. Along with the knives, get a **mud pan** to hold a supply of joint compound (often called mud).

To smooth dried joint compound, use **sanding screens** mounted in a **holder**. For an almost dust-free environment, smooth the walls with a wet **drywall sponge**—it has a tough abrasive plastic layer laminated to one side.

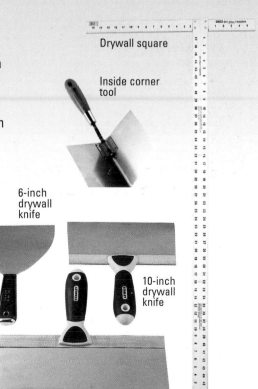

Drywall square

Inside corner tool

6-inch drywall knife

10-inch drywall knife

Sanding screen holder

Mud pan

Drywall sponge

Sanding screens

Surform plane

12-inch drywall knife

PLUMBING TOOLS

For a modest amount of money—probably less than a single visit from a plumber—you can assemble a tool kit that will tackle most plumbing tasks for your basement remodeling project.

General plumbing tools
These tools are useful no matter what material your pipes are made of. An **adjustable wrench** adjusts to grab nuts and bolts. Its one-size-fits-all jaws save you from rooting around in your toolbox for the right size open- or box-end wrench. A **locking adjustable wrench** is a handy variation on the same theme that quickly tightens on stubborn nuts and bolts. Press the lever for a quick release. A pair of **groove-joint pliers** is useful for tightening and loosening all sorts of joints. A 14-inch **pipe wrench** is the ideal size for most projects. (To add to its persuasive force, slip a 1¼-inch steel pipe over the handle to increase your leverage.) If you will be working on steel pipe, buy a pair of pipe wrenches (make one an 18-inch size).

A **putty knife** scrapes away old putty and other hardened debris. You'll need both **phillips** and **straight screwdrivers**—a **screwdriver with interchangeable bits** combines both types. Use a **wire brush** to clean parts and encrusted pipe threads.

A **strainer wrench** will help you tighten the upper part of the drain assembly in a sink or

Adjustable wrench

Groove-joint pliers

Putty knife

Pipe wrench

Locking adjustable wrench

SAFETY FIRST
Tools that protect

Whenever you do work that creates sparks or flying debris, wear **safety goggles.** And preserve your hearing when using power tools—or even a simple hammer—by wearing **ear protectors.**

Protect your hands with **leather gloves** when working with rough framing or cut pipes. When removing traps and toilets, wear long-sleeved clothing and **heavy-duty rubber gloves.**

Plug power tools into a **GFCI-protected extension cord,** which will shut off the moment it senses danger from exposure to water. (Cordless tools are safest.) When sweating joints, have a **fire extinguisher** nearby.

GFCI-protected extension cord

Fire extinguisher

Safety goggles

Ear protectors

Leather gloves

Heavy-duty rubber gloves

tub. To tighten a large nut like the one beneath a kitchen sink basket strainer, a **locknut wrench** is easier to use than groove-joint pliers. When repairing a faucet, you may need to get at the seat, a small part located inside the faucet body. Use a **seat wrench.** A **basin wrench** reaches into tight spaces to loosen or tighten hold-down nuts. Without this tool, removing a kitchen or bathroom faucet is nearly impossible.

Tools for plastic pipe
You can use just about any kind of saw to cut plastic pipe—a hacksaw, a standard backsaw, an ordinary handsaw, a circular saw, or even a power mitersaw. However, an inexpensive **plastic pipe saw** (also known as a PVC saw) cuts easily and leaves few burrs. Use it along with a **miter box** to ensure straight cuts in smaller pipe. For larger pipe mark the cut line and keep the saw perpendicular in all directions.

After cutting, you'll need to remove the burrs completely so the joints will fit tightly and stay that way. A **deburring tool** does the job better and more quickly than a utility knife.

To cut supply pipe (1 inch and smaller), you can also use a scissors-action **plastic pipe cutter.** Be sure to get a heavy-duty model made for PVC pipe. For PEX and other flexible tubing, a **plastic tubing cutter** makes a quick, clean cut.

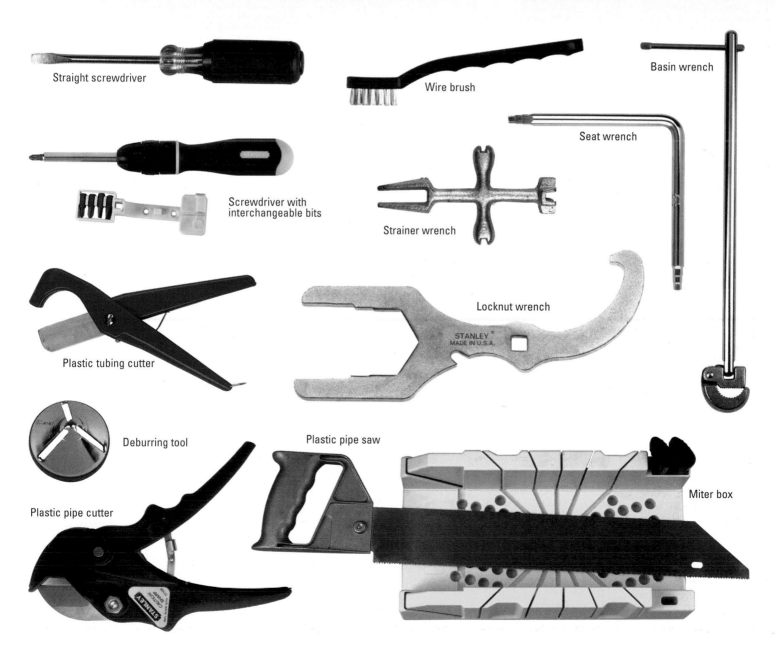

Straight screwdriver

Wire brush

Basin wrench

Screwdriver with interchangeable bits

Seat wrench

Strainer wrench

Plastic tubing cutter

Locknut wrench

Deburring tool

Plastic pipe saw

Plastic pipe cutter

Miter box

PLUMBING TOOLS (continued)

Tools for copper pipe

A **tubing cutter** cuts copper pipe cleanly, quickly, and without bending the pipe out of round. When working in tight spots, you might need a **small tubing cutter** as well. (A hacksaw will cut copper pipe, but it's hard to cut straight and the end is often dented and burred, making it very difficult to add fittings.)

To bend flexible pipe without crimping it, use a **tubing bender.** Choose the size that tightly slips onto the pipe. You might need a **flaring tool** for flare fittings. A **handle puller** smoothly detaches faucet handles without strain or damage.

To sweat copper pipe and fittings, buy a **propane torch.** A model with an **electric igniter** is easiest—and safest—to use. To protect flammable surfaces from the propane torch flame, use a **fiber shield** or prop an old cookie sheet behind the joint being heated.

The ends of copper pipe and the insides of fittings must be burnished before soldering. A **multiuse wire brush** does both jobs. Or buy a **reamer brush** for the fittings and a roll of **plumber's emery cloth** for the pipe ends. Before joining pipes, paint **flux** on the pipes using a **flux brush.**

Reamer brush

Tubing benders

Multiuse wire brush

Plumber's emery cloth

Small tubing cutter

Tubing cutter

Flux

Flux brush

Flaring tool

Handle puller

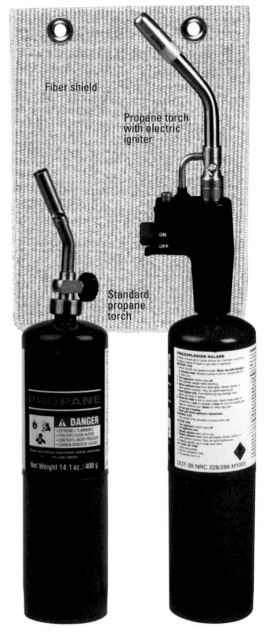

Fiber shield

Propane torch with electric igniter

Standard propane torch

WIRING TOOLS

Assembling a complete kit of quality electrician's tools will cost far less than hiring a professional to do the job.

Wiring tools

A pair of **diagonal cutters** makes working inside a crowded electrical box or snipping off sheathing from nonmetallic cable easier. **Cutting pliers** help with general chores such as snipping armored cable. Use **long-nose pliers** to bend wires into loops before attaching them to terminals. A **combination stripper** with wire holes near the tip is easier to use than those with holes near the handle. Use **lineman's pliers** to twist wires together; no other tool works as well. A **rotary screwdriver** works like a crank to drive screws quickly; use it when you have a number of coverplates to install.

Fishing tools

Tools designed for pulling wires help minimize damage to walls and ceilings when running cable to extend circuits or add new ones. In addition to a standard ¾-inch **spade bit,** buy a **fishing bit,** which can bore through two studs or joists and then pull a cable back through the holes it has made.

You can use a straightened coat hanger wire to fish cable through short runs, but a **fish tape** is easier to use. Occasionally you may need to run one tape from each direction, so buy two. Also use a fish tape when pulling wires through conduit.

Testers

For most work you will need a **voltage tester** to test for the presence of power. A **multitester** tests for voltage, checks devices for damage, and performs other functions. A **receptacle analyzer** shows if a receptacle is grounded and polarized.

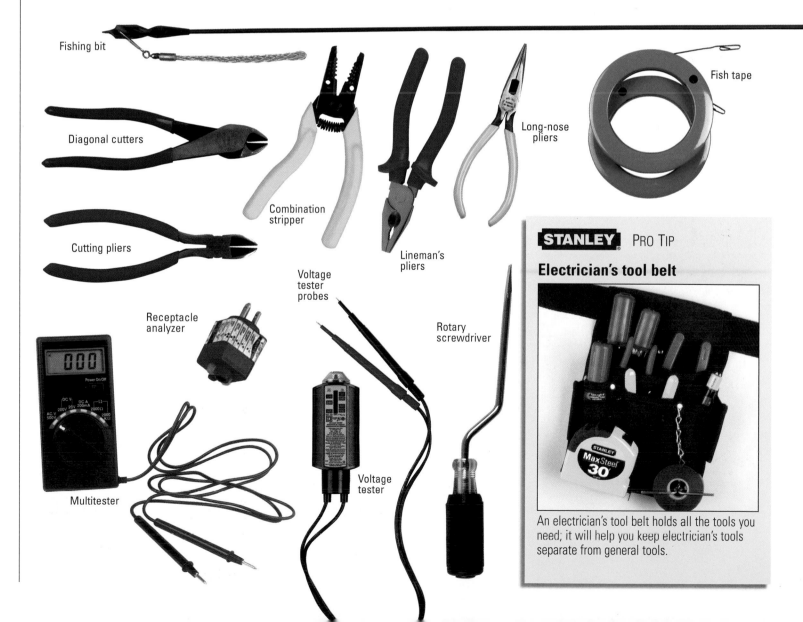

Fishing bit

Fish tape

Diagonal cutters

Long-nose pliers

Combination stripper

Cutting pliers

Lineman's pliers

Voltage tester probes

Receptacle analyzer

Rotary screwdriver

Multitester

Voltage tester

STANLEY PRO TIP

Electrician's tool belt

An electrician's tool belt holds all the tools you need; it will help you keep electrician's tools separate from general tools.

CHOOSING LUMBER

Much of the lumber you'll use in your remodeling project will be 2× (two-by) stock—lumber that when sawed from the tree was about 2 inches thick. A 2×4 is a standard construction size. Because lumber loses some of its thickness to shrinkage and planing, a 2×4 is about 1½ × 3½ inches. Board stock, nominally 1 inch thick, actually measures ¾ inch. The length of lumber is usually as stated or slightly longer.

In addition to 2×4s, your project might require some 2×6s (5½ inches wide),

2×8s (7¼ inches wide), 2×10s (9¼ inches wide), or 2×12s (11¼ inches wide).

Many home centers carry different grades of lumber. The grades indicate the relative quality of the wood. The better the grade, the fewer defects in the pieces and the higher the price. For framing, you can use standard grades of lumber; choose better grades for trimwork.

Along with grade, the species of the wood makes a difference in the price. Douglas fir, hemlock, or Southern pine yield strong

wood. Steel stud dimensions are the same as wooden studs. They are light and fireproof. You cut them with tin snips and join them with screws.

Your remodeling project may also call for sheet stock such as plywood, particleboard, oriented strand board (OSB), medium-density fiberboard (MDF), or medium-density overlay (MDO). These products come in 4×8-foot sheets, in thicknesses from ⅛ to 1¼ inches. Along with full sheets, many home centers sell quarter and half sheets.

Look for defects: Tight knots are no problem for framing. Reject pieces with knotholes, knots you can move with your fingers, checks (splits and cracks), and wanes (missing corners or edges). Sight along the edges to see if the piece is straight. A slight warp is OK, but reject boards that are severely bowed or twisted.

COMMON LUMBER DEFECTS

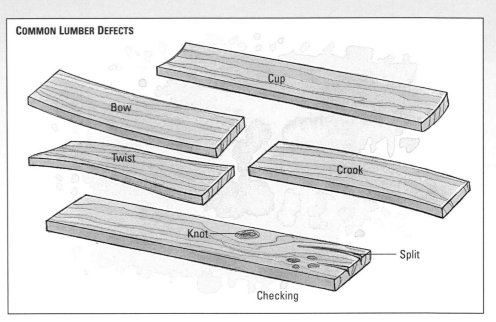

Cup

Bow

Twist

Crook

Knot

Split

Checking

PRO TIP

Buying the right length

Most framing lumber comes in standard lengths that start at 8 feet and increase in 2-foot increments. You may be able to reduce waste with some cutting. If you need a few 5-foot 2×4s, for instance, cut 10-footers into two 5-foot sections rather than cutting down 8-footers and leaving 3-foot scraps.

Which grade to buy?

For framing in most remodeling projects, buying the highest grade of lumber is a waste of money. Just avoid the worst pieces of a lesser grade and pick the best ones.

The grade stamp on a board tells you where the wood came from and what grade it received at the mill. The smaller the grade number, the higher the quality of the wood. Instead of a number, 2×4s are often stamped "STUD" to indicate they are suitable for this purpose. "Hem-Fir" means the wood is either hemlock or fir, two equally strong species. The WWP logo means the wood was graded under Western Wood Product Association rules, and "134" is the number of the mill that processed the wood. KD indicates the wood has been kiln-dried.

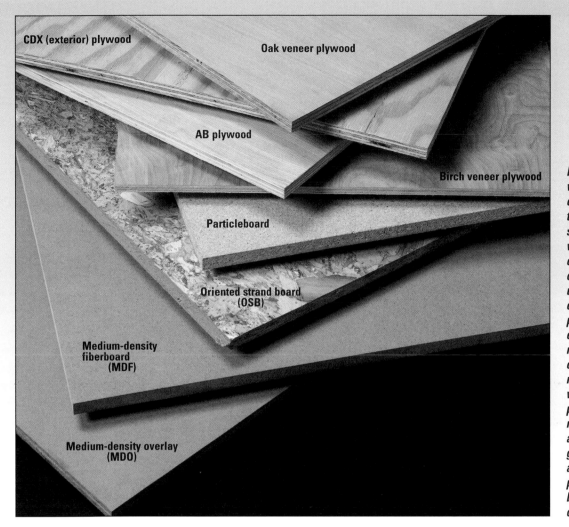

CDX (exterior) plywood

Oak veneer plywood

AB plywood

Birch veneer plywood

Particleboard

Oriented strand board (OSB)

Medium-density fiberboard (MDF)

Medium-density overlay (MDO)

Plywood is made of thin layers of wood called plies, or veneers, each with the grain 90 degrees to the previous layer. The resulting sheet is dimensionally stable and very strong. Particleboard is made of coarser wood particles. It is commonly used as floor underlayment. OSB, another engineered sheet made of bigger pieces of wood, is stronger than either MDF or particleboard but not as strong as plywood. It is commonly used for sheathing and roof decking. MDF is made of fine wood fibers that have been pressed and glued together. The resulting sheets are very smooth and flat. MDF paints well and is a good choice for interior shelving and painted cabinetry. MDO has a paper face designed to take paint beautifully. It is often used to make outdoor signs.

Reading the plywood stamp

When shopping for construction plywood, look for a grading stamp that says "APA The Engineered Wood Association." This stamp's meaning varies according to the intended use of the panel. For example, if the plywood is graded for sheathing outside walls, it will include the stud spacing on which it should be attached. For interior remodeling, the appearance of the face veneers is most important. Here are the characteristics of each face grade:

A—A smooth, paintable veneer free of knots and possessing only neatly made repairs that are parallel to the grain. It can be finished with a clear coat (rather than paint).

B—A solid-surface veneer that allows only small round knots, patches, and round repairs. Acceptable for the inside surfaces of a painted shelving unit.

C—Allows small knots, knotholes, and patches. Probably not used for an exposed face inside the house unless you are going for a rustic look. The lowest grade allowed for permanent exterior exposure.

D—This veneer can include large knots and knotholes. Acceptable only for a hidden face, such as the surface of a sheathing panel that faces inside the wall.

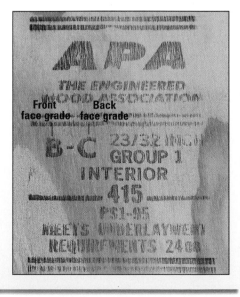

Front face grade | Back face grade

APA
THE ENGINEERED
WOOD ASSOCIATION
B-C 23/32 INCH
GROUP 1
INTERIOR
415
PS1-95
MEETS UNDERLAYMENT
REQUIREMENTS 24 oc

DRYWALL AND TRIM

The wall surface in most modern homes is drywall, a sheet material made of a thick layer of gypsum sandwiched between two layers of paper. The paper and gypsum work together, forming a strong, smooth building material. Mold-resistant paperless drywall is available for use in moisture-prone areas such as basements and bathrooms.

Drywall commonly comes in 4×8-foot sheets (they can be up to 16 feet long) and in ¼-, ⅜-, ½-, and ⅝-inch thicknesses. The ½-inch drywall is standard for most walls, but heavier, stiffer ⅝-inch sheets make a flatter wall and possess higher sound-deadening qualities. On ceilings, ⅝-inch drywall is less likely to sag than thinner

material, especially when attached to 24-inch on-center joists.

The long edges of the sheets are tapered to help create a flat seam at joints. The short edges or cut edges are flat. Recruit a helper or two before you hang drywall—it is heavy, unwieldy material.

⅜-inch drywall: Good for covering old walls and some curves

Moisture-resistant (MR) drywall: For use in humid or damp locations

¼-inch drywall: Good for curved surfaces

⅝-inch drywall: Good for firewalls and top-quality work

½-inch drywall: General purpose for walls and ceilings

Setting-Type Joint Compound

Durabond 45

Lightweight Setting-Type Joint Compound
Weighs up to 25% less.
Easy mixing, smooth applying.
Low shrinkage, excellent bond.

Easy Sand 20

Topping Joint Compound
Ready-Mixed/Non-Asbestos
USG
NET WT. 61.7 LB. (28 kg)

Spackling Powder
NET WT. 4.0 LB. (1.8 kg)

Lightweight All Purpose Joint Compound
Lower Shrinkage
Fewer Coats Over Metal
Easier Sanding
Plus 3
Ready Mixed
4.5 GAL. (17 L)

Lightweight All Purpose Joint Compound
Lower Shrinkage
Fewer Coats Over Metal
Easier Sanding
Plus 3
Ready Mixed
4.5 GAL. (17 L)

Drywall tape

All drywall joints must be taped, generally with either paper or fiberglass mesh tape. Paper tape is more time-consuming to install because you must embed it in a coat of compound. It is also prone to blistering and wrinkling.

Most fiberglass mesh tape is self-adhesive, which makes it easier to install. The nonadhesive variety requires staples to hold it in position. Installing fiberglass tape along inside corners can be a challenge unless you have a special application gun. Backerboard (a substrate for ceramic tile) requires a special type of fiberglass tape that resists deterioration from the chemicals in thinset mortar.

Working the corners

Applying joint compound to inside corners can be a real challenge, but composite and metal tapes help you get sharp corners, even if you're a novice. The folded tape creates a crisp line. For outside corners, use metal or vinyl corner beads. Specialized bead designs allow you to create bullnose inside and outside corners.

Trim lumber

Trim lumber differs in several ways from the lumber used in framing. It's drier (less subject to warping), has fewer defects (the

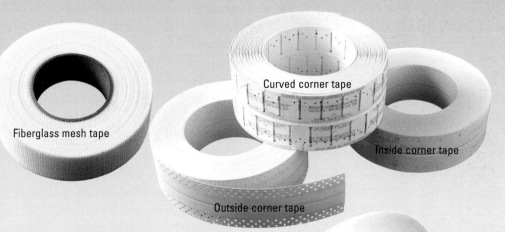

Fiberglass mesh tape

Curved corner tape

Inside corner tape

Outside corner tape

Flexible paper tape

number depends on the grade), and costs more.

Softwoods, such as redwood, cedar, pine, fir, and spruce, are cut from coniferous evergreen trees. They are light and easy to work with.

Hardwoods, such as oak, ash, poplar, walnut, and cherry, are produced by broad-leafed, deciduous trees. They offer stability, strength, machining predictability, and resistance to abuse.

Hardwood trees are not as abundant as softwood trees in North America, so their lumber is more costly.

Avoid using boards that display any of the major defects shown on page 42, especially ones that are warped. To check a board for warp, lay it on the floor and see if it lies flat. Reject boards with loose knots—they'll have a visible dark line around them and will work loose and eventually drop out. Tight knots, on the other hand, are structurally sound but must be coated with a sealer before painting so they don't weep sap and discolor the paint.

Hardwoods (and the best softwood grades) are also kiln-dried at a controlled temperature to reduce their moisture content to 6 to 9 percent, the ideal range for interior projects. Kiln-dried lumber won't readily reabsorb moisture when properly coated with a finish. That means it will remain stable in use and will be less likely to swell, shrink, crack, or warp over time.

Walnut

Philippine mahogany

Cherry

White ash

Red oak

Yellow poplar

STANLEY PRO TIP

Use setting compound for strength

You'll find joint compound packaged two ways: premixed in a bucket or as setting compound in a bag with numbers (90, 45, or 20) that indicate how long it takes to set up. Premixed compound is easier to apply and sand, but setting compound is stronger. You can smooth cured premixed compound with a sponge, which is faster and creates less dust. Setting compound is harder to sand, but you'll want its strength at outside corners, which are vulnerable to damage. Use the 90-minute mix. If you want it to set faster, mix it with warm water.

PIPES AND FITTINGS

When you install new fixtures in your basement remodeling project, you'll need to know what kind and what size of pipe to use. Newer homes usually have drainpipes made of plastic and supply pipes made of copper; a pre-1950 home may have cast-iron drainpipes and galvanized steel water supply pipes.

Plastic

Plastic pipe is inexpensive and easy to work with. Joints are glued together using a primer that cleans the surfaces and a cement that bonds them securely. Four different kinds of plastic are used in residential plumbing.

White or cream-color **PVC (polyvinyl chloride)** pipe is the most common choice for drainpipes. It's strong, lasts nearly forever, and is almost completely impervious to chemicals. PVC is sometimes used for supply pipes, but codes in most communities no longer allow it for hot water lines. That's because heat shrinks it and weakens the joints. To find out the strength (or "schedule") of a PVC pipe, look for stamped printing on it. In most localities schedule 40 is considered strong enough for residential purposes.

CPVC (chlorinated polyvinyl chloride) pipe has the strength of PVC and is also heat-resistant, so many (but not all) codes allow its use for interior supply lines.

Black **ABS (acrylonitrile butadiene styrene)** drainpipe was the first plastic pipe to be used in homes. Most localities no longer permit its use because it deteriorates rapidly. PVC is considered a superior material.

Flexible **PE (polyethylene)** supply pipe is the newest kind of plastic pipe, but many codes restrict its use. **PEX (cross-linked polyethylene)** is stronger and can handle hot as well as cold water.

Copper

Copper pipe is long-lasting and resists corrosion, making it ideal for water supply pipes. It is more expensive than plastic but still reasonably priced.

Rigid copper pipe comes in three wall thicknesses. The thinnest, rated "M," is considered by most local codes to be strong enough for residential purposes. Thicker pipes, rated "L" or "K," are used outdoors. To join rigid copper pipe, you sweat-solder the joint—heat it with a propane torch until molten solder flows freely into the joint.

Flexible copper tubing is used primarily to supply water to appliances or fixtures. You'll find small-diameter tubing carrying water to an icemaker. Larger tubing supplies a

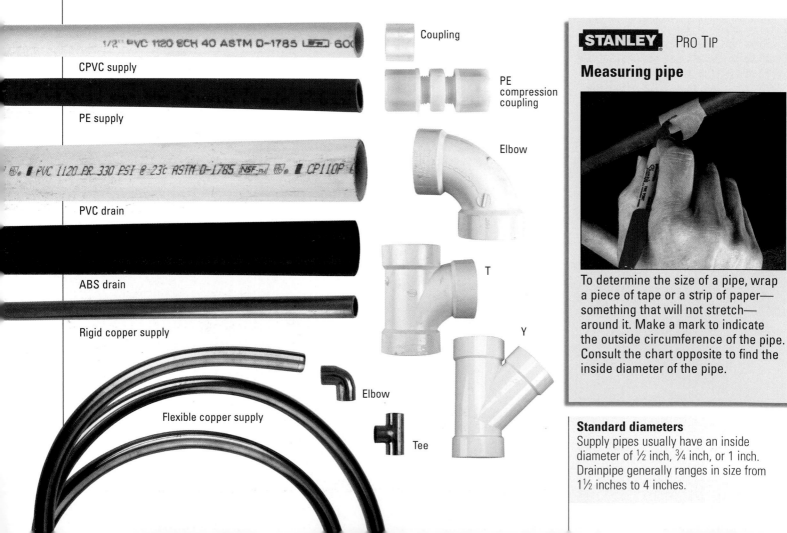

CPVC supply

PE supply

PVC drain

ABS drain

Rigid copper supply

Flexible copper supply

Coupling

PE compression coupling

Elbow

T

Y

Elbow

Tee

Measuring pipe

To determine the size of a pipe, wrap a piece of tape or a strip of paper—something that will not stretch—around it. Make a mark to indicate the outside circumference of the pipe. Consult the chart opposite to find the inside diameter of the pipe.

Standard diameters

Supply pipes usually have an inside diameter of ½ inch, ¾ inch, or 1 inch. Drainpipe generally ranges in size from 1½ inches to 4 inches.

dishwasher. The tubing is easily bent to make fairly tight turns. If it gets kinked, however, there's no way to fix it; the piece must be replaced. It is joined to fittings and valves using compression fittings.

Steel

Many older homes have **galvanized steel pipes** (also called galvanized iron pipe) for supply lines, and sometimes for branch drain lines as well. It has a dull gray color. Galvanized pipe is strong—a nail has a hard time piercing it—but its useful life is only 50 years or so. Joints rust and, more importantly, the galvanized surfaces attract minerals that build up in the pipe. The minerals clog the pipe, restricting the flow of water. Galvanized drainpipe rarely gets clogged enough to stop water from flowing, but the joints may leak.

Black steel pipe (also called black iron pipe) is used for gas lines only. It should not be used for water supply lines because it rusts quickly. (In some areas black steel is allowed for lines that supply a boiler that heats the house.) Black pipe with a yellow coating is used for underground gas lines.

To join steel pipe you must first wrap the threads with white PTFE tape (yellow for gas pipes) or brush them with pipe dope (a thick sealant that may be gray, white, or yellow), then tighten it. The joints must be very tight so they cannot be loosened without a long pipe wrench. Inadequately tightened joints will leak eventually.

Cast iron

Used only for drain lines and vents, **cast-iron pipe** is heavy and strong. Many people prefer it over plastic drainpipe because cast iron deadens the sound of running water, while plastic seems to amplify it.

Cast iron can last for more than a hundred years. However, it's not unusual for one or two sections to rust through while the rest of the pipe remains in good shape.

Traditionally cast-iron pipe is joined by first stuffing oakum (a loose rope of greasy fiber) into the recess of one pipe, fitting in the end of the next pipe, then pouring molten lead into the recess. Newer cast-iron pipe and no-hub fittings are joined with neoprene sleeves and clamps.

Fittings

Whenever pipe turns a corner or branches off, a fitting is required. **Elbows** (or Ls) make 90- or 45-degree turns. **Ts** and **Ys** are used where pipes branch off. **Couplings** join two pipes together.

PIPE SIZES

Material	Outside Circumference	Inside Diameter
Copper	2"	½"
	2¾"	¾"
	3½"	1"
Steel (galvanized or black)	2"	⅜"
	2⅜"	½"
	3⅛"	¾"
	4"	1"
	4¾"	1¼"
	5½"	1½"
	7"	2"
Plastic (PVC, CPVC, or ABS)	2¾"	½"
	3½"	¾"
	4¼"	1"
	5⅛"	1¼"
	6"	1½"
	7½"	2"
	10½"	3"
	14"	4"
Cast Iron	7"	2"
	10⅛"	3"
	13⅜"	4"

Coupling

Elbow

Union    T

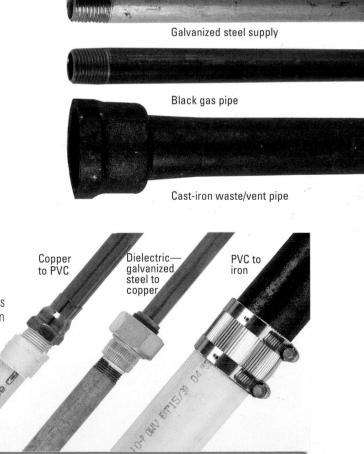

Galvanized steel supply

Black gas pipe

Cast-iron waste/vent pipe

Transition fittings

When changing from one pipe material to another, transition fittings are used. A steel-to-copper transition will corrode quickly unless a dielectric fitting is used—it has a plastic washer that separates the metals. Other transition fittings join copper to plastic, plastic to steel, and plastic to cast iron.

Copper to PVC

Dielectric— galvanized steel to copper

PVC to iron

CABLE AND WIRE

Most house wires—the wires that run from the service panel through walls to receptacle and switch boxes—are **solid-core**, meaning they are made of a single, solid strand. Light fixtures and some switches come with **leads**—wires made of many strands of thin wire, which are more flexible. The thicker a wire, the lower its number; for instance, #12 wire is thicker than #14.

Cable refers to two or more wires encased in a protective sheathing. Cable packaging tells the gauge and number of wires. For example "12/2 WG" means two (black and white) 12-gauge wires, plus a ground wire.

Nonmetallic (NM) cable, sometimes called Romex, has two or three insulated wires, plus a bare ground wire, wrapped in plastic sheathing. Many local codes permit NM cable inside walls or ceilings, and some codes allow it to be exposed in basements and garages. **Underground feed (UF) cable** has wires wrapped in solid plastic for watertight protection. Use it for outdoor projects and buried supply cable to outbuildings.

Armored cable encases insulated wires in metal sheathing for added protection. **Metal-clad (MC)** has a ground wire. **BX (also called AC)** has no ground wire, only a thin aluminum wire unsuitable as a ground; the metal sheathing provides the path for grounding. Some local codes require armored cable or conduit (below) wherever wiring is exposed.

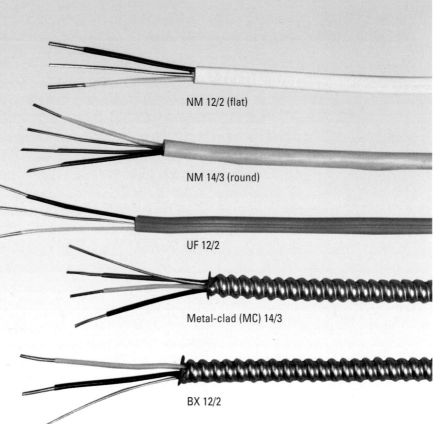

NM 12/2 (flat)

NM 14/3 (round)

UF 12/2

Metal-clad (MC) 14/3

BX 12/2

Conduit types

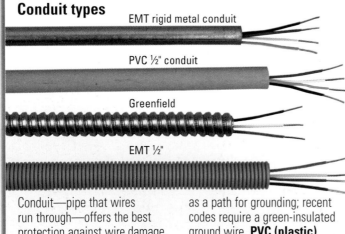

EMT rigid metal conduit

PVC ½" conduit

Greenfield

EMT ½"

Conduit—pipe that wires run through—offers the best protection against wire damage. It also makes it easy to change or install new wires in the future: Pull the wires through the conduit rather than cutting into walls to run new cable.

Metal conduit once was used as a path for grounding; recent codes require a green-insulated ground wire. **PVC (plastic) conduit** is cheaper but not quite as strong. Metal **Greenfield** and plastic **EMT tubing** are flexible types of conduit. They are expensive but useful when working in tight spots.

Wire colors and sizes

The thicker the wire, the more amperage (amps) it can carry without overheating. A 14-gauge wire carries up to 15 amps; a 12-gauge wire up to 20 amps; and a 10-gauge wire up to 30 amps. Never overload a wire; for instance, never place a 14-gauge wire on a 20-amp circuit.

Wires with insulation that is black, red, or another color are hot wires, carrying power from the circuit breaker in the service panel to the receptacle or switch box. (White neutral wires connect to the neutral bus in the service panel.) Green or bare wires are ground wires. **Beware, however: Electrical work might have been done incorrectly, so the wires could be the wrong color.**

HOT WIRES

14-gauge red

12-gauge blue

10-gauge brown

12-gauge black

GROUND WIRES

12-gauge green

12-gauge copper

ELECTRICAL BOXES

Wiring installation in a remodeling project usually begins by adding a box. All connections—whether splices or connections to terminals—must be made inside a code-approved box. (Some fixtures, such as fluorescent and recessed lights, have self-contained electrical boxes approved by most building departments.)

Plastic or metal?
Check with your building department to see whether plastic boxes are acceptable. Some municipalities require metal boxes, which are more expensive but usually no more trouble to install.

In older systems that use conduit or armored-cable sheathing as a grounding path, the boxes must be metal because they are part of the grounding system. Homes with NM or MC cable use green-insulated or bare copper wires for grounding and don't require metal boxes. However, some local codes call for metal boxes, which provide a more secure connection for the ground wire.

Remodel and new-work boxes
A remodel box has fittings that secure it to a finished wall. Plastic boxes have wings. Metal boxes feature expandable clips or bendable ears that hold them in the wall. Remodel boxes all have internal clamps that clasp the cable to the box.

New-work boxes install quickly in framing that has not been covered with drywall or plaster. To install most models, hold the box in place (the box should extend beyond the framing by the thickness of the wall material) and drive in two nails.

Octagonal box with nailing bracket

Single-gang box

Remodel box with wings

Two-gang box with stud catcher

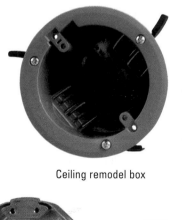

Gangable switch box

Ceiling remodel box

Remodel ceiling fan box with brace

STANLEY PRO TIP: **Buy boxes that are big enough**

Capacity label

To make sure a box will not be overcrowded, always buy as big a box as will fit the space available. The cubic-inch capacity of electrical boxes is usually marked on the box or the store bin. To calculate whether a box will be crowded, use these figures: A 14-gauge wire takes up 2 cubic inches; a 12-gauge wire takes up 2¼ cubic inches. Count the fixture or device as one wire. For instance this box contains eight 12-gauge "wires," two blacks, two whites, three grounds, and one receptacle—for a total of 18 cubic inches.

FASTENERS AND CLAMPS

In addition to cable and boxes, electrical jobs call for a few other supplies: tape, staples—or straps to secure cable to framing members—and clamps that hold cable to boxes.

Light fixtures usually come with all the necessary hardware for fastening to a ceiling box. If you have old boxes, you may need to buy extra hardware.

Cable fasteners

Codes require that all exposed cable be tightly stapled to the wall, ceiling, or a framing member. Also use staples when running cable in unfinished framing. For NM cable buy plastic-insulated staples that are the right size for the cable.

To anchor metal conduit, hammer in drive straps every few feet. For PVC conduit or armored cable, use one- or two-hole straps; make sure they fit snugly around the cable or conduit.

Avoid the black drywall (or all-purpose) screws because they break easily. Bugle-head woodscrews cost more but are more reliable and easier to drive.

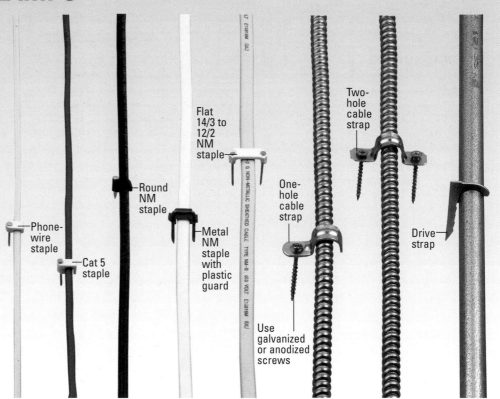

Phone-wire staple

Cat 5 staple

Round NM staple

Metal NM staple with plastic guard

Flat 14/3 to 12/2 NM staple

One-hole cable strap

Use galvanized or anodized screws

Two-hole cable strap

Drive strap

Clamp types

Built-in clamp

Armored cable clamp

NM cable clamp

New-work plastic boxes have holes with plastic flaps that lightly grab NM cable. With that type of box, you must staple the cable to a framing member near the box. Use these only in unfinished framing. When installing a remodel box or a box that will be exposed, the cable or conduit must be firmly clamped directly to the box.

A cable clamp comes in two parts: the clamp and the locknut. An NM clamp holds the cable using a strap with two screws; an armored-cable clamp holds the cable using a single setscrew.

For instructions on how to clamp cable to a box, see pages 104–105.

WIRE NUTS

In old installations wire splices often were covered with thick electrician's tape. That is not only a slow way to cover a splice, but it is also a code violation now. Cover every splice with an approved wire nut.

Assemble various sizes of nuts so you will be ready for any splice. Wire nuts are color-coded according to size. The colors and sizes may vary according to manufacturer. Read the containers to make sure the nuts you buy will fit over your splices. The most common arrangement is like this:

■ The smallest wire nuts—which usually come with a light fixture—are often white, ivory, or blue. If these have plastic rather than metal threads inside, throw them away and get orange connectors with metal threads for a secure connection.
■ Orange nuts, the next size up, can handle splices of up to two 14-gauge wires.
■ Midsize yellow wire nuts are the most common. Use them for splices as small as two 14-gauge wires or as large as three 12-gauge wires.

■ Red wire nuts, the largest size, can handle a splice of up to four 12-gauge wires.
■ Green wire nuts are used for ground wires. They have a hole in the top, which allows one ground wire to poke through and run directly to a device or box.
■ Gray twisters are designed as all-purpose wire nuts—they can handle the smallest to the largest splices. However, they are bulky and expensive.
■ B-cap wire nuts are slim, which makes them useful if a box is crowded with wires.

Two 16-gauge stranded wires

Two 14-gauge solid wires

Two 14-gauge solid ground wires

Three 12-gauge wires

Four 12-gauge wires

All-purpose twister wire nuts

Space-saving B-cap wire nuts

STANLEY PRO TIP: **Use high-quality tape**

Professional-quality electrician's tape costs more than bargain-bin tape, but it sticks better and is easier to work with.

You should cut pieces of tape rather than ripping them off the roll; ripped pieces have rippled ends that do not stick. Cutting with a utility knife is often awkward and time-consuming, so buy tape in a dispenser—just pull out and down to make a clean cut.

Grounding pigtail

Grounding screw

Grounding pigtail

If codes require you to attach grounds to metal boxes, save time and work by buying grounding pigtails. If your boxes do not already have them, buy green grounding screws that fit into threaded holes in the boxes.

RECEPTACLES

The 120-volt duplex receptacle (a receptacle with two outlets) is the workhorse of any residential electrical system. Because household wiring has remained standardized almost from the time it was first introduced, you can plug even the oldest tools and appliances into a new duplex receptacle.

Receptacles are easy to replace, so install new ones if your old receptacles are damaged, paint-encrusted, or simply ugly. However, do not replace an older, ungrounded receptacle with a three-hole receptacle unless you can be sure it will be grounded.

If the wires connecting to a receptacle are 12-gauge or thicker and it is protected by a 20-amp circuit breaker or fuse, you can safely install a 20-amp receptacle. Otherwise, install a standard 15-amp receptacle. Amp ratings are printed or stamped on the side of the receptacle.

Some people prefer to mount the receptacle in the box with the ground hole on top; others prefer it on the bottom. In terms of safety, it does not matter. For appearance, be consistent.

Standard receptacles are fine for most purposes. But if a receptacle will receive a lot of use or is in a high-traffic area—a busy hallway, for example—purchase a spec-rated or commercial receptacle, which is stronger and more resistant to damage.

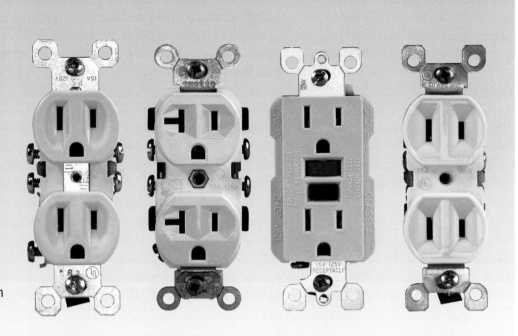

The most common electrical device in your home is probably a **grounded 15-amp, 120-volt receptacle.** It supplies adequate power for all but the most power-hungry appliances and tools.

If a receptacle's neutral slot (the longer one) has a horizontal leg, the receptacle is rated at 20 amps. Codes often call for **20-amp receptacles** in kitchens or work-shops, where power use is heavy.

A **GFCI** (ground fault circuit interrupter) receptacle provides extra protection against shocks and is required by code in damp areas.

An **ungrounded receptacle** has two slots and no grounding hole. One slot is longer than the other on a polarized receptacle.

240-volt receptacles

Appliances that use 240 volts are all rated for certain levels of amperage and have plugs configured to fit only one type of receptacle. Here are the common types:

A **dryer receptacle** supplies the heating element with 240 volts and the timer and buzzer with 120 volts. The receptacle shown requires four wires; older models use only three wires.

An **electric range receptacle** also provides both 240 volts and 120 volts.

This single-outlet **air-conditioner receptacle** provides 240 volts only. Check your air-conditioner to make sure its amperage and plug configuration match the receptacle.

SWITCHES

Turn a switch on and it completes the circuit, letting electricity flow through it. Turn it off, and the circuit is broken; the switch creates a gap that stops the flow.

Essential switches

The most common household switch, a single-pole, has two terminals and simply turns power on or off.

A three-way switch has three terminals; a four-way has four. These are used to control a light from two or three locations, such as in a stairwell, at either end of a hallway, or in a room with more than one entrance.

A dimmer switch controls a light's intensity. Usually you can replace any single-pole switch with a dimmer. However, buy a special fan or fluorescent dimmer switch to control a fan or a fluorescent light.

Special switches

In addition to the familiar toggle and rotary switches, specialty switches can do everything from turning on when you walk into a room to varying the speed of whole-house fans. You'll also find special-duty switches that can be time-programmed or that let you know if a remote light is on or off. Decorative switches include styles that rock back and forth or slide up and down rather than toggling.

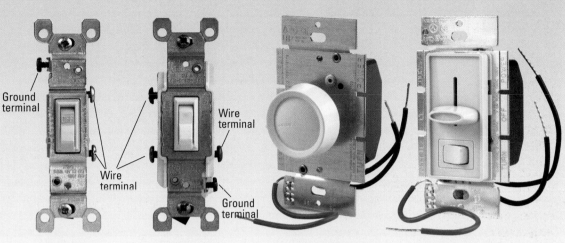

Ground terminal

Wire terminal

Wire terminal

Ground terminal

Wire terminal

A **single-pole** switch has two terminals and a toggle labeled ON and OFF. Always connect two hot wires to it, not two neutrals.

A **three-way** switch has three terminals, and its toggle is not marked for on or off.

A **rotary dimmer** switch is the most common type. Some styles look like toggle switches.

A **sliding dimmer** with an on/off toggle turns a light on to the brightness you left the last time the light was on.

Two ways to wire a switch

End-line switch wiring: If power goes to the fixture first and then to the switch, you have end-line wiring. Only one cable enters the box, coming from the fixture. Here, the white wire is taped or painted black to indicate that it is hot.

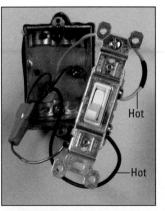

Hot

Hot

Power through switch: With through wiring, power enters the switch box. The feed wire (the hot wire coming from the service panel) runs to the switch before it goes to the fixture. Two cables enter the box—one coming from power and one going to the fixture.

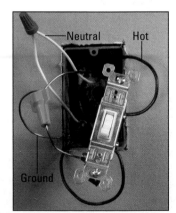

Neutral

Hot

Ground

The neutrals are spliced, and a hot wire connects to each terminal.

To ground or not to ground?

Your switches may not have a grounding screw terminal—the ground wire may travel past the switch to the light fixture. This is not unsafe, but recent building codes call for switches to be grounded.

PREPARATION & DEMOLITION

If you're remodeling existing finished spaces in your basement, the first stage of your project might include some demolition. Demolition is hard, messy work, but it can be rewarding. It moves along quickly, progress is instantly visible, and knocking things apart can be fun—remember how flattening a sand castle was usually more fun than building it?

Demolition with forethought

Before you start tearing things down, decide whether you want to salvage any building materials. Wood moldings, for example, can be difficult to match. But even if they are readily available, you can save money by reusing the old ones. You can also reuse framing lumber after you remove the nails. After deciding what to salvage, your primary objective will be to contain dust and debris.

Dust control

Some easy methods will help you isolate the work site from the rest of the house.
■ If you are tearing out a wall or doing other dirty work in a room where you want to save the carpet, protect it with reinforced-plastic tarps. Tape the tarp to the floor to keep it in place.
■ Lay tarps at the top of the basement stairs to keep from tracking dust and debris onto upstairs floors.
■ Tape plastic over doorways you won't use or tack up an old bedsheet as a curtain for doorways you will go through.
■ If the demolition room has a window, open it and set a box fan in it to blow airborne dust out.
■ Keep dust from spreading into other rooms by taping cardboard over heat and return-air ducts. Or you can remove them, wrap them with plastic, and replace them.

■ Set a small rug (a carpet sample works well) just outside the door of the work area to remove debris from your shoes. Slip into a pair of slippers and leave your work shoes behind at the end of the day.

Cleanup

If the work area is small, bag debris and put it out with the trash. Construction debris is heavy; don't overfill containers. Use heavyweight or doubled bags. Rent a roll-off waste container for debris if your project is large.

A shop vacuum makes quick work of construction dust, but most standard filters can't deal with the fine dust generated by demolition. To trap fine particles, some vacuum manufacturers make bags that fit over the regular filters. You might be able to retrofit your vacuum with an aftermarket filter.

In some places you can donate salvaged building materials to groups that recycle them.

CHAPTER PREVIEW

Is this wall structural?
page 56

What's in the wall?
page 57

Removing old surfaces and framing
page 58

Keeping the water out
page 60

Plan your demolition and preparation work in sections and do the easy tasks before the hard ones. Remove the trim and molding before taking up any old flooring material. Then make sure the basement floor is level and flat before starting any renovation activities.

Installing a sump pump
page 62

Preparing a slab floor
page 64

IS THIS WALL STRUCTURAL?

When you plan a remodeling job you will probably encounter details of your home's construction that you hadn't noticed before. Things you considered permanent before—walls, for example—may not seem that way anymore. You'll soon realize that almost any alteration is possible if you are willing to do the work and bear the expense. Before you start knocking down walls, however, you need to understand that there are two kinds of walls in a building: bearing (or structural) walls and nonbearing (or partition) walls.

Bearing walls help carry the weight of the structure and contents of the upper stories to the ground. **Partition walls** simply divide interior space. It is far simpler to remove or relocate a partition wall than it is to alter a bearing wall. Removing a bearing wall is costly and time-consuming. If not done correctly, it can weaken the structure of the house and make it unsafe. In many cases it would be better to redesign your project than to remove or modify a bearing wall.

How to spot the difference

One of the first steps in planning a remodeling project is to determine whether an interior wall is a bearing wall.

If a basement wall runs parallel to the ceiling joists above it, it is probably not a bearing wall. Short closet walls, for example, or those surrounding a basement bath or shower are usually not bearing walls. If the wall runs perpendicular to the ceiling joists, there is a good chance it is a bearing wall.

How can you tell which way the joists run if the ceiling is covered? One way is to look at the direction of the ridgeline of the roof.

In most houses, joists run perpendicular to the ridgeline. If you're still not sure, you can look for fasteners in the ceiling or take down part of the ceiling material.

Another test is to determine whether there is a wall running the same direction exactly above the one you want to remove or modify. If there is, the basement wall is probably a bearing wall. If the wall is built under an overhead beam or incorporates posts or piers, you can assume it's a load-bearing wall.

If you still have doubts, hire an engineer to inspect the wall. A small fee will buy you a lot of comfort. If you do decide to remove a bearing wall, you'll have to build a temporary support wall a few feet away from it, tear out the old wall, and install a post-supported beam in its place. You may want to have professionals do this work.

IDENTIFYING A BEARING WALL

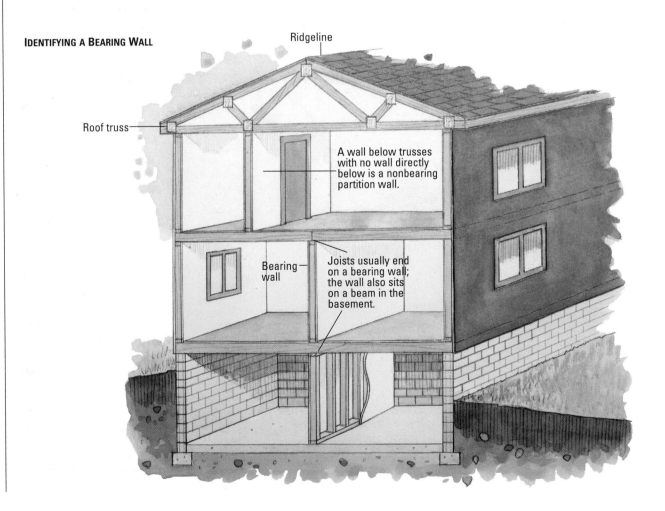

Ridgeline

Roof truss

A wall below trusses with no wall directly below is a nonbearing partition wall.

Bearing wall

Joists usually end on a bearing wall; the wall also sits on a beam in the basement.

WHAT'S IN THE WALL?

When you start thinking about modifying existing frame walls in your basement, first consider what might be running through them, hidden behind the drywall. The walls in most houses, even basement walls, are often strung with a network of wires, pipes, and ductwork. Moving or taking out a wall may require rerouting one or more of these hidden systems.

At the very least, most walls contain some electrical wiring—a certainty if there are receptacles or switches on the wall. Even without those indicators, wiring might be routed through the wall, so use caution when poking through or cutting the surface.

Before you remove the drywall, do a little sleuthing to figure out what you might run into. Go upstairs and see what's immediately above the basement wall. Look for electrical outlets, switches, heat registers, cold-air returns, and plumbing fixtures. Any of these items may mean there are wires, ductwork, or pipes in the basement wall below. Look for wires, ducts, or pipes entering the wall in the basement.

Mark new routes for wires, ducts, and pipes on your plan. If you decide not to reroute the lines yourself, leave them in place and call in a trade professional. Most plumbers and electricians will want to see the original layout before tearing it out.

 PRO TIP

Schedule the pros

If you discover something in a wall you don't feel qualified to tackle, hire a professional to do the job. If you do hire a plumber, electrician, or HVAC (heating, ventilation, and air-conditioning) contractor, schedule the first visit before you start demolition. Altering utility systems usually requires more than one working session— one to disconnect and a second to reconnect after you frame the new walls.

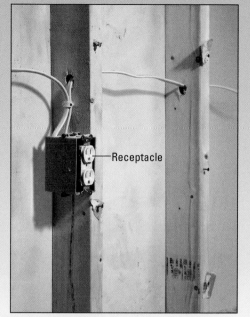

Electrical wiring is found in most walls. Most receptacles are wired to circuits in other walls, so you may have to reroute the wiring in more than one room. Check both sides of a wall as well as those in neighboring rooms.

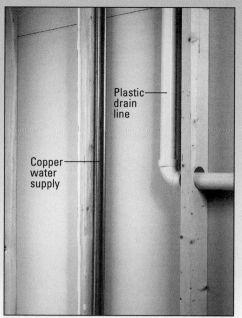

Plumbing can be hidden behind the surface too. If a bathroom or kitchen is located directly above the wall you intend to work on, you will probably find pipes in that wall.

Heating and air-conditioning ductwork is difficult to trace. Often second-floor vent lines and return-air lines pass through stud bays but are difficult to spot from underneath because other ducts block them from view.

Drain-waste-vent lines can be trickier to locate than plumbing supply lines; they take less direct routes. Besides being much larger than supply lines, drains and vents often run from the basement through the roof—moving the wall can require extensive rerouting.

REMOVING OLD SURFACES AND FRAMING

Taking off trim and baseboards is the first step in demolition. Slide a wide putty knife under the trim and pry it until you can insert a flat pry bar behind the wood. Move along the trim with the pry bar, keeping the putty knife behind it for added leverage.

Before you remove any old drywall, make sure you won't damage any hidden utility lines. Tap the wall with a screwdriver handle to find a spot that sounds hollow. That's the place to make your first hole with the hammer.

Use a heavy-duty paint scraper or chisel to remove construction-adhesive residue. Soften up stubborn spots with construction-adhesive remover.

When taking out old framing, you can beat the studs with a sledgehammer, but cutting the nails will allow you to reuse the lumber. After removing the studs, pry off the top and bottom plates.

PRESTART CHECKLIST

☐ **TIME**
 Trim and molding: About 10 minutes per lineal foot
 Drywall: 1 to 2 hours per 4×8 sheet
 Framing: From 5 to 15 minutes per framing member
 Flooring: From 30 to 45 minutes per square yard

☐ **TOOLS**
 Hammer, pry bar, utility knife, groove joint pliers, cordless drill, reciprocating saw, floor scraper, small sledge, cold chisel, putty knife, heat gun, spray adhesive remover

☐ **SKILLS**
 Prying, pulling nails, removing screws, cutting, scraping

☐ **PREP**
 Isolate the work site to contain the mess; determine what utilities may be contained within the wall

Removing wood shoe molding and baseboards

1 Starting at a corner, slide a small pry bar behind the shoe. Loosen the shoe until you can insert the pry bar next to a nail. Pry the nail out a little at a time. To avoid splits, loosen at least two nails before pulling the molding completely off the wall.

2 Begin at a corner or at a mitered joint, working a wide putty knife behind the baseboard. Loosen each nail with a pry bar. Keep the putty knife behind the bar to increase your leverage. Loosen all nails before removing a baseboard section.

Removing drywall

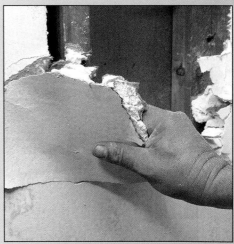

1 Use a hammer to punch a hole in the drywall between the studs. (If the surface is tiled, it may help to shatter one or two tiles in the center of the wall first.) Enlarge the hole until you can put your hand or the end of a pry bar into it.

2 Grab an edge of the hole you have made and pull off the drywall. To remove large sections, space your hands as far apart as possible. Use a pry bar if necessary. Pull the remaining nails. Check for rot and mold.

Removing wood framing

1 Cut through the nails between the bottom of the stud and the plate with a reciprocating saw. Be sure to use a metal-cutting blade.

2 Knock the bottom of the stud sideways with a hammer to free the bottom. With the bottom loose, twist and lever the stud free of the nails that hold it to the top plate. Remove the nails as you go.

Removing resilient tile

Warm the adhesive with a heat gun. If you don't have a heat gun, use a hair dryer set on high heat. Warm a corner first, insert a floor scraper or wide putty knife, and with the heat on, lift up the tile. Scrape the adhesive from the floor with a floor scraper.

Removing sheet flooring

Insert a floor scraper or wide putty knife under the sheet at a corner and pry it up. Work down each strip of the material, rolling the strip as you go, using a hair dryer to soften the adhesive. Then spray adhesive remover, let it work, and scrape the residue from the floor.

Removing ceramic tile

Crack one tile with a small sledge and cold chisel to make a starting point in the middle of the floor. Break out the remaining area and chip out the grout along the edge of an adjacent tile. Tap a wide chisel under the edge of the tiles and pop them off the floor.

Removing carpet

Grab a corner of the carpet with groove-joint pliers and pull it off the tack strips. Then pull it up off the entire floor. Cut the pad into strips with a utility knife and pull the strips from the floor. Then work a pry bar under the tacking strips and pry them up.

KEEPING THE WATER OUT

Basement walls and floors are especially vulnerable to moisture damage, which can ruin a floor. Don't install any kind of flooring until you fix water problems.

Condensation on water pipes and walls occurs in hot weather and is not technically a water problem. Increasing the ventilation, insulating the pipes, or installing a dehumidifier can relieve condensation.

To control seepage from the groundwater, install new gutters or fix the existing ones, then slope the soil away from the foundation for about 4 feet so water runs away and doesn't seep through the walls. Sealing the interior surface of the walls with hydraulic cement and patching the holes can also cure seepage problems. If neither method helps, consult a drainage specialist.

Moisture seeping up through the slab is more difficult to correct. For minor problems, a waterproofing membrane on the slab will often eliminate water migration through it. The best way, however, is to install a sump pump, removing some of the slab to install drainpipes (pages 62–63).

PRESTART CHECKLIST

☐ **TIME**
About 1 hour to seal a 6-foot wall

☐ **TOOLS**
Wire brush, small sledge and cold chisel, trowel, paint brush

☐ **SKILLS**
Brushing walls, keying cracks, and applying liquid waterproofing agents

☐ **PREP**
Check for moisture and eliminate outside seepage

☐ **MATERIALS**
Hydraulic cement or urethane caulk, muriatic acid, waterproofing agent, foam backer rod

1 Using a wire brush, remove as much loose mortar and paint as you can. Remove efflorescence (salts that leach to the surface of the wall and appear as a white deposit) with muriatic acid, following the manufacturer's instructions. Rinse the wall and let it dry.

2 Using a small sledge and cold chisel, key the cracks in the wall—hold the chisel at an angle and undercut the edges of the crack so the bottom of the crack is wider than the opening. Keyed cracks help keep the patching cement in place. Vacuum the crack to remove the dust.

SOLVING MOISTURE PROBLEMS

Preventing Condensation

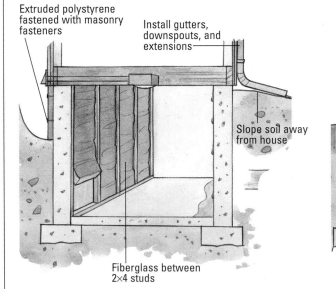

Extruded polystyrene fastened with masonry fasteners

Install gutters, downspouts, and extensions

Slope soil away from house

Fiberglass between 2×4 studs

Venting Crawlspaces

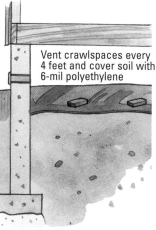

Vent crawlspaces every 4 feet and cover soil with 6-mil polyethylene

Caulking wide cracks

3 If the area is not already wet, mist it with a spray bottle. Then force a small amount of hydraulic cement into the crack with a trowel and smooth it down. Apply hydraulic cement where the wall meets the floor also.

4 When the hydraulic cement cures, brush on two coats of a high-quality interior waterproofing paint.

You can plug wide cracks with hydraulic cement or a high quality urethane caulk. Press foam backer rod into a wide crack before applying caulk.

Interior Drainage System

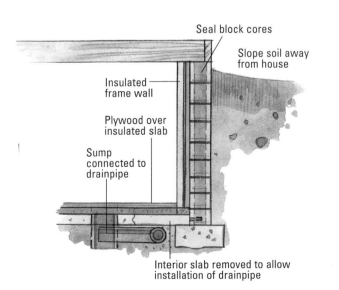

Seal block cores

Slope soil away from house

Insulated frame wall

Plywood over insulated slab

Sump connected to drainpipe

Interior slab removed to allow installation of drainpipe

Exterior Drainage System

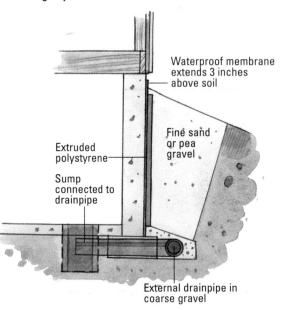

Waterproof membrane extends 3 inches above soil

Fine sand or pea gravel

Extruded polystyrene

Sump connected to drainpipe

External drainpipe in coarse gravel

INSTALLING A SUMP PUMP

If your basement floods or gets damp in wet weather, even after you divert water away from the foundation walls, a sump pump may be the solution.

Choose from two types of installations:

If your basement has no drainpipes beneath it designed to handle rainwater, then dig a hole at a low point of the basement floor and install a perforated pit liner (you may have to perforate it yourself using a ⅜-inch spade bit and electric drill). Water under the basement floor will slowly percolate into the liner.

If your floor already has rainwater drainpipes, it probably also has a pit for a sump pump with a drainpipe running into it. Purchase a nonperforated pit liner and cut a hole for the drainpipe. If you want to install drain lines, break out the slab along the perimeter of the floor and bed the pipes in gravel. Add a rechargeable battery backup unit to power the pump if the power goes out. A pump-failure alarm is also a good addition.

PRESTART CHECKLIST

☐ **TIME**
About half a day to dig a pit and install a sump pump

☐ **TOOLS**
Sledgehammer or electric jackhammer, cold chisel, drill with masonry bit and spade bit, hole saw, PVC saw, small level, screwdriver, groove-joint pliers

☐ **SKILLS**
Basic carpentry skills, cutting and joining PVC drainpipe

☐ **PREP**
Locate a low spot in the basement near a wall so the pump won't take up usable space. If necessary, install a GFCI receptacle nearby.

☐ **MATERIALS**
Sump pump, pit liner, PVC drainpipe, primer, cement

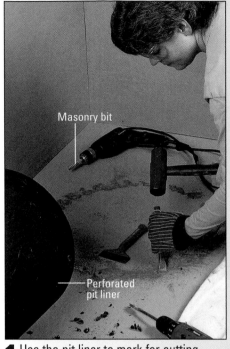

1 Use the pit liner to mark for cutting a hole in the basement floor. Using a masonry bit, drill a series of holes around the perimeter. (A concrete basement floor is usually 3 inches thick.) Chip out the concrete with a sledge and cold chisel or an electric jackhammer (page 94).

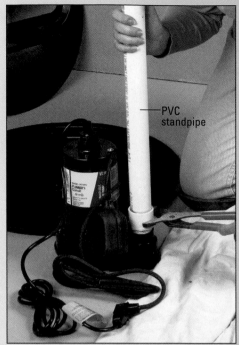

2 Dig the hole deep enough for the pit liner and set the pit liner in place. Make sure the liner is resting solidly on the ground so it can support the pump. Attach a PVC standpipe to the unit, using the adapter parts supplied by the manufacturer.

INSTALLING A
SUMP PUMP

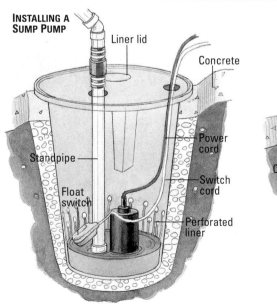

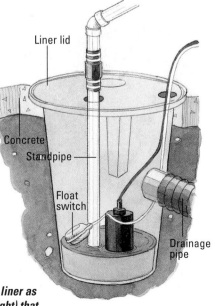

A retrofit sump pump (above) empties a perforated pit liner as water seeps in. Newer homes have drainage pipes (right) that feed into the pit liner. Both can use the same sump pump setup.

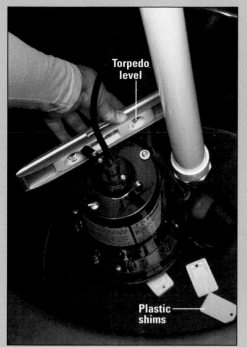

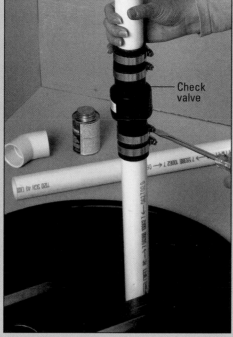

3 Set the pump on the bottom of the liner. It should be near the center so the float won't touch the side of the liner. Check to make sure the pump is level; insert plastic shims underneath it if necessary. Place the lid on the liner.

4 Just above the level of the floor, install a check valve, which ensures that water does not backflow into the pump. Run PVC pipe up and toward the exit point. Clamp the electrical wires to the side of the pipes. Plug the unit into a GFCI receptacle.

5 Cut a hole through the rim joist for the pipe to exit the house. Run PVC pipe out of the house and extend it so it carries water at least 6 feet away from the house. Water that is discharged near the house will seep back into the basement.

BREAK OUT THE SLAB

To add drain lines for your sump pump, break out 15 to 18 inches of the slab along the wall. Dig a trench to the depth required for your pit liner and install drain lines in a bed of gravel. Install the pit liner, backfill the trench with gravel, and repour the concrete.

Pedestal sump pump

A pedestal-type sump pump has its motor above the water and is not waterproof. Use this kind for a basement that needs frequent draining; its float can be adjusted. This type is less expensive than a submersible but is also noisier.

Ejector pump for gray water

If your drain lines are above floor level and you want to install a utility sink, the simplest solution is a gray-water sump box. It must be connected to the house's drain and vent lines. To provide drainage for a toilet as well, install an upflushing unit (page 177).

PREPARING A SLAB FLOOR

No matter what kind of finished flooring you plan to install in your new basement rooms, the slab must be solid, smooth, and level. Inspect its condition before you build new framing and install any flooring materials. First look for large cracks and sagging sections. If they're present, the base is not adequate—you'll need to remove sagging sections and pour new concrete.

Cover isolated, inactive cracks with an isolation membrane. Completely cover new concrete and any floors you suspect might develop cracks. Fix active cracks—those that are growing longer or wider—instead of covering them up. Active cracks can be an indication of serious structural problems and can pull the floor apart.

PRESTART CHECKLIST

☐ **TIME**
From 30 to 45 minutes per square yard

☐ **TOOLS**
Repair or degloss surface: 4-foot level, sledgehammer, cold chisel, margin and mason's trowels, grinder, masonry-grit abrasive wheel, vacuum, brush, mop
Repair structural defect: sledge, crowbar, wheelbarrow
Install membrane: roller, mason's trowel

☐ **SKILLS**
Using a level, troweling, grinding with power grinder

☐ **PREP**
Remove finished flooring

☐ **MATERIALS**
Repair/degloss surface: hydraulic cement or thinset, muriatic acid, rubber gloves
Repair structural defect: gravel, reinforcing wire, concrete mix, 2×4 screed
Install membrane: membrane, adhesive

1 Divide the slab into imaginary 6-foot sections and check each section with a 4-foot level. Mark cracks, high spots, and other defects with a carpenter's pencil.
Cracks may be a sign of a structural defect. Some may be repairable. Others may require professional help.

2 Use a small sledge and a cold chisel to open small cracks so you can fill them. If possible, angle the chisel into each side of the crack to create a recess wider at the bottom of the crack than on top. This will help hold the patching cement securely.

Self-leveling compounds

Self-leveling compounds, technically not a substrate, are used to level depressions in slabs and subfloors. Most call for only light mixing with water and level themselves when poured. Quick-setting brands allow tiling within hours.

Self-leveling compounds work best when applied in thicknesses of less than 1 inch. If using a compound to fill a deeper depression, make more than one pour, but check the manufacturer's directions first.

Pour the compound after completing all other repair work. Doing so ensures that the compound stays clean and ready for tiling.

Commercially applied gypsum-based compounds are excellent for leveling floors on which surface radiant heating systems have been installed.

3 Wash out the crack with water and fill it with quick-setting hydraulic cement or thinset. Use a margin trowel or mason's trowel and feather out the edges until the patch is level with the surrounding surface.

4 To fill depressions in the slab, pour a small amount of thinset or self-leveling compound into the depression and trowel it level. Add thinset or compound until the surface is level and feather the edges of thinset even with the floor.

5 Grind down high spots you have marked using a grinder equipped with a masonry-grit abrasive wheel. A right-angle grinder makes this job go quickly. Hold a vacuum hose near the grinder to remove the dust as you work. Vacuum and damp-mop the surface thoroughly.

Repairing structural defects

Large holes, cracks with uneven surfaces, and sunken areas are signs of structural defects in a slab. Repair these defects before installing new flooring materials.

For most repairs, you'll have to break the concrete into manageable pieces and remove it. The remaining hole must be excavated an additional 4 inches and filled with a 4-inch gravel layer. New concrete calls for reinforcing wire and screeding (leveling) with a long 2×4. Let the patch cure for three to seven days.

Fixing structural defects in a slab is a formidable job. Consult with a specialist before tackling it yourself. Contracting the work is often more cost-effective.

Apply an isolation membrane (slip sheet) over cracks

1 Apply the membrane adhesive equally on both sides of a crack or expansion joint. Use a roller to apply the adhesive and spread on a light but even coat.

2 Follow the manufacturer's instructions to apply the membrane to cured or wet adhesive. Apply the membrane over the adhesive, following the contour of the crack across the surface.

FRAMING
FLOORS & WALLS

When you start framing floors and walls, the pieces go together quickly so you instantly see signs of progress. The actual assembly of a floor or wall frame is the easiest part of the job. What takes time is accurately laying out the parts. An accurate layout assures you of a structure that is straight, with joists or studs on 16-inch centers. Framing that's properly laid out makes flooring and drywall installation easier.

Choosing lumber
Quality framing starts in your lumberyard or home center by buying the straightest and most defect-free stock you can find.

Examine each board carefully. A few tight knots are acceptable, but a board with several defects (see page 42) should be rejected. Lumber is inspected and graded, but within most stacks of lumber you'll find some boards you should avoid. With a little patience, you'll go home with lumber that won't cause you problems during construction.

Partition walls (the most common ones in a remodeling project) are typically framed with 2×4 studs between 2×4 top and bottom plates. If your basement remodeling plan calls for a new wall thick enough to house large drainpipes, use 2×6 or larger stock throughout that wall.

Wood or metal framing
Wood is the traditional material for interior walls. It's easier to preassemble a wood wall than to build it in place if you have enough floor space to lay out all the pieces. If you're short on floor space, build a wood wall in place or use metal framing. Lightweight, galvanized steel framing is easy to handle, won't burn, and is rust-resistant. Besides, there's no tedious lumber-sorting in the quest for straight studs. Metal studs are formed straight at the factory and stay that way. After you've run the utility lines in a wood or metal wall, add insulation between the studs for soundproofing.

You'll see your progress quickly when you are framing new rooms.

CHAPTER PREVIEW

Framing sleeper floors
page 68

Framing a wood stud wall
page 70

Framing a wall with metal studs
page 72

Framing for masonry walls
page 76

The easiest way to build a partition wall is to preassemble the plates and studs on the floor, then stand the wall in place.

Building soffits and chases
page 78

Adding an egress window
page 80

FRAMING SLEEPER FLOORS

You can install laminate, engineered wood, resilient flooring, and many other finished flooring materials directly over a dry concrete slab, but a wooden subfloor helps insulate the flooring from the cold concrete. It also adds a little cushion to the hard surface of the concrete. A wooden subfloor will not cure moisture problems however. Moisture that comes up through the slab will ultimately find its way into your finished floor. Cure the moisture problem before you install the floor.

Headroom in most basements is at a premium. To make low floor framing that will conserve headroom, lay pressure-treated 2×4s (sleepers) flat and cover them with ¾-inch tongue-and-groove OSB underlayment or exterior plywood.

Prepare the slab by vacuuming it thoroughly, then seal it with an asphalt primer and a layer of asphalt mastic. Lay a moisture barrier (6 mil polyethylene is often used) and mark the plastic sheet with a felt marker so you can position the sleepers on 16-inch centers.

PRESTART CHECKLIST

☐ **TIME**
About 8 hours for a 10×10 floor

☐ **TOOLS**
Circular saw, level, powder-actuated gun, cordless drill

☐ **SKILLS**
Measuring and marking, cutting lumber, installing mastic and waterproofing membrane using powder-actuated fasteners

☐ **PREP**
Clean and repair floor

☐ **MATERIALS**
Polyethylene membrane, tape, powder-actuated fasteners, shims, screws, ¾" tongue-and-groove OSB underlayment or exterior plywood, pressure-treated 2×4s

1 Prepare the floor by vacuuming it and installing a waterproofing membrane on asphalt mastic. Overlap the seams of the plastic sheet at least 6 inches and tape the seams with the tape recommended by the manufacturer. Starting with a ¼-inch gap along the walls, mark the sheet with a felt marker at 16-inch intervals, and snap chalk lines to help you position the sleepers. Set out the sleepers along the perimeter of the room and in their approximate locations across the rest of the floor, cutting them to length where necessary.

TYPICAL SLEEPER SUBFLOOR INSTALLATION

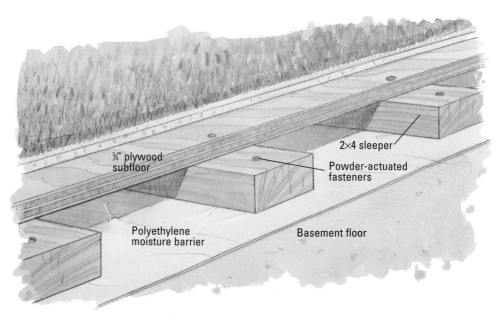

¾" plywood subfloor

2×4 sleeper

Powder-actuated fasteners

Polyethylene moisture barrier

Basement floor

Asphalt mastic

2 After making sure that the floor is level, use cedar shims to level the sleepers. Fasten the sleepers (through the shims) with powder-actuated fasteners.

3 Set the first sheet of underlayment (tongue to the wall) with the long side perpendicular to the sleepers and ½ inch from the wall. Fasten the sheet with 2½-inch coated screws every 6 inches along the walls and every 8 inches across the sheet. Don't drive screws at the grooved edge yet.

4 Install the remaining sheets in the first row along the wall with a ⅛-inch gap between the ends. In the second row, start with a half sheet (then a full sheet for the third row) so the joints will be offset. Fit the tongue of one sheet in the groove of the other and screw it to the sleepers.

Level the sleepers

Lay a 4-foot level across the sleepers all across the floor to make sure they lie on the same plane. Insert a pair of cedar shims to raise the sleepers at low spots.

Work faster and easier with a powder-actuated nailer

A powder-actuated nailer drives nails into concrete quickly and easily. There's less chipping of the concrete surface too.

You can buy a powder-actuated nailer at most home centers or rent one from rental outlets. A nailer is handy for anchoring both wood or metal framing to masonry.

An explosive charge drives a hardened nail into the concrete. Some types operate by pulling a trigger, others by hitting the firing pin with a hammer. Concrete nails (which break or bend if not hit squarely) and hardened screws (which take some time to install) are slower and less secure than powder-driven nails.

Wear ear and eye protection when using a powder-actuated nailer. Plant the tip of the nailer firmly against the wood before pulling the trigger or striking the firing pin.

STANLEY PRO TIP

Locating the first sheet

Because walls are seldom perfectly straight, measure out 49 inches from the wall and snap a chalk line. Position the edge of the first sheet along the line.

This will give you enough clearance along the length of the room so you can line up the inside edges (the grooved edges) of the plywood sheets.

In some places you will have more than a ¼-inch gap along the wall, but you can cover that with baseboard and shoe molding.

FRAMING A WOOD STUD WALL

When you add a wall in your basement, it will run either across the joists—perpendicular to them or at an angle—or parallel with them.

Building a wall across the joists is easier because the joists provide convenient nailing points for the top plate.

Building a wall parallel to the joists usually requires adding blocking between the joists. You can avoid adding blocking if you can place the wall directly under a joist, but make sure that location suits the overall use of the space.

Preassembling the wall on the floor is the most efficient way to frame it, but if the basement floor space is cramped, you'll have to build the wall in place. To do that, plumb the top and bottom plates to each other, and fasten the studs to the plates by toenailing (driving fasteners at an angle).

PRESTART CHECKLIST

☐ **TIME**
If you have a helper, allow at least one hour for a simple 8-foot-long wall that runs perpendicular to the joists. Framing a doorway or other opening will add time to the project.

☐ **TOOLS**
Tape measure, stud finder, chalk line, plumb bob with nylon line, hammer or power screwdriver, level, circular saw, ladders, powder-actuated gun

☐ **SKILLS**
Measuring; snapping a chalk line; crosscutting; driving fasteners; using a stud finder, plumb bob, and level

☐ **PREP**
Draw project plans and locate joists

☐ **MATERIALS**
2×4 studs, 2×4 top and bottom plates, 16d (3½-inch) nails or 3½-inch screws, tapered shims, powder-actuated fasteners

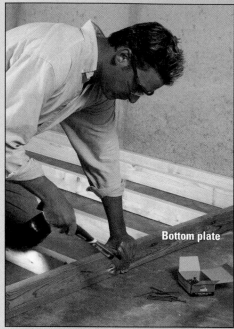

1 Snap a chalk line across the joists to mark the location of the cap plate. With a helper, hold the top plate on the line and fasten it. If the plate isn't quite straight, fasten part of it, then push the end into line. The wall top plate fastens to the cap plate.

2 Mark the stud locations on both the top and bottom plates and set the studs on edge between them. Fasten them one by one, keeping the edges of the studs flush with the edges of the plates.

ANATOMY OF A TYPICAL WALL

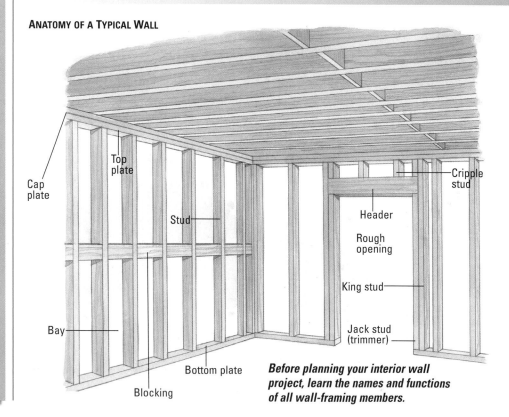

Cap plate
Top plate
Cap plate
Stud
Cripple stud
Header
Rough opening
King stud
Bay
Jack stud (trimmer)
Bottom plate
Blocking

Before planning your interior wall project, learn the names and functions of all wall-framing members.

Cap plate

Plumb bob

3 Hang a plumb bob from the corner of the cap plate to transfer the wall location to the floor. If you are working alone, hang the plumb bob from a nail in the plate. Repeat at the other end.

4 Position the bottom plate and fasten it to the slab with powder-actuated fasteners or masonry nails. For greater holding power, apply a bead of construction adhesive on the slab before driving the fasteners.

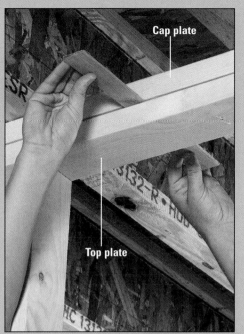

Cap plate

Top plate

5 If there is a little space between the top plate and the cap plate, slip a pair of shims between the two before nailing. Drive the nails through the shims to keep them from slipping out.

WHAT IF...
There's no room to preassemble the wall?

If you don't have room to preassemble the wall, build it in place. Mark the stud locations on the top and bottom plates, then fasten them to the floor and ceiling. Measure each stud length at the marks and cut it. Toenail the studs while a helper plumbs them.

Running a wall parallel to the joists

Cut 2×4 blocking to fit between the joists and fasten the pieces to the joists on 16-inch centers. Then preassemble and attach the wall or build the wall in place.

6 Anchor the wall by nailing up through the top plate into the cap plate. Make sure the edges of the two plates are flush. Use a carpenter's level to check the wall for plumb as you go.

FRAMING A WALL WITH METAL STUDS

Metal studs are a good choice for a remodeling project. Metal studs are straight when you buy them and stay that way. They won't burn or rot, and termites and other insects can't eat them. They're also lightweight and easy to cut and fasten—you can tuck the parts for an entire wall under your arm and carry them down the basement stairs. Factory-punched knockouts eliminate drilling for wiring and plumbing.

Most walls in remodeling projects are nonloadbearing, meaning that they don't help support the weight of the house. If you need to build a load-bearing wall, make sure that your metal studs are rated for that use.

If you're accustomed to building with lumber, metal studs may initially seem flimsy. That's because they're not designed for strength on their own—instead, they combine with the drywall to form a system that makes a sturdy wall.

PRESTART CHECKLIST

☐ **TIME**
When working with a helper, allow at least one hour for a simple 8-foot-long wall that runs perpendicular to the joists. Framing openings such as doorways or windows will add time to the project.

☐ **TOOLS**
Gloves, metal snips, chalk line, plumb bob with nylon line, tape measure, level, stud finder (if joists are concealed), power screwdriver, C-clamp self-locking pliers, powder-actuated fastener gun, compound-leverage aviation snips

☐ **SKILLS**
Measuring; snapping a chalk line; cutting metal; driving fasteners; using a stud finder, plumb bob, and level

☐ **PREP**
Draw project plans and locate joists

☐ **MATERIALS**
Metal studs and tracks, fasteners to attach track to floor and joists, assembly screws, plastic grommets

1 Snap chalk lines on the floor to mark the edges of the track. Cut the track at the edge of door openings and attach it to the floor, using panhead or flathead wood screws when working on a plywood sleeper floor. Use powder-actuated fasteners, concrete screws or nails, or screws driven into expansion plugs when the floor is concrete.

2 Transfer the location of the track on the floor to the ceiling by inserting a stud into the floor track and holding a level against it. Mark the stud's edges on the ceiling at each end of the wall, and join the marks by snapping a chalk line.

Steel framing terminology

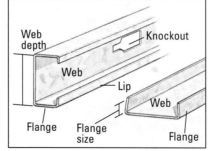

Web depth — Knockout — Web — Lip — Web — Flange — Flange size — Flange

Steel track and stud sizes match standard lumber sizes. For example, a nominal steel 2×4 has a web depth of $3\frac{1}{2}$ inches, and a steel 2×6 has a $5\frac{1}{2}$-inch web. The minimum flange size is $1\frac{5}{8}$ inch, and the maximum is 2 inches. The lip on steel studs improves their rigidity. The flanges of the track usually toe in slightly so that they firmly grip the flanges of the studs.

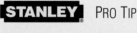 PRO TIP

Add plywood blocking

If you will be hanging cabinets or trim on a wall that's framed with metal studs, install $\frac{3}{4}$-inch plywood blocking between the studs to provide a fastening surface. Likewise, you can insert 2×4s into headers and studs at door openings for attachment of doorjambs.

3 Attach the track to the ceiling by driving screws into the joists. If the wall runs parallel to the joists, add blocking as shown on page 71. If you attach ceiling drywall to the underside of a roof truss system, professionals recommend a special resilient track design that accommodates the potential movement of the truss. Ask the steel-framing supplier for more information.

4 Lay out the stud locations on the edge of the bottom track, using a permanent marker and a length of wood that equals the stud spacing. Although you could mark the centerline of the studs, you'll probably find it less confusing to mark one edge, then mark a quick X where the stud goes. You don't need to mark the upper track. Double-check the spacing of the layout before you attach any studs.

5 Cut the studs to length if necessary. Insert a stud into the upper and lower track with a twisting motion. Make certain that the open side of all studs faces the same direction. Align the edge of the stud with the mark on the floor track, and clamp it with C-clamp self-locking pliers designed for welders. Drive a self-drilling screw to secure the stud to the track.

Splicing a track

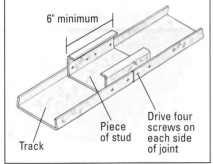

6" minimum

Piece of stud

Drive four screws on each side of joint

Track

Join lengths of track by using the simple method shown in the drawing. Make sure that the splice doesn't land at a stud location, and offset joints in the upper and lower tracks by at least 12 inches for maximum wall strength.

Cut the studs to length

Compound-leverage aviation snips are the most practical tools for cutting metal tracks and studs. The snips usually have color-coded handles. Red is for left-curving or straight cuts, green is for right-curving and straight cuts, and yellow is for straight cuts or slight curves either way. To make a smooth cut, don't let the tips of the blades come together until the end of the cut. To cut a metal stud or track, cut through both flanges, then cut the web.

Self-drilling screw

Join steel studs to the track with #8×½-inch modified truss-head self-drilling screws with phillips drive. You'll find these screws (or a similar design) where you buy your metal framing. The self-drilling screw drills a pilot hole through both pieces before the threads engage. The large-diameter truss head spreads the holding force and has a low profile so it doesn't create a hump under the drywall.

Framing a wall with metal studs (continued)

6 To make a header, cut a length of track 4 inches longer than the opening. Draw a line square across the web 2 inches from each end to mark the length of the opening. Cut V-notches into the flanges, aiming at the lines on the web. Bend the track along the lines, and drive a screw through each tab into the king stud.

7 Create an attachment surface for wall cabinets by notching a length of track and screwing it to the flanges of the studs. Consult your cabinet installer to make sure you place the track at the correct height and so the installer knows to bring sheet metal screws for the installation.

8 Add blocking of solid wood or plywood to simplify the installation of baseboards, crown moldings, shelves, and accessories like towel bars. This also is another way to prepare for hanging cabinets. With blocking, you can drive nails or screws just as you would with a wood-stud wall. Without wood backing, install moldings with construction adhesive and trimhead screws.

WHAT IF...
You want to install a door?

To fasten wood doorjambs or molding to steel framing, use trimhead screws. These fasteners have heads barely larger than a countersunk nail. Drive them about 1/32 inch below the wood's surface and fill the hole with putty. Another strategy is to line the opening with wood trimmer studs and a header as shown in the drawing. This provides a solid target for nailing. Substitute wood for the two full-length king studs that flank the opening to gain a broader nailing surface for the door molding.

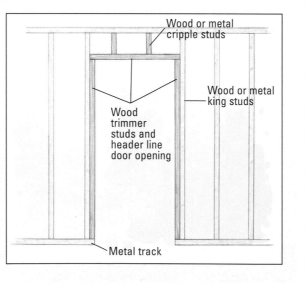

Wood or metal cripple studs

Wood or metal king studs

Wood trimmer studs and header line door opening

Metal track

Align the knockouts

When you install studs, align the knockouts with each other to simplify the task of pulling wires or installing plumbing lines.

9 Snap plastic grommets into the knockouts to prevent the sharp edges of the stud from slicing the insulation on electrical wires. You could use armored cable or conduit instead. The grommets also prevent metal-to-metal contact with water pipes, which could cause an electrolytic reaction that would corrode the pipes and studs. If you can't find grommets, use lengths of foam pipe insulation.

10 Install the drywall by driving type S fine-threaded screws into the studs. For best results, drive the screws all along one stud before moving to the next one. Start at the edge of the drywall sheet that is on the open side of the flange.

Building a curved wall

1 Fasten the bottom track to the floor and use it as a template for the top track. Clamp one end of the top track to the first with locking-grip pliers, form the curve, then clamp the other end with locking-grip pliers.

2 Use a plumb bob to position the top track. Support the top track with a few temporary studs. Check the alignment of the top and bottom tracks at both ends and at the middle with plumb bob. Then attach top track to the joists.

3 Twist either wood or metal studs into the tracks and plumb them before driving screws through the track to secure them. For the smoothest wall surface, space the studs close together.

Another way to fasten metal framing

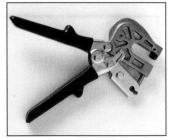

If you have a large project, a punch lock stud crimper will make the job go faster and easier. This tool uses compound leverage to create a rectangular crimp that mechanically locks the stud and track together, forming a strong bond. The tool is easy to maneuver into tight quarters, and you never need to worry about running out of screws.

FRAMING FOR MASONRY WALLS

Most basement remodeling projects call for an attractive wall surface—usually drywall. No matter what wall material you choose, it will often need to be fastened to a concrete or masonry block wall.

When installing framing along such a wall, you have two choices—you can either add furring to the wall with 2×2s or Z-channel or build a 2×4 (or 2×6) stud wall. In both cases, the construction techniques are the same as framing an interior partition wall with top and bottom plates, except that 2×2 furring strips need to be attached to the wall.

One of the primary benefits of framing a block wall is that it gives you a way to insulate the wall and keep your new rooms more comfortable. Use 1½-inch rigid insulation board between furring strips (or Z-channel); fiberglass batts in 2×4 or 2×6 stud walls.

If possible, rip your 2×2 furring strips from 2×4s or 2×6s. You'll end up with straighter boards than buying manufactured 2×2s, and ripping will actually take less time than straightening a strip during installation.

PRESTART CHECKLIST

☐ **TIME**
About 4 hours for an 8-foot wall

☐ **TOOLS**
Circular saw, tape measure, cordless drill, powder-actuated fastener gun, utility knife, level, electrical tools, chalk line

☐ **SKILLS**
Measuring, marking, cutting, using powder-actuated fastener gun

☐ **PREP**
Clean and seal wall and install vapor barrier

☐ **MATERIALS**
2× lumber, 2½-inch screws, vapor barrier, powder-actuated fasteners, electrical boxes, and protective plates, construction adhesive, shims, tape, fiberglass or foam insulation

1 Install vapor barrier if codes require it. Measure and cut a 2×2 top plate, and fasten it to the joists, flush with the surface of the block. Butt-join sections and cleat the joints with 2×2 scrap. Mark the furring-strip locations on the bottom of the plate at 16-inch centers.

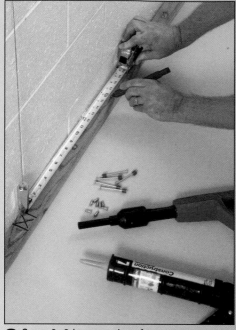

2 Cut a 2×2 bottom plate from pressure-treated lumber, coat the bottom and rear with construction adhesive, and fasten the plate to the floor with a powder-actuated fastener gun. Transfer at least one of the furring-strip locations from the top plate with a plumb bob. Measure and mark the remaining locations.

FRAMING A 2×4 EXTERIOR STUD WALL

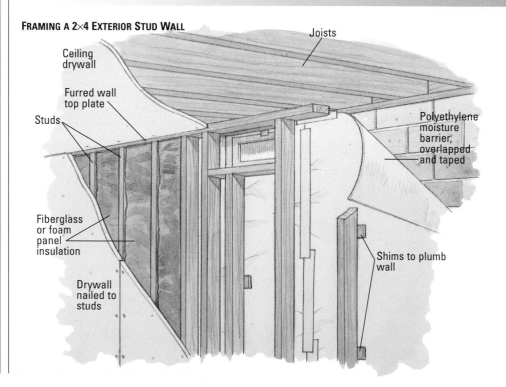

Joists

Ceiling drywall

Furred wall top plate

Studs

Polyethylene moisture barrier, overlapped and taped

Fiberglass or foam panel insulation

Shims to plumb wall

Drywall nailed to studs

Notch in furring strip and protective plate for electric cable

Notch foam insulation for cable

3 At each mark, measure the length of the furring strip and cut it to fit between the plates. Apply construction adhesive to the back of each strip, and using masonry screws or a powder-actuated fastener gun, fasten the strips to the wall at the marks. Drive fasteners at 16-inch intervals and use a carpenter's level to keep the strips plumb and straight. If a furring strip is bowed, fasten it at one end with two fasteners and force it in line as you drive the rest of the fasteners.

4 If your wall will house electric cable, snap two level chalk lines across the furring strips and notch them with a circular saw set just under 1½ inches. Run the cable and cover the notches with protective plates, then fill the cavities between the strips with rigid foam insulation, notching the foam at the location of the cable. Make sure the foam fits snugly and install a vapor barrier on the surface if building codes require it.

WHAT IF…
Your furred wall runs parallel to the joists?

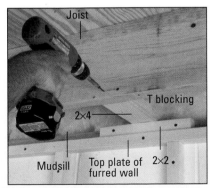

Joist

2×4

T blocking

Mudsill

Top plate of furred wall

2×2

Walls parallel to the joists require support for the ceiling drywall. Assemble T-shape blocking from 2×4s and 2×2s and fasten the pieces to the joists and the mudsill on top of the foundation wall. Align the 2×4 flush with the bottom of the joists.

Installing rigid foam with Z-channel

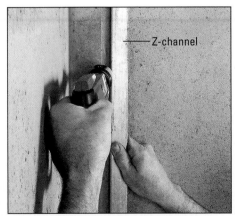

Z-channel

Powder-actuated nailer

1 Install Z-channel in one corner, with the flange facing the wall. Leave enough room for a sheet of foam and a piece of drywall along the adjacent wall. Attach the channel with power-actuated fasteners. Use a #3 load with a ½-inch pin, five per channel.

2 Slip a piece of foam under the Z-channel and trap it in place with a second channel on the other side. The flanges are made with a slight angle that grips the insulation. Continue this pattern until you reach the next corner.

BUILDING SOFFITS AND CHASES

A soffit is an architectural element that's often utilized to fill the space between the top of wall-mounted cabinets and the ceiling. In a basement remodeling project, a soffit can hide wiring, heat ducts, and plumbing lines.

If you're installing wall cabinets, you can either build a soffit the same depth as the cabinets or make the soffit 1½ inches deeper than the cabinets to help disguise minor alignment discrepancies. This also allows installation of a small molding strip. Build the soffit level and square to simplify cabinet installation.

When you're designing your soffit, allow for an overhang at the exposed ends of soffit runs. Also be sure to allow for the thickness of the drywall on the front and bottom. Heavy construction is not necessary because the soffit is not a structural feature.

A chase is somewhat like a vertical soffit. Build a chase around pipes, ductwork, or supporting posts to hide them and add an architectural element to the room.

1 Nail or screw 1×4s to the back of the upper and lower 2×2 runners, creating a ladderlike construction. Place a vertical support at each end and about 16 inches on center along the side. Keep the assembly straight, square, and flat.

2 Snap a chalk line onto the bottom of the joists parallel to the wall. To run a soffit parallel to the joists, add nailers between the joists or build the soffit inside the joists as shown on page 79. If you're framing a soffit that runs on adjacent walls, install the first part parallel to the longest wall, then square the other soffit legs to it.

PRESTART CHECKLIST

☐ **TIME**
About an hour for a 6-foot length

☐ **TOOLS**
Circular saw, cordless drill, hammer, carpenter's level, chalk line

☐ **SKILLS**
Measuring, cutting, and fastening lumber

☐ **PREP**
Lay out soffit and draw plans

☐ **MATERIALS**
1×4, 2×2, and 2×4 lumber, construction adhesive, drywall, screws or nails, shims

HIDING PLUMBING IN A FINISHED ROOM

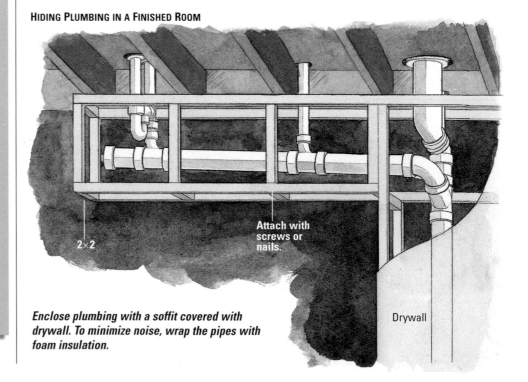

2×2

Attach with screws or nails.

Drywall

Enclose plumbing with a soffit covered with drywall. To minimize noise, wrap the pipes with foam insulation.

3 Tack the runner assembly to only two joists. Check for level along the length of the lower runner. Add tapered softwood shims, if necessary, between the upper runner and joist to level the assembly and to eliminate any gaps. Drive the fastener through the shim to make sure it stays in place. Otherwise, smear a dab of constructive adhesive on both sides of the shim near its tip to secure it to the framing. Let the adhesive dry before you trim the shims.

4 Use a level to transfer the position of the bottom runner onto the wall studs. You need to mark only the ends, and then join the marks with a chalk line. Screw or nail the 2×2 wall runner to the studs.

5 Screw 1×4 horizontal supports to the top edge of the wall runner and the lower runner. You can space these about 48 inches on center. Make sure the soffit stays square. Cover the face and bottom of the soffit with drywall. Install corner bead on outside corners (see page 123) and tape the inside corners (see page 127).

WHAT IF…
Your soffit runs parallel to the joists?

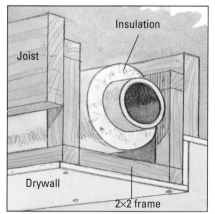

To run a soffit parallel to the joists, you can add blocking between the joists and hang the soffit on the blocking, or you can screw the soffit frame to the inside faces of the joists.

Saving headroom

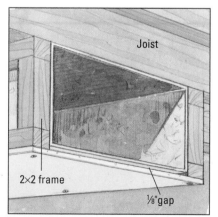

Save a little headroom where the ceiling is low by building the side frames ⅛ inch lower than the utility line or duct. Then fasten the drywall to the frame. The drywall stabilizes the structure—but limit this construction to soffits a foot wide or narrower.

Chasing a pipe or column

Construct chases with 2×4 frames instead of 2×2s. The heavier lumber will make a sturdier chase. Use pressure-treated wood for the bottom frame on concrete floors, standard lumber for the top frame and sides. Set the top and bottom plates as you would to build a wall in place (page 71) and then add the corners. Frame openings for access panels where required for shutoffs, cleanouts, and the like. Cover with drywall.

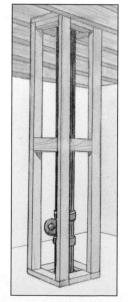

ADDING AN EGRESS WINDOW

A bedroom or apartment in your basement will require a sufficient opening for egress (see page 8). Whether you enlarge an existing window or cut a completely new opening, the techniques are the same. One of the most important aspects of window installation is getting the rough opening right. If you've ordered but haven't received the window yet, follow the manufacturer's specifications when marking the rough opening.

Because exterior basement walls are load-bearing walls, you must provide adequate support for the wall above the window. If you're not changing the width of an existing window, that support will already be in place. But enlarging the width or cutting a new opening will require building a temporary support wall and installing a wood header or steel lintel that spans the top of the opening. Before you cut into the wall, excavate a new window well or enlarge the existing one. This could require moving a lot of dirt, so be sure to allow sufficient time for the excavation and installation of the well.

PRESTART CHECKLIST

☐ **TIME**
About 6 to 8 hours to remove an existing window and enlarge the opening

☐ **TOOLS**
Carpenter's pencil, level, small sledge, brick set, circular saw with masonry blade, mason's trowel, caulk gun, drill

☐ **SKILLS**
Measuring and marking, using a small sledge and brick set, using a drill

☐ **PREP**
Excavate and line the window well and install temporary support wall if necessary

☐ **MATERIALS**
2× lumber, concrete mix, caulk, shims, polyurethane foam, concrete screws

Making the opening

1 Remove the old window and frame and mark the new rough opening, keeping the lines plumb with a carpenter's level. Score the line with a brick set and small sledge and cut along the line with a circular saw and masonry blade. Start with a shallow cut, making the cuts deeper with several passes.

2 Break out the center block of the new rough opening with a small sledge and brick set. First, break the mortar joints around the block then break the face of the block and chip the large pieces. Remove the remaining blocks and chisel the edge of the opening smooth.

BUILDING A TEMPORARY SUPPORT WALL

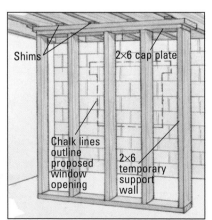

Shims

2×6 cap plate

Chalk lines outline proposed window opening

2×6 temporary support wall

Cutting a new opening or increasing the width of an existing window will weaken the support provided by a basement wall. Before you start, build a temporary support wall several feet away from the wall.

TYPICAL WINDOW WELL CONSTRUCTION

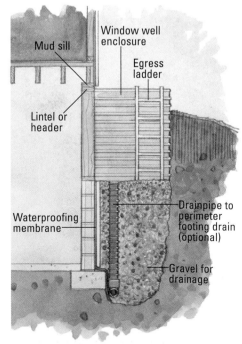

Mud sill

Window well enclosure

Egress ladder

Lintel or header

Waterproofing membrane

Drainpipe to perimeter footing drain (optional)

Gravel for drainage

3 Fill the voids of the remaining block with pieces of concrete broken from the original opening. Trowel in and smooth fresh concrete. Let the concrete cure.

4 Cut pressure-treated 2× stock to the dimensions of the rough opening and spread a generous bead of construction adhesive on the back of each one. Fasten the frame with predrilled self-tapping masonry screws. Caulk the edges of the frame on both sides of the wall.

Installing the window

1 Center the new window in the rough opening and fine-tune its position by shimming it from the inside.

Fitting a window well

1 Whether you're enlarging a window for egress or to increase the light, a window well liner holds back the soil. Place its top edge 6 inches above the soil line. Mark the fastener holes on the wall. Drill the block for masonry fasteners and attach the liner.

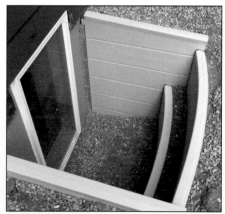

2 Install the gravel and drainpipe. Fit a ladder in the well if the window has been installed to provide egress.

2 Following the manufacturer's instructions, fasten the window flanges to the outside of the wall. Then caulk the outside edges of the flange and fill in gaps on the inside of the frame with expanding polyurethane foam.

PLUMBING

One look at the pipes running through a basement is usually enough to make a homeowner start looking for a professional plumber. At first glance, plumbing often seems difficult and messy. But the plumbing associated with basement remodeling is mostly new work, so you'll find it more novice-friendly and straightforward—especially when you consider potential do-it-yourself savings. Installing your own plumbing for a new basement bathroom, kitchen, or laundry room can save a lot of cash.

Learning the basics
Even if you've never before lifted a pipe wrench or fixed a faucet, you can learn how to add a new sink, toilet, or tub. But like every home improvement project, these installations rely on a firm grasp of some basic techniques. That's what you'll find in this chapter—a look at the basics of plumbing systems, pipes, and fittings, and how to work with them. Step-by-step instructions make it possible for any do-it-yourselfer to complete the projects.

Building codes
Even if you have extensive knowledge and confidence, you will probably not be able to carry out your remodeling project without consulting a building inspector. This is especially true when you install a plumbing fixture where there was none before—whenever you need to run new pipes. New plumbing work must conform to building codes and must be inspected by your local building department.

Plumbing affects health and safety, so building departments are usually sticklers for ensuring that plumbing is done properly. You'll probably have to take out a building permit, file plans, and arrange for inspections. If you are unsure whether you need a permit, consult your building department before you start the work.

Working safely and comfortably
Before attempting any project, turn off the water and turn on an upstairs faucet to make sure the water supply is off. Take care not to touch nearby electrical outlets, especially if you are wet.

Plumbing is sometimes physically challenging, not because of heavy lifting, but because you often have to exert force in cramped places. Take a break to relieve cramped muscles and strained joints.

Use kneepads or even an old pillow to make the work area more comfortable. Spread drop cloths around and keep a bucket and some old towels handy to catch the small amounts of water that will inevitably dribble out of existing pipes.

Position a flashlight or work light so you can see clearly. Keep tools within reach or have a helper to hand them to you.

Practical planning
Plan your time carefully; your family will not be able to use the bathroom or kitchen until you can turn on the water again. Organize the job so you can keep water-service interruptions to a minimum. Even a well-planned project can run into unforeseen problems and delays, however, so it's a good idea to make contingency arrangements with neighbors or friends.

CHAPTER PREVIEW

Before tackling a project, understand plumbing in general and your system in particular.

Understanding the systems
page 84

Plumbing a bathroom and kitchen
page 86

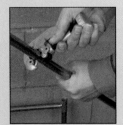
Working with copper pipe
page 88

Installing plastic drainpipe
page 90

New plumbing lines are relatively easy to install, but the work must be done according to established building codes. A building inspector might want to inspect this drain-and-vent system before the wall is covered.

Working with PEX tubing
page 92

Building a wet wall
page 94

Running drain lines
page 96

Running copper supply lines
page 98

UNDERSTANDING THE SYSTEMS

The pipes running from your basement through your walls and floors have two different functions—the **supply system** brings water into the house, and the **drain-waste-vent system** carries wastewater and sewer gases out of the house.

Supply system

A single supply pipe, usually ¾ to 1¼ inches in diameter, brings water into the house. This water is supplied by a utility company, which is responsible for its purity.

Soon after entering the house, most supply pipes connect to a water meter, which records the amount of water you use. If your water bill is the same from month to month, your water is probably unmetered.

The supply pipe then travels toward the water heater. There the pipe splits into two branches. One supplies cold water to the house and the other fills the water heater. The pipe that emerges from the water heater supplies hot water to the house.

These two pipes run in pairs to supply hot and cold water to various rooms and fixtures. Vertical supply pipes are sometimes called risers. Older systems usually have pipes made of galvanized steel, while newer homes have pipes made of copper, plastic pipe (either PVC or CPVC), or plastic tubing.

Somewhere near the water heater, pipes usually reduce to ¾ inch in diameter. Farther on, as they turn into branch lines, the pipes step down in size to ½ inch. If your water pressure is low, the problem may be calcium buildup or supply pipes that are too small.

Water flow can usually be shut off before it enters the house, at a main shutoff just inside the house, at branch lines, and near the individual plumbing fixtures.

Drain-waste-vent system

Carrying water out of a house smoothly is the job of the drain-waste-vent (DWV) system. These pipes must be installed according to precise specifications found in national and local plumbing codes. Never install a DWV pipe until you check with your building department and are sure you comply with local codes.

Drain water for every fixture must run through a trap made of plastic or chromed brass. The walls of such traps are thinner than supply and DWV pipe, and the trap is made to be dismantled easily.

Traps are shaped like a P or an S. This shape traps water in a bend so fumes and gases cannot escape into the house. A toilet has its own built-in trap. A trap usually connects to a branch drainpipe, typically 1½ or 2 inches in diameter. A branch drain carries water to the main stack.

Drainpipes must slope properly so water can run freely through them. Plumbing codes require DWV fittings to make sweeping turns rather than abrupt ones so that waste matter does not get stuck.

The center of a DWV system is the main stack, a fat pipe usually 4 to 6 inches in diameter, which runs straight up through the roof. It carries wastewater out to the local sanitary sewer system or septic tank, keeps water flowing smoothly, and also carries noxious fumes out of the house. Often a home has one or more secondary stacks, perhaps 2 or 3 inches in diameter, that serve the kitchen or another part of the system.

Older homes have stacks made of cast iron, while newer homes use ABS or PVC plastic pipe. Drain lines and stacks often have cleanouts, which are elbowed pipes with a plug that can be temporarily removed to allow a clog to be augered out.

The drain for every fixture must be connected in some way to a vent pipe, which usually extends up through the roof. In the most common arrangement, a stack extends upward so that its upper portion acts as a vent, while its lower portion is a drain. Sometimes a separate pipe called a revent is used to vent a section of a system. A revent reaches up and over its fixture connection to tie into a stack.

Vent pipes need not be as large as drainpipes, but they must be kept clear. A vent may become clogged by a bird's nest or debris from reroofing. If so, be sure to clear it out with an auger.

Whenever you install new service, it is important to have the venting installed and operating correctly.

A bathtub access panel

Bathtub plumbing is complicated, so many homes have an access panel to allow you to reach it. To find an access panel, look in the adjacent room or closet, on the wall directly behind the tub faucet.

FIXTURE TRAPS

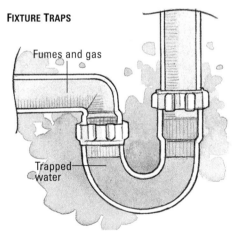

Fumes and gas

Trapped water

The drain water for every fixture must pass through a trap—a section of pipe shaped like a sideways P or S. Because of its shape, it holds water, creating a seal that keeps fumes and gases from entering the house. A toilet has a built-in trap. Sink traps are made of chrome-plated brass or plastic, with joints that can be taken apart easily.

HOUSEHOLD SUPPLY LINES, VENTS, AND DRAINS

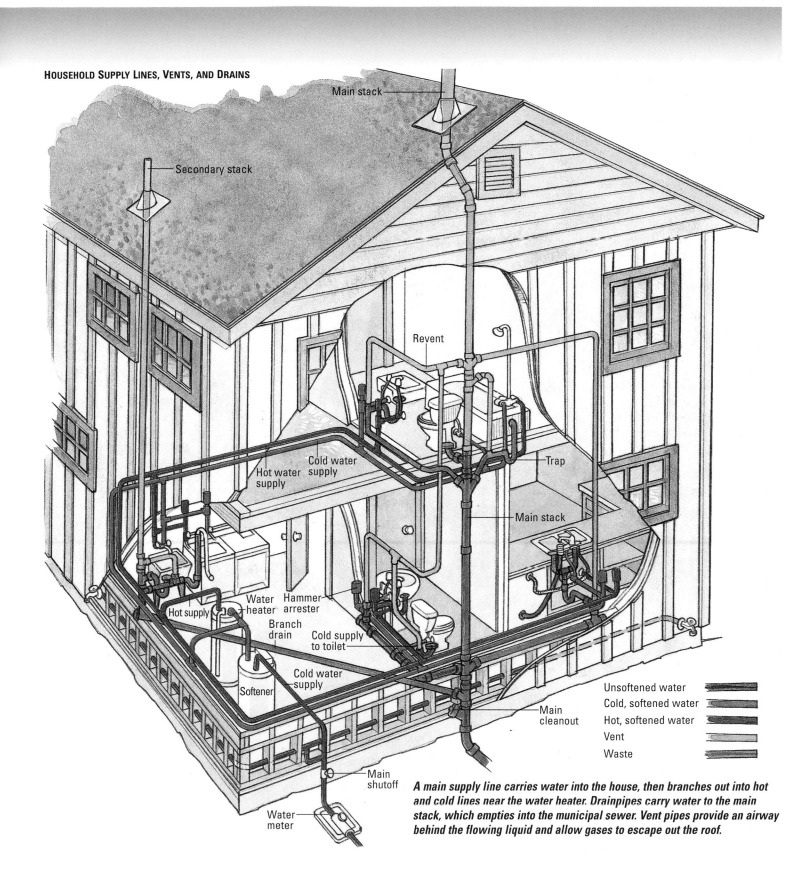

Main stack

Secondary stack

Revent

Trap

Main stack

Cold water supply

Hot water supply

Water heater

Hammer arrester

Hot supply

Branch drain

Cold supply to toilet

Cold water supply

Softener

Main cleanout

Unsoftened water

Cold, softened water

Hot, softened water

Vent

Waste

Main shutoff

Water meter

A main supply line carries water into the house, then branches out into hot and cold lines near the water heater. Drainpipes carry water to the main stack, which empties into the municipal sewer. Vent pipes provide an airway behind the flowing liquid and allow gases to escape out the roof.

PLUMBING A BATHROOM AND KITCHEN

Although you will use the same general techniques when plumbing either a basement bathroom or kitchen, there are different specific requirements for each of these rooms.

Plumbing a bathroom

Where you place the toilet, sink, and tub or shower may depend on the location of the existing drain lines and main stack. You can save time and money by placing the bathroom where these lines are already located. Or you could extend the lines to another part of the basement and build a new wet wall to house them (pages 94–95). In general, it's best to minimize long horizontal runs of vent pipes and drainpipes.

Plan a layout that is comfortable and convenient. Most codes require placing any fixture at least 15 inches from the toilet centerline. There must be at least 24 inches of space in front of the toilet. (It's OK for a door to swing into this space.)

Sinks and vanity sink tops range from 20 to 30 inches wide. A standard bathtub measures 60 by 32 inches. If your plans call for a larger tub, alter the layout to fit it.

The framing—not the finished wall—must be 60 inches wide to accommodate a standard tub length. If the opening is any smaller, the tub will not fit; if the opening is more than ¼ inch too long, making a tight seal along the wall will be difficult. Framing must be almost perfectly square.

Most codes call for 3-inch PVC pipe for the main drain and 2-inch PVC for the other drain lines and the vents. Local codes may call for a 4-inch main drain, and some plumbers prefer to run larger vent pipes.

Cast-iron drainpipe is making a comeback in some areas because it muffles noise better than plastic pipe. However, cast-iron should be installed by a pro. (You can reduce the noise of water draining through PVC by wrapping the pipe with insulation.)

Rigid copper is the most common pipe for supply lines, but PEX or other plastics might be allowed in your area. Bathrooms are usually supplied with ½-inch pipe. For maximum water pressure, however, run ¾-inch supply pipe and use ½-inch for short runs only.

TYPICAL BATHROOM PLUMBING INSTALLATION

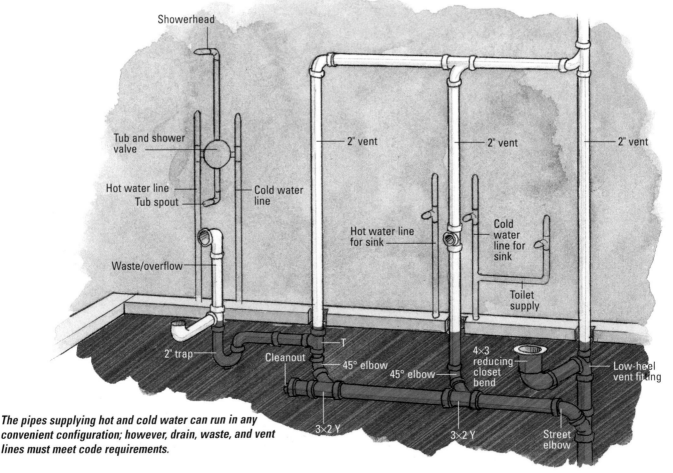

Showerhead

Tub and shower valve

Hot water line
Tub spout

Cold water line

2" vent

2" vent

2" vent

Hot water line for sink

Cold water line for sink

Waste/overflow

Toilet supply

2" trap

Cleanout

T

45° elbow

45° elbow

4×3 reducing closet bend

Low-heel vent fitting

3×2 Y

3×2 Y

Street elbow

The pipes supplying hot and cold water can run in any convenient configuration; however, drain, waste, and vent lines must meet code requirements.

Plumbing a kitchen

The easiest kitchen installation includes the standard trio of kitchen appliances—a double-bowl sink, a garbage disposer, and a dishwasher. You can add other appliances, such as an undersink filter or a hot-water dispenser, without much trouble during the initial installation.

The sink trap connects to the sanitary T of a 2-inch drain line. The ideal height of the T varies, depending on the depth of the sink. (If the T is lower than the ideal height, you can simply extend the trap downward. If the T is too high, you may need to install a new T at a lower point.)

Although you can connect the drain to a separate smaller stack that runs to the roof, reventing the line is the best method to use in a basement, unless prohibited by local codes.

The hot-water pipe supplies both the hot-water faucet and the dishwasher; there should be a stop valve for each. The cold-water pipe supplies the faucet as well as a line that runs to the icemaker; there is a stop valve for each.

A standard base cabinet topped with a countertop is 36 inches high. A sink base cabinet has no drawers or shelves to make room for the sink and the plumbing.

A hole must be cut in the countertop to accommodate the sink (page 183). You can do this yourself if the countertop is plastic laminate. If the top is granite or solid-surface, hire a pro.

The dishwasher is usually installed right next to the sink base to simplify running the drain and supply lines. (It is also the most convenient location for handling the dishes.)

A 24-inch-wide opening in the cabinet houses a standard dishwasher.

Kitchen designers often speak of a "work triangle," meaning that the sink, range, and refrigerator should all be within easy reach of one another. This is easily accomplished in a kitchen that is U-shape. If the kitchen is long and narrow, it's usually best to place one of the three elements on the wall opposite the other two. Make sure you can open the refrigerator without interfering with cooking or washing dishes.

Place the range at least 12 inches away from the sink. And leave 36 inches of counter space on either side of the sink for food preparation and draining dishes. The range should have a range hood above it with an exhaust fan that vents to the outside.

TYPICAL KITCHEN PLUMBING INSTALLATION

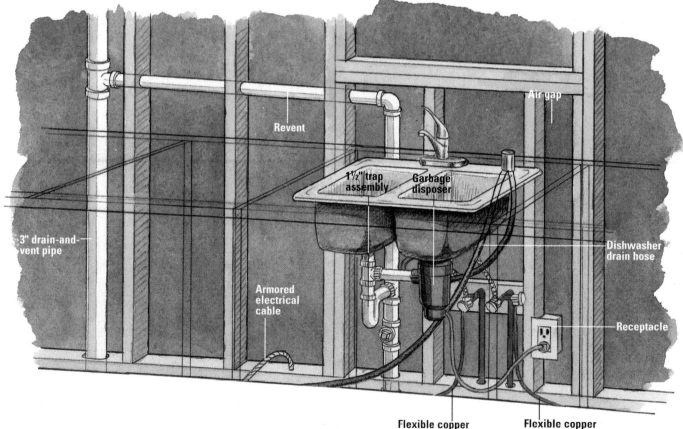

Revent

Air gap

1½" trap assembly

Garbage disposer

3" drain-and-vent pipe

Dishwasher drain hose

Armored electrical cable

Receptacle

Flexible copper supply line for dishwasher

Flexible copper supply line for icemaker

WORKING WITH COPPER PIPE

A properly soldered (or "sweated") pipe joint is as strong as the pipe itself. A poorly soldered joint will leak. It might not leak until the next day, or in a year or two, but it will leak.

The key to making a strong joint is to work systematically. You must cut the pipe square and remove all the burrs. The inside of the fitting and the outside of the pipe must be sanded to a shine. Flux must be applied to both surfaces or the solder won't adhere. Then you must heat the pipe evenly so the solder will be fully drawn into the joint. Even wiping is essential—a droplet of solder can weaken a joint.

Keep it round

Pipe ends and fittings must be perfectly round. If the pipe is dented even slightly you can't restore it to its original shape. Cut the pipe again or buy a new fitting.

Cutting with a tubing cutter ensures roundness. If space is tight and you must cut with a hacksaw, do it slowly and gently. If you must bend a pipe to move it away from a wall, work carefully.

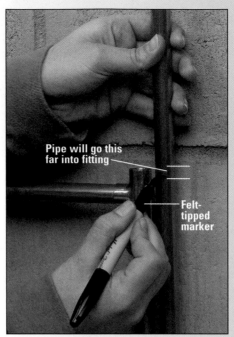

1 Hold the pipe against the fitting to mark the cut, or measure its length with a tape measure. Be sure to include the distance the pipe will travel into the fitting. Mark the cut with a felt-tipped marker.

Pipe will go this far into fitting
Felt-tipped marker

2 Use as large a tubing cutter as space permits. Line up the cutting wheel on your mark. Twist the knob until the wheel starts to bite into the pipe. Rotate the cutter once around the pipe, tighten a half turn or so, and repeat until the pipe is cut. Assemble all the parts of a joint in a dry run.

Tubing cutter

PRESTART CHECKLIST

☐ **TIME**
About 15 minutes to cut a pipe and join a fitting

☐ **TOOLS**
Tubing cutter or hacksaw, multiuse wire brush, propane torch (preferably with a trigger igniter), flux brush, flame guard

☐ **SKILLS**
Cutting pipe, soldering

☐ **PREP**
Protect any flammable surfaces with a fiber shield or a cookie sheet

☐ **MATERIALS**
Copper pipe and fittings, flux, solder (95 percent tin for drinking water supply), damp rag

Sweating a brass valve

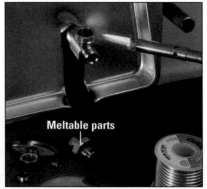

Meltable parts

If a valve has any plastic parts—most stop valves do—disassemble the valve and remove all the parts that could melt. Heat the brass valve body as you would a fitting. It may take a bit longer to heat than a fitting. After sweating the joint, wait for the valve to cool before replacing the plastic parts.

STANLEY PRO TIP

Protect walls and framing from the torch flame

While sweating a copper joint you may not notice that the flame is charring a nearby joist or wall surface. Protect flammable surfaces with a fiber shield or use an old cookie sheet. **Keep a fire extinguisher handy.**

If you can't pull a pipe more than a half inch away from a wall or framing member, don't worry about heating all around the fitting. As long as you heat two opposite sides, the solder will draw evenly around the joint.

MAPP gas, an alternative to propane fuel, produces an extremely hot flame and is not recommended for most residential work.

After the job is complete, **check the area an hour later to be sure no flammable surfaces are smoldering.**

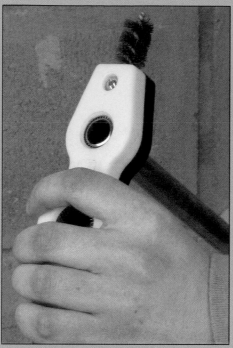

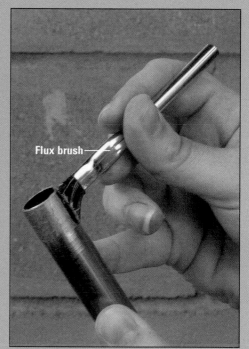

3 Clean out every fitting opening until it is shiny using a wire brush equal to the size of the fitting. Even oil from your hand may weaken the joint. If you accidentally touch a brushed opening, ream it again.

4 Insert the pipe in the multiuse brush and spin the brush a few times until the pipe's outside surface shines. You can brighten the surface with emery cloth or a flexible sanding material too. Rebrush or resand if you touch the shiny area.

5 Apply flux to all inside openings of the fitting and to the outside of the pipe with a flux brush (available with the flux or sold separately at your home center). Take care to keep the flux brush away from any debris; clean off any particles that stick to it.

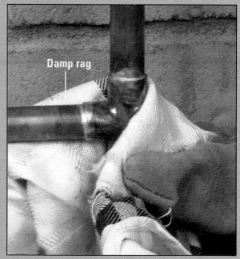

6 Light your propane torch and point the flame at the fitting—not at the pipe or the joint itself. The tip of the blue portion of the flame should just touch the fitting. Move the flame back and forth to heat two opposite sides of the fitting.

7 When the fitting starts to smoke, remove the flame and touch the tip of the solder to the joint. If it does not melt, heat again. Once the fitting is hot enough, the solder will be drawn into the joint. Move the solder around so the entire joint fills with solder.

8 Immediately repeat the process for any other joints in the fitting. This will go quickly because the fitting is already hot. Once all the joints are soldered, quickly wipe all the joints with a damp rag. Avoid bumping the fitting for 10 to 15 minutes.

INSTALLING PLASTIC DRAINPIPE

Plastic PVC pipe and fittings are inexpensive and easy to install. However, a good PVC joint takes a little planning. Once glued, a joint is rock-hard and cannot be adjusted. If you make a mistake, you'll have to cut out the section and start over.

Making a dry run

To prevent a mistake, cut the pipes and assemble them without glue to make sure everything fits correctly and points in the right direction. When joining multiple sections, cut and assemble all of them to make sure that the last pipe in the run is facing the right direction. Mark and number the pipes with a felt pen so you can reassemble them correctly. Disassemble them, apply primer to each end and fitting, apply the cement, and join the pipes and fittings in order.

PRESTART CHECKLIST

☐ **TIME**
About one hour to cut and assemble five or six pipes and fittings

☐ **TOOLS**
PVC saw or backsaw, miter box or power mitersaw, deburring tool, felt-tipped marker

☐ **SKILLS**
Sawing, measuring, working methodically

☐ **PREP**
Make a drawing of the drain/vent assembly; clear a path for the pipes

☐ **MATERIALS**
Primer and cement for your type and size of pipe

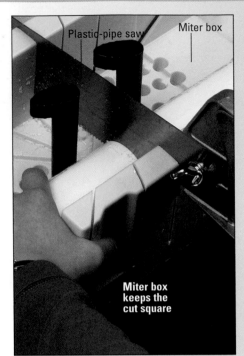

1 Mark the cut with a felt-tipped marker—include the length of the pipe inside the fitting. A plastic-pipe saw is designed to cut the pipe, but a hacksaw or backsaw will work. A power mitersaw with a fine-cutting blade will produce the most accurate cuts.

2 Remove the burrs from the cut pipe end. A deburring tool cleans up the end of the pipe quickly and easily, or you can scrape burrs off with a knife. Assemble cut pipes and fittings in a dry run (below).

DRY RUN FOR DRAINPIPE

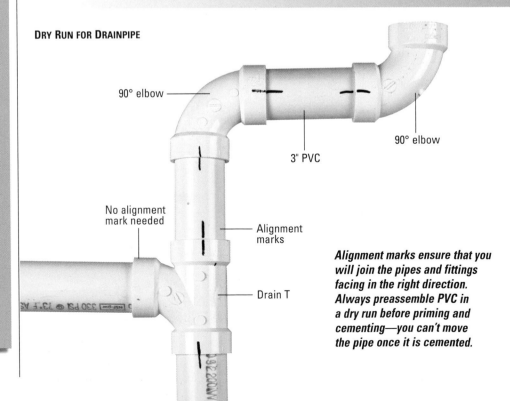

Alignment marks ensure that you will join the pipes and fittings facing in the right direction. Always preassemble PVC in a dry run before priming and cementing—you can't move the pipe once it is cemented.

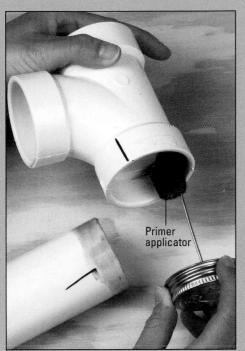

Primer applicator

PVC cement

3 Apply primer to the pipe ends and the inside of the fitting. Wet the applicator enough to produce a fairly dark line, but not so much that the primer drips. Place the pieces where they will not get dirty. If debris sticks to the primer, it will be difficult to join the pipes.

4 Apply cement to the inside of one fitting opening and to the end of one pipe. Work quickly—the cement starts to set in a few seconds.

5 Push the pipe into the fitting and twist so the alignment marks line up. Hold for a few seconds, then wipe with a damp cloth. In a minute the joint will be strong enough that you can assemble the next piece. After 15 minutes you can run unpressurized wastewater through the pipes.

WHAT IF...
You are connecting ABS pipe?

Most codes require PVC for drain lines, but if you already have black ABS pipe in your home, local codes may allow you to add the same material to your system instead of replacing it with PVC.

Cut and assemble the black ABS pipe in the same way as you would PVC pipe. Use a plastic-pipe saw or backsaw with a miter box, remove the burrs, and put pipe and fittings together in a dry run. Use a sharpened, light-color crayon to make alignment marks.

Instead of primer, apply ABS cleaner to pipe ends and fitting openings, then glue the pieces together with ABS cement. Push the pieces together and twist.

To connect PVC pipe to existing ABS pipe, use a no-hub fitting (pages 96–97).

ABS cleaner applicator

Use the right products

Check the label on a can of primer or cement to make sure it's made for your type of pipe. Local inspectors might not accept all-purpose cement. The larger the pipe diameter, the bigger the applicator should be so you won't have to dip it more than once; in general an applicator should be about half the diameter of the pipe to be joined.

WORKING WITH PEX TUBING

The supply pipe of the future may already be here. Older PE (polyethylene) tubing has long been used for irrigation systems, but it must be buried for protection and can carry only cold water. Cross-linked polyethylene (PEX) is stronger and can handle hot as well as cold water. It is approved for use in many areas of the country—especially the South—and is gaining acceptance elsewhere.

PEX is an installer's dream. It's easy to cut and flexible enough to make gentle bends around corners. Joints in the run are made with compression fittings that require no special tools or materials—just a pair of pliers or an adjustable wrench. Rigid fittings require a special crimping tool (see Steps 2 and 3). Where approved by local codes, PEX is an ideal replacement for old galvanized pipes because it is easy to snake through walls.

Another advantage of PEX is that you can use a manifold fitting (Step 2), which allows you to pull one water supply line to a location and then add branch lines to various fixtures.

PRESTART CHECKLIST

☐ **TIME**
About an hour to run and install about 50 feet of pipe with five fittings

☐ **TOOLS**
Plastic tubing cutter or plastic-pipe cutter, crimping tool, adjustable wrench, reaming tool, drill

☐ **SKILLS**
Understanding of supply pipes

☐ **PREP**
Bore holes for running pipe through joists or studs

☐ **MATERIALS**
PEX tubing, compression fittings, crimp rings

Flexible tubing cutter

1 Holes for PEX tubing need not be carefully laid out in a straight line. PEX can be bent around corners, but don't make the bend too sharp or kink the tubing. In most cases you can run the pipe through the holes and then cut it in place. Drill 1-inch holes for ½-inch tubing.

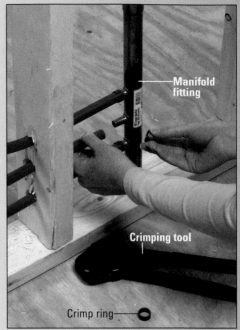

Manifold fitting

Crimping tool

Crimp ring

2 Make sure the tubing end is cut square and that the cut is free of burrs. To make a crimped connection, slide the crimp ring onto the tube, then slip the tube onto the fitting.

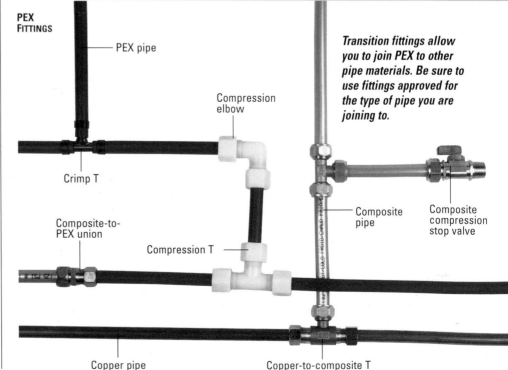

PEX FITTINGS

PEX pipe

Crimp T

Composite-to-PEX union

Compression elbow

Compression T

Transition fittings allow you to join PEX to other pipe materials. Be sure to use fittings approved for the type of pipe you are joining to.

Composite pipe

Composite compression stop valve

Copper pipe

Copper-to-composite T

3 Grasp the ring with the crimping tool and squeeze until you feel the ring compress. Tug on the connection to make sure it is rock-solid.

4 To install a stubout, temporarily screw the drop-ear elbows, mark the tubing for cutting, and cut with a tubing cutter.

5 Remove the elbow, attach it to the tubing using the crimping tool, and reattach the elbow. To prevent rattling when the water is turned on and off, clamp the pipe firmly every couple of feet. Where pipe runs through a hole, gently tap in a wooden shim.

Installing composite pipe

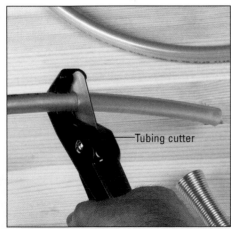

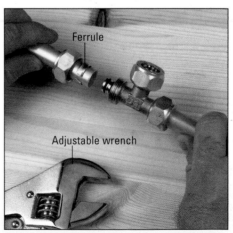

In addition to straight polyethylene pipe, composite pipe, with an aluminum core sheathed in plastic, is approved in some areas for water supply and for gas lines. Cut it with a tubing cutter.

Use a reaming tool to true the tubing into round and to clean out the inside of the cut end. Insert the tool and give it a couple of twists. Make sure no scrapings are left inside the tube.

Slip a nut and a ferrule onto the tube end, then slip the tube onto the fitting. Finger-tighten, taking care not to cross-thread. Then tighten the nut with one full turn (no more), using an adjustable wrench or pliers.

BUILDING A WET WALL

To build a new bathroom, half-bath, shower unit, kitchen, or laundry room in your basement, you'll probably have to build a wet wall to enclose the pipes. This is an undertaking which sounds formidable, but the work is not complicated, just heavy. In many homes you will have to break out the concrete to expose the existing drain line. In some homes, drain stub-ins may already be in place so you won't have to remove the concrete.

You can save some money by tearing out the concrete with a sledge hammer (trim the edge neatly with a cold chisel) but you'll find a rented electric jackhammer well worth the expense. Be sure you have an easy way to remove the old concrete—trash bags won't do.

When you install the drain lines, make sure to slope them for proper flow—¼ inch per running foot is standard, but check your local codes. They may require a steeper fall.

PRESTART CHECKLIST

☐ **TIME**
About 2 days to frame and plumb an 8-foot wall

☐ **TOOLS**
Tape measure, chalk line, small sledge and cold chisel, cordless drill, hammer, electric jackhammer or 12-pound sledge, wheelbarrow, mixing hoe, level, reciprocating saw

☐ **SKILLS**
Measuring and marking, breaking concrete, installing PVC and copper pipe

☐ **MATERIALS**
PVC and copper pipe, stakes, protective plates, 2× lumber, PVC primer and cement, concrete mix

1 Snap chalk lines to mark the areas to remove. Using a sledge and brick set or circular saw and masonry blade, score the lines. Then break out the concrete with an electric jackhammer or sledge. Dig a trench 2 inches deeper than the main drain.

2 Make a connection to the main drain line (see below). Dry-fit and mark the new drain and vent lines and cut them to fit. Support the new lines with stakes to slope them properly.

STANLEY PRO TIP: **Building a branch drain**

If you want a new bathroom in the basement but your chosen location is some distance from the existing main drain, you may have to install a branch line. This means breaking up the concrete and installing new lines and fittings as shown above. Before you tear into the floor, make sure you know exactly where the existing line runs.

Mark the position of the existing drain line and the proposed run of the branch line on the floor with a chalk line. Set the new shower and toilet in place to help you mark the exact location of the lines.

Score the lines with a masonry blade in your circular saw, then break up the concrete between the lines with a sledge or rented electric jackhammer. After you get the first chunk out, dig out the soil as far as you can

under the remaining sections as you go—concrete is easier to break if there's nothing beneath it.

If you aren't sure of the nominal size of the existing line, measure it so you will know what size fittings to buy. Mark the position of the new fitting carefully on the old line. Cut the line with a chain cutter, reciprocating saw, or hacksaw.

Install the new fitting with no-hub connectors (pages 96–97) on both sides of the cut line. Adjust the fitting with a torpedo level to ensure the correct fall, then tighten the no-hub clamps.

Install the new drain line, then recheck the fall of the line over its length; adjust it at either end if necessary. Pour concrete into the excavated trench and finish the surface.

3 Cement the fittings to the pipe with solvent cement, keeping the fittings aligned. Recheck for proper drain slope, and place aggregate around the line to hold it in position. After the line passes inspection from your local building department, backfill the trench with soil and pour concrete. Finish the concrete to match the floor.

4 Using the techniques on pages 70–75, frame a stud wall to enclose the drain and vent lines. Predrill holes in the studs for horizontal pipe runs. Assemble the remaining parts of the drain-waste-vent system. Connect the vent to the main stack.

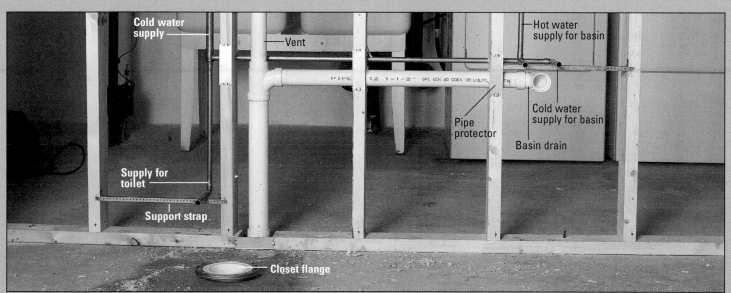

Cold water supply

Vent

Hot water supply for basin

PIPE 12 1-1/2" IPS SCH 40 COEX CELLULAR

Pipe protector

Cold water supply for basin

Basin drain

Supply for toilet

Support strap

Closet flange

5 Install shutoff valves on the supply lines closest to the new wet wall and extend copper supply lines to the wall, using the techniques shown on page 98. Install blocking or straps where necessary so the supply lines are supported properly and tack protective plates where the lines pass through the studs. Plug the lines to keep construction debris out. Leave the wallcovering off until the building inspector has approved the installation.

RUNNING DRAIN LINES

If you need to run a new drainpipe, draw a simple plan to show how it will be vented and where it will connect to the house's drain. Have your plan approved by a local plumbing inspector.

Because it needs to house only a 2-inch drain/vent pipe, a kitchen usually does not have wet wall as thick as a bathroom's (pages 94–95). If you run supply plumbing through an unheated crawlspace, it pays to insulate the pipes.

Remove wallcovering, cabinets, or other obstructions that are in the way to make the job easier. Cover other nearby surfaces and the flooring to protect them from scratches.

If wiring is in the way, **shut off the power to the circuit** and test to make sure power is off. You may need to remove a cable or move a box before working on the drain.

PRESTART CHECKLIST

☐ **TIME**
About a day to run a new drain line with a revent

☐ **TOOLS**
PVC saw or holesaw, level, drill with hole saw, reciprocating saw, layout square, hex-head driver

☐ **SKILLS**
Cutting and joining PVC pipe, running pipes through walls, connecting new pipe to old

☐ **PREP**
Clear the room of all obstructions; have your plans approved by an inspector

☐ **MATERIALS**
PVC pipe and fittings to suit local codes, fitting for joining to the drainpipe, PVC primer and cement, pipe straps, riser clamps, 2× blocks

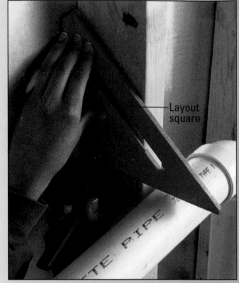
Layout square

1 Sometimes it's easiest to dry-fit all or part of the new drain and vent runs, then mark existing pipes for cutting. Use a level to check the vent and drain lines for correct slope—¼ inch per foot. Fasten the dry run in place with duct tape. This allows you to accurately mark the joints and check the slope and the final location of the drain stubout.

2 Once you've put together a dry run of the drain and vent lines, mark the framing for holes you'll need to cut. Using a layout square, strike a line even with the top of the pipe. Then mark the center of the pipe at the center of the stud.

Connecting new drain lines to the old

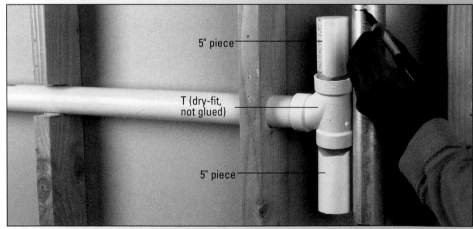
5" piece

T (dry-fit, not glued)

5" piece

1 To join a new plastic drainpipe to an old steel pipe, run new pipe into the room. Prime and glue two 5-inch pieces of pipe to a T fitting. Temporarily run pipe—longer than it needs to be—so it comes near the old pipe. (When running pipe across a stud wall, you may need to cut some of the holes into notches using a reciprocating saw.) Dry-fit the T assembly onto the new pipe and hold it next to the existing pipe. Mark the existing pipe for cutting. You may need to cut out a section slightly longer than the T assembly to accommodate the neoprene sleeves on the no-hub couplings.

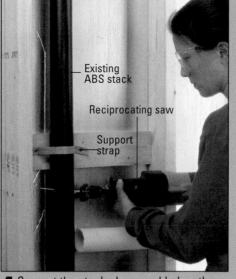

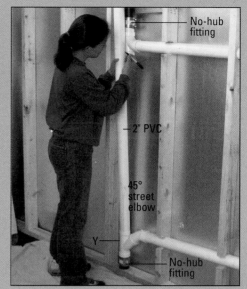

3 For 2-inch pipe, drill through the studs with a 2½-inch holesaw. When possible, cut until the guide bit pierces the stud, then bore from the opposite side to prevent tear-out. Assemble the pipes in the wall, notching the studs where necessary.

4 Support the stack above and below the cutting point you marked earlier with pipe straps. Then cut away the section to make way for the new fitting.

5 If the stack is ABS (shown in Step 4) or cast iron, use short lengths of PVC pipe and no-hub fittings to connect a sanitary T for the vent and a Y and 45-degree street elbow for the drain. Then mark and cut a section of 2-inch PVC pipe to fit between them to complete the stack.

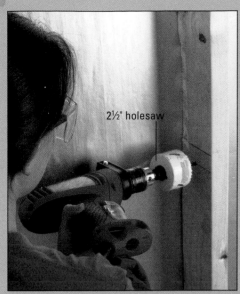

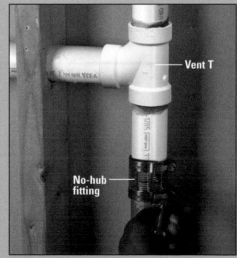

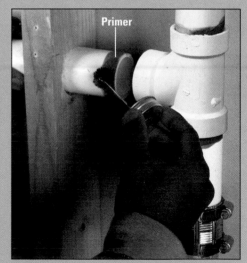

2 Support the pipe above and below the cut with riser clamps so it cannot drop as you work. The support also takes the weight of the drain stack above so the PVC fitting will not have to bear it. You will probably need to install a new stud or two as well as blocking for the upper clamp.

3 Slide a no-hub fitting onto each end of the old pipe, slide back the banded coupling, and fold down the neoprene sleeves. Position the T assembly. Fold the neoprene sleeves over the PVC pipe stubs and slide the metal bands over the sleeves. Tighten the nuts with a hex-head driver.

4 Cut the new pipe to exact length and test that it fits into the T fitting; you may need to loosen the nuts and rotate the fitting slightly. Prime and glue the pipe to the fitting.

RUNNING COPPER SUPPLY LINES

Rigid copper is the preferred material for supply lines in most localities, although flexible or rigid plastic might be permitted. An hour or two of practice will prepare you to cut copper pipe and sweat joints quickly and securely (pages 88–89).

Supply lines can be routed along almost any path, although extending a pipe run and adding bends will lower water pressure slightly. Some plumbers prefer to run pipes so that they do not cross drainpipes or vents. In most cases it's easier to make the horizontal runs below the room in the crawlspace or basement.

Installing hammer arresters (Step 3) eliminates the banging noise when you turn a faucet on or off.

Copper pipe can last for many decades. However, it is easily punctured or dented. Position it out of harm's way and install protector plates where pipes pass through the studs to protect against errant nails.

As you face the wall, hot water supply lines always come out on the left, cold water on the right.

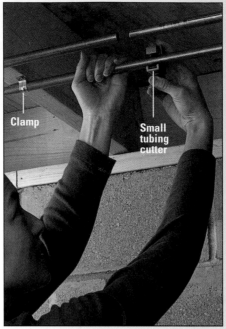

1 To tap into existing copper lines, shut off the water. With a tubing cutter, cut an opening in each pipe that is about an inch shorter than a T fitting. Dry-fit the Ts. If the pipes are rigidly installed, remove a clamp or two so you can pull the ends apart slightly.

Labels: Clamp, Small tubing cutter

2 Dry-fit the pipes that will be inserted into the Ts and draw alignment marks. Disassemble, wire-brush the fittings and pipe ends, brush on flux, and sweat the joints (pages 88–89).

Label: T

PRESTART CHECKLIST

☐ **TIME**
About half a day to run supply lines for a sink and toilet

☐ **TOOLS**
Drill, bit and bit extender, propane torch, tubing cutter, multiuse wire brush, flame guard, groove-joint pliers, carpentry tools for installing braces, flux brush

☐ **SKILLS**
Accurate measuring and drilling, working with copper pipe

☐ **PREP**
Install all or most of the drain and vent pipes; determine the supply routes

☐ **MATERIALS**
Copper pipe and fittings, flux, solder, damp rag, nailing plate

Running and securing supply pipes

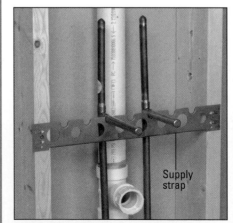

A copper supply strap attaches to the face of the studs. Pipes fit into notches or holes, sized and spaced for correct placement. The pipes can be soldered onto the strap using the same techniques as for sweating fittings.

Label: Supply strap

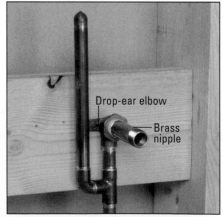

A drop-ear elbow makes the most secure attachment. If you use one, the hammer arrester must be connected to a T and an elbow just below the drop-ear elbow. Insert a brass threaded nipple into the elbow.

Labels: Drop-ear elbow, Brass nipple

Hammer
arrester

8–10"

19"

Toilet
supply

8"

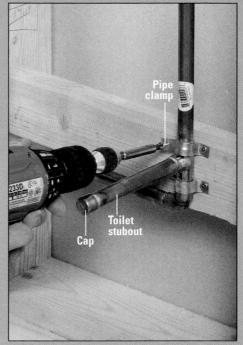

Pipe
clamp

Toilet
stubout

Cap

3 Hot and cold stubouts should be 8 to 10 inches apart and 19 to 23 inches above the floor; consult the fixture manufacturer's instructions to be sure. A toilet stubout is usually 8 inches above the floor. Dry-fit a complete assembly for the sink and the toilet. For each stubout use a T fitting, a 6-inch length of pipe (which you will cut off later), and a cap to protect the pipe. Install a hammer arrester to each.

4 Sweat all the parts following instructions on page 89. Anchor the pipes with one or two clamps at each stubout as shown.

STANLEY PRO TIP

Tap into shower supplies

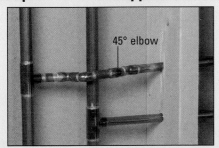

45° elbow

Rather than run sink supply lines from below, you may want to run them horizontally from the tub or shower. If the shower lines are ¾ inch, use reducer Ts to tap into the lines. Use 45-degree elbows to snake one line past the other (in this case the hot past the vertical cold-water line). If the sink is used at the same time as the shower, water temperature will change.

WHAT IF...
Supply lines must run past drain or vent pipes?

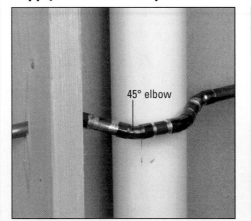

45° elbow

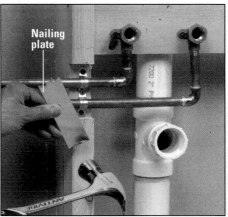

Nailing
plate

Run supply lines around an obstruction such as a drain or vent pipe with four 45-degree elbows. This arrangement allows smoother water flow and less loss of water pressure than using 90-degree elbows.

Cut notches rather than holes and run supply pipes in front of the vent pipes. If you do this, install protective nailing plates to prevent the pipes from being punctured by a nail when the drywall is installed.

WIRING

Although some homeowners fear working with electricity, a handy person who carefully follows instructions can install wiring and fixtures safely and with good results. Attention to detail is the key to success.

Approach household electrical work with caution and respect. Professional electricians take steps to ensure they have double and even triple protection against electric shocks. You should be just as careful while doing the work.

Shut off the power
Before starting any electrical project, always shut off power to the circuit you will be working on. Then test to make sure there is no power present in the electrical box or wires you'll be working with. Check all the wires in a box—even the white neutral wires—in case wiring was done incorrectly in the past.

You may be tempted to save a trip to the service panel. Or you might think you can change a receptacle or light without touching any wires. Don't risk it. It takes only a few minutes to protect yourself against shock.

Insulate yourself
The seriousness of an electric shock varies with the amount of power present, how well insulated you are from it, and your physical condition. Of these three variables, you can control the first two. Turn off the power, then insulate yourself by wearing rubber-soled shoes and removing jewelry. Keep yourself dry. If the floor of your work area is damp or wet, lay dry boards or a rubber mat to stand on. Use tools with insulated handles.

If you are wearing dry clothes and rubber-soled shoes, a 120-volt shock might jolt you but probably not harm you. If you have a heart condition or are particularly sensitive to shock, however, the effects could be more serious. If you haven't taken proper precautions, a shock is more likely to cause injury.

Don't take chances: Turn off the power and insulate yourself for any electrical work. If you feel uncomfortable about doing any task, don't do it. Call a pro.

Put your plans on paper
Before you tackle the wiring for your remodeling, make rough drawings showing the lighting and electrical service you want to install. Start planning ways to run cable with minimal damage to existing walls.

Next figure out whether your existing service can support new circuits. You may be able to connect to existing circuits. Or you may need to add a circuit or two to your existing service panel, add a subpanel, or install a new service panel.

Why codes count
Electrical work must meet standards established by the National Electrical Code and local building codes. Codes protect you and everyone in your home from shock and fire. They also standardize installations to make it easier to work on the electrical system in the future. Anyone who works on your home's wiring later will understand the system if it is installed according to standards.

Good planning will not only make wiring your bathroom easier, it will also help keep you safe.

CHAPTER PREVIEW

Wiring a bathroom, kitchen, and laundry room
page 102

Stripping and clamping cable
page 104

Working with metal conduit
page 106

Working with PVC conduit
page 108

A do-it-yourselfer can safely install new wiring and fixtures by following simple safety rules and working carefully.

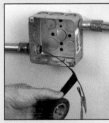

Pulling wires through conduit
page 109

Running cable in framing
page 110

Installing switches and receptacles
page 112

Installing electric radiant heat
page 114

Hooking up a new circuit
page 116

WIRING A BATHROOM, KITCHEN, AND LAUNDRY ROOM

Wiring for a bathroom, kitchen, or laundry room must meet specific requirements to ensure proper function, convenience, and safety,

Wiring a bathroom

Because bathrooms are often damp, all receptacles should be protected by a ground fault circuit interrupter (GFCI). You should have at least one 20-amp GFCI receptacle within a foot or so of the sink. Some codes require separate circuits for bathrooms; others permit bathrooms to share receptacle and light circuits with other rooms. An exhaust fan is essential; a fan with a heater may use enough electricity to require its own circuit. The lights and fan must be on a different circuit from the receptacles. For comfort, install lighting over the sink and in the shower (use an approved moisture-proof fixture), with the switch at the doorway or by the sink.

Wiring a kitchen

A kitchen needs a lot of electrical services: abundant lighting, receptacles to run six or seven appliances at once, and separate circuits for some appliances. Where possible, position light switches near their lights (typically on 15-amp circuits) to minimize confusion about which fixture each switch controls. Install three-way switches to turn lights on and off from two different entrances. Many codes require a separate refrigerator circuit, and a large microwave oven may need its own circuit too. Electric ranges, stove tops, and ovens must be wired to a dedicated 120/240-volt circuit. You should also have two circuits for countertop receptacles. Check local codes for details.

Wiring a laundry room

Codes are specific about laundry-room wiring. If the dryer is electric, you need a separate 120/240-volt receptacle. If the dryer is gas, it can plug into a receptacle on the same circuit as the washer. There should be an extra receptacle so you won't have to reach back and unplug the washer or dryer to plug in something else. Laundry-room receptacles must be on a dedicated 20-amp circuit. The lights, however, can share a circuit with lights in another room.

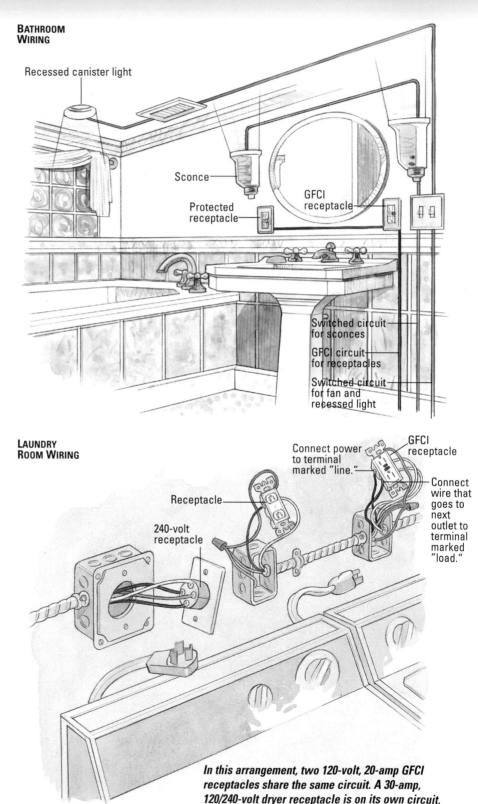

BATHROOM WIRING

Recessed canister light

Sconce

GFCI receptacle

Protected receptacle

Switched circuit for sconces

GFCI circuit for receptacles

Switched circuit for fan and recessed light

LAUNDRY ROOM WIRING

GFCI receptacle

Connect power to terminal marked "line."

Connect wire that goes to next outlet to terminal marked "load."

Receptacle

240-volt receptacle

In this arrangement, two 120-volt, 20-amp GFCI receptacles share the same circuit. A 30-amp, 120/240-volt dryer receptacle is on its own circuit.

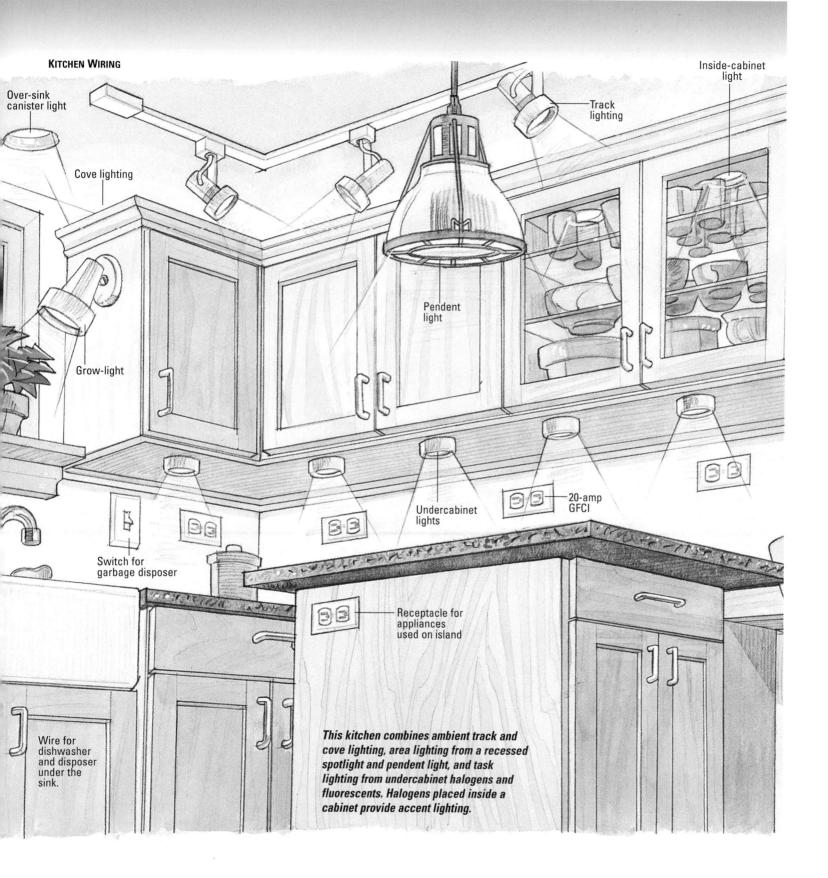

KITCHEN WIRING

Over-sink canister light

Cove lighting

Grow-light

Inside-cabinet light

Track lighting

Pendent light

Undercabinet lights

20-amp GFCI

Switch for garbage disposer

Receptacle for appliances used on island

Wire for dishwasher and disposer under the sink.

This kitchen combines ambient track and cove lighting, area lighting from a recessed spotlight and pendent light, and task lighting from undercabinet halogens and fluorescents. Halogens placed inside a cabinet provide accent lighting.

STRIPPING AND CLAMPING CABLE

Nonmetallic (NM) cable is easy to work with and inexpensive, so it's not surprising that it is the most common type of cable used in household wiring.

NM cable is usually sold in 25-, 50-, or 100-foot lengths. When in doubt buy the larger package—it doesn't cost much more and it may come in handy later.

NM's plastic sheathing does not offer much protection to the wires, so the cable must be protected from damage. Run NM cable through holes in the center of studs so drywall nails cannot damage it. If the cable is less than 1¼ inches from the edge of a framing member, install a protective nailing plate (page 111). Some codes require this even for cable in the center of a stud.

Take care not to damage the wire insulation when working with NM cable. Slit the sheathing right down the middle with a sharp utility knife or a sheathing stripper. To avoid slicing the wire insulation, don't cut too deep with a knife.

When cutting cable leave yourself an extra foot or two. If you make a mistake while stripping, you can recut the cable.

Armored cable
Armored cable (MC cable) is required in some instances. Its coiled metal sheathing offers better protection against physical damage than the plastic on NM cable.

Wherever cable will be exposed—where you've run a new bathroom circuit through an open basement, for instance—many local codes call for armored cable or conduit (pages 106–110). You could also run armored cable behind moldings where it comes near nails.

Armored cable costs more than NM, takes longer to strip and clamp, and can't make tight turns. However, with practice you can install armored cable nearly as quickly as you can run NM cable.

BX cable has no ground wire (page 48). It is common in older homes and is still available in some areas. Local code may limit use of BX to no more than 6 feet; then ground wire must be used. MC cable has a green-insulated ground wire that works like the bare ground wire in NM cable.

Stripping NM cable

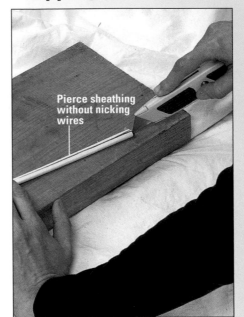

Pierce sheathing without nicking wires

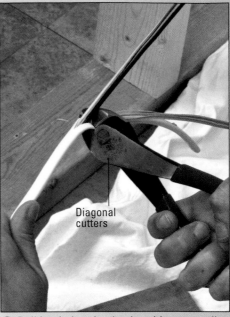

Diagonal cutters

1 Lay the cable on a flat work surface, such as a small piece of scrap wood. Starting 8–10 inches from the end, insert the tip of a utility knife blade into the center of the cable, pushing just hard enough to cut through the sheathing. Slice the sheathing, exerting even pressure.

2 Pull back the plastic sheathing, as well as the paper wrapped around the wires, exposing 6–8 inches of wire. Snip back the sheathing and paper with diagonal cutters or a knife. If you use a utility knife, cut away from the wires to avoid cutting or nicking the insulation.

Grounding NM cable

Metal boxes must be grounded. The surest method is to connect both the device and the box to the ground wire in the cable with pigtail leads.

If the box is plastic, simply connect the ground wire to the device's grounding terminal.

Clamping NM cable

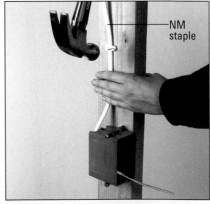

NM staple

With this type of box, push the wires through the hole and the tab will grab the cable. About ½ inch of sheathing should show inside the box. Staple NM cable to framing so it's out of reach of nails. Fasten it within 8 inches of the box and every 2–4 feet thereafter.

Stripping armored cable

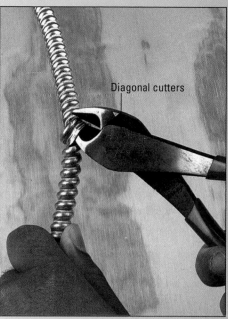

1 Bend the cable about 10 inches from its end and squeeze with your hand until the coils of the armor come apart. If you can't do this by hand, use a pair of pliers. Firmly grip the cable on each side of the cut and twist until the split-armor coil pops out, away from the wires.

2 Using diagonal cutters, cut the exposed coil of sheathing. You may have to grab the coil with the cutters and work it back and forth to open and make the cut.

3 If you are cutting a piece to length, slide back the sheathing and cut through the wires. Otherwise slide the waste piece off and throw it away. Cut off any sharp points of sheathing. Remove the paper wrapping and any thin plastic strips. If the cable is BX, cut the thin metal bonding strip to 2 inches.

Grounding MC cable

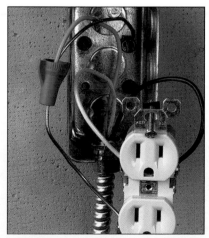

MC cable has a ground wire. Attach it the same way you would the ground wire in NM cable (opposite page) except strip the green insulation first.

STANLEY PRO TIP: **Clamp armored cable**

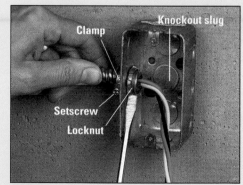

1 Most metallic cable comes with a bag of bushings; if not, purchase some. Slip a bushing over the wires and slide it down into the sheathing so it protects wires from the cut end of the armor. Remove the locknut from the armored-cable clamp and slide the clamp over the wires and down onto the bushing. Then tighten the setscrew.

2 Remove the knockout slug from the box. Guide the wires and the clamp through the hole. Slip the locknut over the wires and screw it onto the clamp. Tighten the nut by levering it with a screwdriver or tapping it with a screwdriver and hammer.

WORKING WITH METAL CONDUIT

Conduit offers superior protection and safety for wires. Even if local codes permit NM cable for basement and crawlspace runs, consider installing conduit to protect the wiring.

Choosing conduit

Metal conduit comes in several thicknesses. For most interior home installations, EMT (also called "thinwall") is strong enough. In some areas PVC conduit meets local codes for indoor use.

Metal conduit may serve as the path for grounding, or local codes may require you to run a green-insulated ground wire. If you install metal conduit without a ground wire, make sure all the connections are tight; one loose joint could break the grounding path. PVC conduit always requires a ground wire, either green-insulated or bare copper wire.

Conduit fittings

A conduit bender used by professional electricians is a tool that takes time to master. Unless you will be running lots of metal conduit, you'll save time by buying prebent conduit sections and fittings. A coupling joins two pieces of conduit end to end. A sweep makes a long turn through which you can easily pull wires. Install a pulling elbow where you need to make a sharper turn.

The setscrew fittings shown at right are commonly used with EMT conduit. They make firm but not waterproof joints.

Flexible metal conduit

Flexible metal conduit, also called "Greenfield," is like armored cable without the wires. It is costly, so it is typically used only in places where it would be difficult to bend conduit to fit.

When installing a hardwired appliance, such as an electric water heater, buy an electrical whip, which is a section of armored cable equipped with the correct fittings for attaching to the appliance.

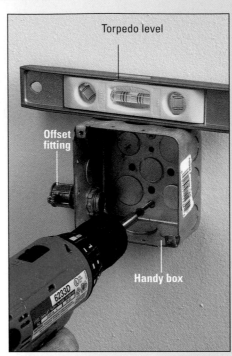

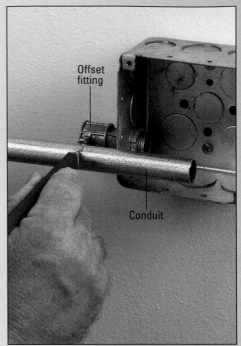

1 Anchor metal boxes to the wall with screws (use concrete screws for block walls). For exposed wiring use handy boxes, which have rounded edges and metal covers. An offset fitting allows the conduit to run tight up against the wall.

2 Once the boxes are installed, measure the conduit for cutting. The surest method is to hold a piece in place and mark it rather than using a tape measure. Remember that the conduit will slide about an inch into each fitting.

Metal conduit

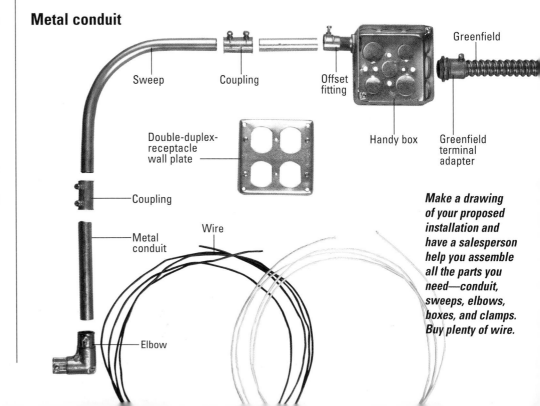

Make a drawing of your proposed installation and have a salesperson help you assemble all the parts you need—conduit, sweeps, elbows, boxes, and clamps. Buy plenty of wire.

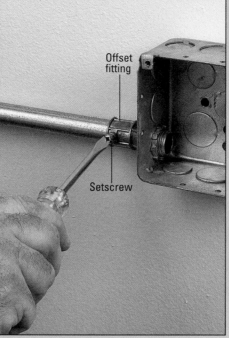

3 Cut the conduit to fit with a hacksaw. Do not use a tubing cutter, which creates sharp edges inside the conduit that could damage wire insulation. Remove the burrs inside and out. A conduit-reaming attachment on a screwdriver makes this easy.

4 Slide the conduit all the way into the fitting and tighten the setscrew. Test to make sure the connection is tight. (If you will not be installing a ground wire, these connections are critical for grounding.)

5 Anchor the conduit with a one- or two-hole strap at least every 6 feet and within 2 feet of each box. The larger the conduit, the closer the straps need to be. Check with local codes. Screws should be driven into joists or studs, not just into drywall.

Conduit that's large enough

Make sure the wires have ample room inside the conduit to slide through easily. Local codes have detailed regulations regarding conduit size, but in general, 1/2-inch conduit is large enough for five or fewer wires; 3/4-inch conduit is used for more than five wires. When in doubt, or if you might run more wire in the future, buy the larger size—it doesn't cost much more than the smaller one.

Anchoring conduit
Anchor conduit with one- or two-hole straps every 6 feet and within 2 feet of each box.

A pulling elbow every fourth turn

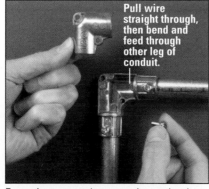

Pull wire straight through, then bend and feed through other leg of conduit.

Every time you make a turn, it gets harder for the wires to slide through. If the conduit will make more than three turns before entering a box, install a pulling elbow so you can access the wires. Never make a splice here, just use it as an access point when pulling wires.

STANLEY PRO TIP: **Anchor to masonry**

To attach boxes and straps to concrete, block, or brick, buy masonry screws and a masonry bit of the correct size. Level the box and drill pilot holes.

Drive a masonry screw into the pilot hole, being careful not to overtighten it. The combination of proper hole and screw provides a much more secure attachment than a plastic anchor.

WORKING WITH PVC CONDUIT

Plastic conduit is nearly as durable as metal conduit and it costs less. Some local codes permit it for exposed indoor wiring.

When installing PVC conduit, connect four or five pieces in a dry run, make alignment marks, then dismantle and glue the pieces together. When making a turn, take care that the elbow or sweep is facing in exactly the right direction when you glue it. Once the glue sets, you will not be able to make adjustments. Work in a well-ventilated area when using PVC primer and cement—the fumes are powerful and dangerous.

Consult local codes for the correct PVC cement. You may be required to apply purple-color primer to every piece before you apply the cement. **Always run a green-insulated ground wire through PVC pipe.**

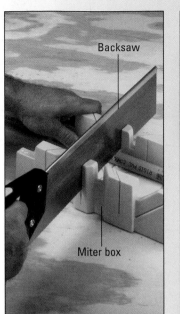

1 Install PVC boxes, then measure and cut the conduit. Cut with a backsaw and miter box, a hacksaw, a circular saw or mitersaw equipped with a blade for cutting plywood, or a tubing cutter.

Backsaw

Miter box

2 Use alignment marks to ensure that the pieces will face in the right direction. Apply PVC primer (if needed) and cement to the outside of the conduit and to the inside of the fitting.

Alignment mark

Primer

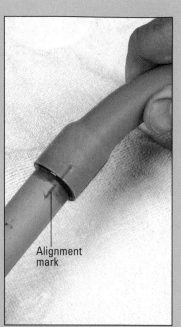

3 Immediately push the conduit into the fitting, twisting it enough to align the marks. Hold the pieces together for about 10 seconds; wipe away cement that squeezes out.

Alignment mark

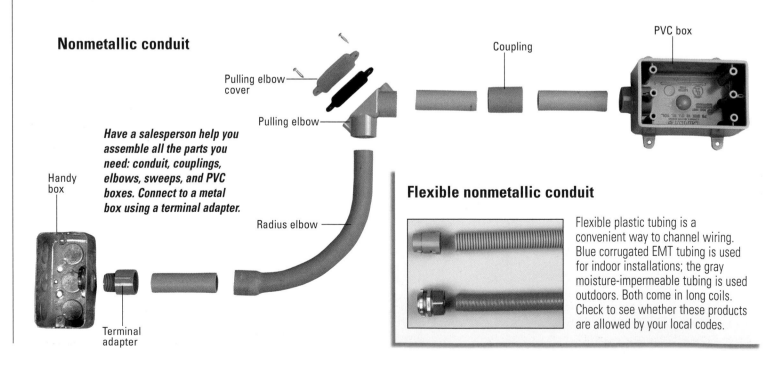

Nonmetallic conduit

Pulling elbow cover

Pulling elbow

Coupling

PVC box

Have a salesperson help you assemble all the parts you need: conduit, couplings, elbows, sweeps, and PVC boxes. Connect to a metal box using a terminal adapter.

Handy box

Radius elbow

Terminal adapter

Flexible nonmetallic conduit

Flexible plastic tubing is a convenient way to channel wiring. Blue corrugated EMT tubing is used for indoor installations; the gray moisture-impermeable tubing is used outdoors. Both come in long coils. Check to see whether these products are allowed by your local codes.

PULLING WIRES THROUGH CONDUIT

If wires travel less than 6 feet through conduit and make only one or two turns, you may be able to just push them through. For longer runs pull them through with a fish tape.

If wires become kinked while you work they will get stuck, so have a helper feed the wire carefully from one end of the conduit while you pull at the other end. If you must work alone, precut the wires (leave yourself an extra 2 feet or so) and unroll them so that they can slide smoothly through the conduit.

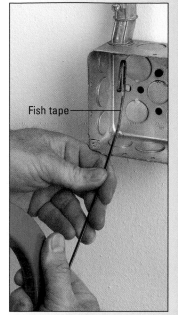

1 At a box or pulling elbow, push the fish tape into the conduit and thread it back to the point of entry.

Fish tape

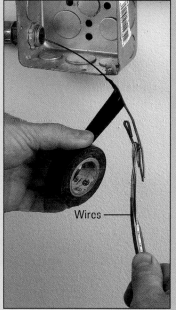

2 Strip 6 inches of insulation from one wire, 8 inches from another wire, 10 inches from a third wire, and so on. Fold the wires over the fish tape as shown and wrap tightly with electrician's tape.

Wires

3 Pull smoothly, using long strokes to avoid stopping and starting. If the wires get stuck, back up a foot or so and start again.

TEAM UP TO PULL WIRE THROUGH CONDUIT

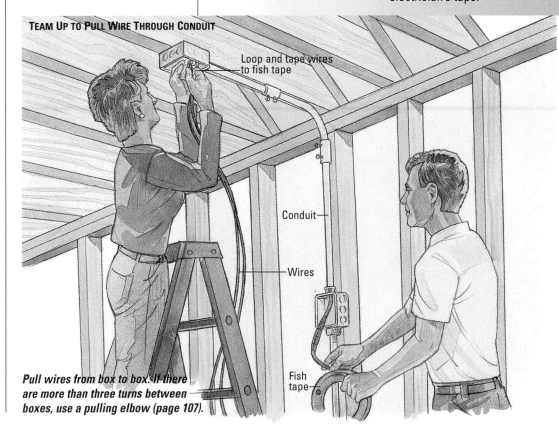

Loop and tape wires to fish tape

Conduit

Wires

Fish tape

Pull wires from box to box. If there are more than three turns between boxes, use a pulling elbow (page 107).

(page 107).

STANLEY PRO TIP

Use pulling lubricant

If the pulling gets tough, try squirting some pulling lubricant on the wires. Don't use soap, detergent, oil, or grease, which can damage wire insulation.

RUNNING CABLE IN FRAMING

Under most building codes, nonmetallic (NM) cable is acceptable for framing runs, but some localities require armored cable or conduit. Armored cable is run much like the NM cable shown, though you may need to drill larger holes and you'll have more difficulty turning corners. To run conduit through framing, use a level or a chalk line to make sure the holes are aligned for straight runs.

A wayward nail could pierce NM cable and damage the wires or insulation. Place holes in the framing out of reach of drywall nails and attach protective plates at every hole.

PRESTART CHECKLIST

☐ **TIME**
About 3 hours to run cable and attach to seven or eight wall or ceiling boxes

☐ **TOOLS**
Drill, ¾-inch spade bits, screwdriver, wire stripper, lineman's pliers, hammer, tape measure, level

☐ **SKILLS**
Drilling, stripping cable sheathing and wire insulation, attaching staples

☐ **PREP**
Double-check that all the boxes are correctly positioned; clear the room of all obstructions

☐ **MATERIALS**
Correct cable (page 48), staples, nailing plates, boxes

1 Set the box as shown, about a hammer length from the floor and extended beyond the stud by the drywall thickness. Drive the box nails into the stud or joist. Drive screws or nails to anchor a flanged box.

Drill with ¾" spade bit

Staple

2 Mark and drill level holes in the studs about 12 inches above the box. Uncoil the cable and pull it through the holes. Staple the cable within 8 inches of a plastic box or 12 inches of a metal box, then every 2 feet.

3 Mark where you will strip sheathing and cut the cable. About ½ inch of sheathing should enter the box, and the wires inside the box should be at least 8–12 inches long (you can always trim them later).

INSTALLING NM CABLE

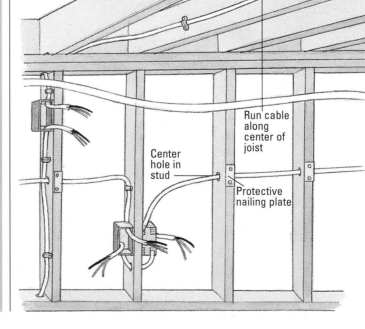

Run cable along center of joist

Center hole in stud

Protective nailing plate

NM cable should be routed where it won't be hit by nails later pounded into the wall. Where possible add protective nailing plates. When working with engineered joists, check the manufacturer's information before cutting, drilling, or nailing. You could void the warranty for the joists.

Placing receptacles: Most codes call for receptacle boxes 12 inches from the floor and switch boxes 46 inches high. Run cable about a foot above the boxes where possible.

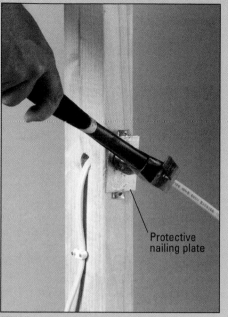

Turning a corner

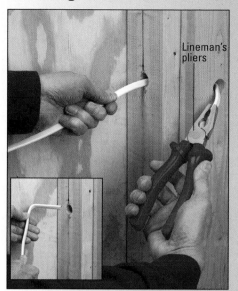

Lineman's pliers

4 With a hammer and screwdriver, open the knockout. On some plastic boxes, you remove the knockout entirely. On the one shown, one end of the tab cracks open so it can grab the cable. A metal box may have a built-in clamp, or you may have to add a clamp before sliding in the cable.

5 Wherever a nail might accidentally pierce the cable, attach a protective nailing plate. Tap the plate in place and hammer it in. Attach plates on both sides of the stud, if needed.

Protective nailing plate

When you reach a corner, drill a hole in each stud. Bend the cable into an L shape. Poke the cable through the first hole and wiggle it into the next hole. When the cable starts to stick out the second hole, grab it with pliers and pull.

STANLEY PRO TIP: **Mount a ceiling light fixture box**

Using a mud ring

Mud ring

Decide where you want a ceiling light fixture to go (usually the center of a room). Attach a flanged box directly to a ceiling joist (above). For more precise placement, install a box attached to a hanger bar; the box slides along the bar. A hanger bar cannot support a ceiling fan; for that, you must use a fan-rated box.

Adapter rings, also called mud rings, are typically ½ inch or ⅝ inch thick. Choose a ring that matches the thickness of the drywall or paneling to be installed. Attach the box flush with the front edge of the framing member, then attach the ring to the box.

INSTALLING SWITCHES AND RECEPTACLES

Bathrooms, kitchens, and laundry rooms require GFCI receptacles, and installing them is a simple matter.

A single-pole switch is the most common type of switch. It has two terminals (not counting the ground), and its toggle is marked with "on" and "off." If three wires attach to it (not counting the ground), it's a three-way switch.

PRESTART CHECKLIST

☐ **TIME**
About 2 hours to run cable and make connections (not including cutting a pathway for the cable and patching the walls)

☐ **TOOLS**
Voltage tester, drill, saw, hammer, fish tape, screwdriver, wire stripper, long-nose pliers, lineman's pliers, utility knife, stud finder, torpedo level, tape measure, pry bar, perhaps a drywall saw or jigsaw

☐ **SKILLS**
Stripping and connecting wires to terminals; installing boxes; running cable through walls and ceilings

☐ **PREP**
Lay a drop cloth on the floor

☐ **MATERIALS**
New receptacle or switch, cable, remodel box and clamps, wire nuts, electrician's tape, protective nailing plates, cable staples

Installing switches

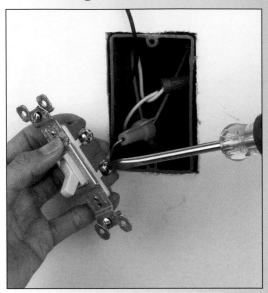

1 If you're replacing a switch, check the wires and terminals. Cut and restrip damaged wire. Loosen the terminal screws and pull off the wires. If you're installing a new switch, run cable and install the box.

2 Form loops in the wire ends with long-nose pliers. Wrap the loops clockwise around terminals and tighten screws. Wrap the switch with electrician's tape to cover terminal screws and any bare wire. Install the switch and coverplate.

Stripping wires

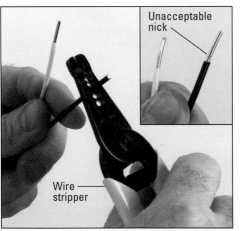

Unacceptable nick

Wire stripper

Open the stripper, place the wire in the correct slot, and squeeze it shut. Give a slight twist, then slide the insulation off.

If you have to pull hard or the stripper nicks the wire, be sure you are using the right slot for the wire gauge. If the problem persists, buy a new wire stripper.

Using wire nuts

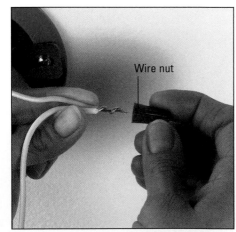

Wire nut

Strip 1¼ inches of insulation from the wires and twist them tightly. Poke the wires into a wire nut as far as possible. Twist the nut tight. Tug on the wire to check the connection. Wrap the bottom of the nut with electrician's tape.

Installing receptacles

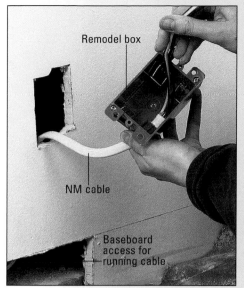

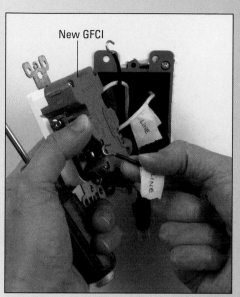

1 Cut a hole for a remodel box and cable access, if necessary. Run cable to the hole, clamp the cable to the box, and install the new box.

2 A GFCI wired in the middle of a circuit will protect all receptacles down the line. Connect the wires that bring power to the box to the line terminals and those that go to receptacles to load terminals.

3 Wrap the receptacle with tape and push it back into the box. Because a GFCI is bulkier than a standard receptacle, take extra care folding the wires into the box behind it.

Attaching wires

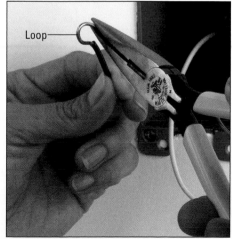

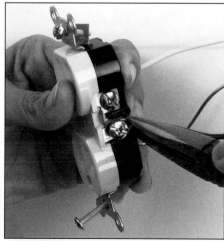

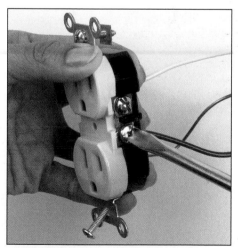

With the tip of a pair of long-nose pliers, grab the bare wire just past the insulation and twist it to the left. Slide the pliers up a little and bend to the right, forming a partial circle.

Unscrew the terminal screw until it becomes hard to turn. Slip the looped wire end over the screw threads. Grab the wire on either side of the screw with long-nose pliers and tighten around the terminal screw.

Check that the loop is on the terminal screw clockwise. Tug to make sure the wire cannot come loose. Tighten the terminal screw until the wire is snug between the screw head and the surface of the terminal.

INSTALLING ELECTRIC RADIANT HEAT

Consider installing electric radiant heat in your basement floor. Installed directly over the substrate (cement board, plywood, a mortar bed, or a concrete slab), this system uses a plastic mat with interwoven heater cable. You can use it under most finish flooring. The mat is embedded in thinset before the final flooring material is installed. Controlled by a wall-mounted thermostat or timer, the heating mat radiates warmth at a preset temperature.

The 120-volt circuit or power source for the radiant heat mats must be GFCI protected. Mats are available in a variety of lengths. Check the manufacturer's specifications for the wattage your situation will require. It will increase as the size of the room increases.

PRESTART CHECKLIST

☐ **TIME**
About 8 hours to install mat, wire, and tile for an average bathroom

☐ **TOOLS**
Digital ohmmeter, drill, ½-inch bit, drywall saw, fish tape, chisel, hot-glue gun, ⅜-inch trowel, screwdriver, stripper, long-nose pliers, lineman's pliers, tools for laying the flooring

☐ **SKILLS**
Stripping, splicing, and connecting wires to terminals; installing boxes; running cable into boxes; using ohmmeter; setting tile

☐ **PREP**
Rough in the plumbing; install the subfloor

☐ **MATERIALS**
12/2 cable, mat, box, armored power cable, thermostat and/or timer, thinset, flooring, mortar or grout

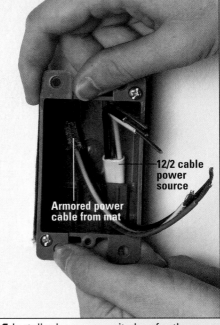

1 Install a large-capacity box for the thermostat 60 inches above the floor. Using 12/2 cable, add a new circuit or extend an existing circuit, but **do not connect the power source.** Provide a route to pull the power cable and sensor cable from the mat into the box.

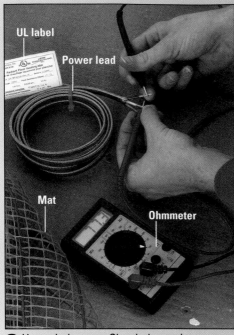

2 Unpack the mat. Check the resistance using an ohmmeter. The reading should be within 10 percent of the rating shown on the UL label. Write the reading on a piece of paper. This will be your benchmark for confirming that the heat cable has not been damaged during installation.

INSTALLING UNDER-FLOOR ELECTRIC RADIANT HEATING

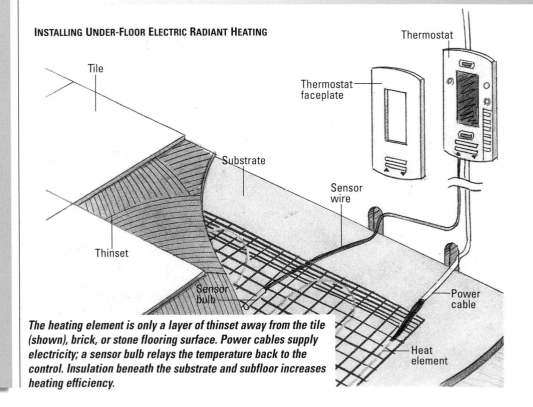

The heating element is only a layer of thinset away from the tile (shown), brick, or stone flooring surface. Power cables supply electricity; a sensor bulb relays the temperature back to the control. Insulation beneath the substrate and subfloor increases heating efficiency.

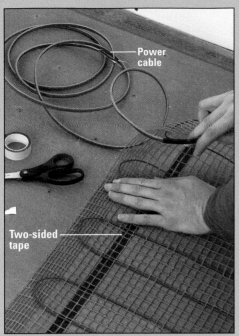

Power cable

Two-sided tape

3 Clean the floor of debris and tighten any protruding screw or nailheads. Roll out the mat so it's at least 3 to 6 inches away from walls and fixtures. Staple the mat to the floor with ½-inch staples or fasten it with double-sided tape every 12–24 inches.

Hot-glue gun

4 Hot-glue the power cable to the substrate. Mark along the power cable and slide it to one side. Working a few feet at a time, run a continuous bead of hot glue. Press the lead into the bead of hot glue. Make sure the lead wires don't cross each other or run perpendicular to a heater wire.

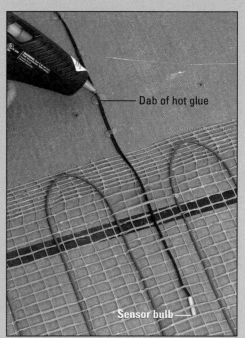

Dab of hot glue

Sensor bulb

5 If your system uses a thermostatic sensor, weave the sensor bulb between two heating elements. Adhere the bulb wire with dots of hot glue. Now check the mat resistance with an ohmmeter. If the reading falls outside the manufacturer's tolerance, find the damaged area and replace it.

Thinset

6 With the flat side of a ⅜-inch notched trowel, apply thinset over an area of the mat. Then turn the trowel over and rake the thinset to ¼-inch uniform depth. Be careful not to snag the mat. Do not clean the trowel by banging it on the mat. Tile the area of the floor covered with thinset.

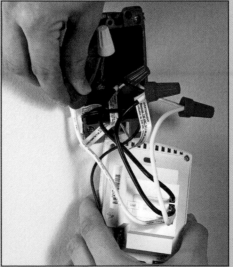

7 Attach the black control lead marked "line" to the incoming black wire. Connect the white control lead "line" to the incoming white wire. Attach the black and white control leads marked "load" to the black and white wires that run to the mat. Fold the wires into the box.

8 Attach the faceplate. Connect to the power source or connect the line to a new breaker. Turn on the power and follow the manufacturer's instructions for setting the temperature and timer.

HOOKING UP A NEW CIRCUIT

Though it may seem complicated, connecting a new circuit is a relatively straightforward project. You'll spend most of your time running cable from the new service to the service panel.

Make sure that adding a new circuit will not overload your electrical system. To make sure you have all the details right, talk with an inspector or an electrician about your plans. If the service panel cannot accept another circuit, install a subpanel. If your system cannot accommodate a new circuit, have an electrician install a new service panel.

If there is an available slot for a new circuit breaker in your service panel, you can add a breaker there. If not, you may be able to replace a regular circuit breaker with a tandem breaker (below right).

PRESTART CHECKLIST

☐ **TIME**
About two hours to make connections for a new circuit once cable has been run

☐ **TOOLS**
Flashlight, hammer, screwdriver, strippers, lineman's pliers, long-nose pliers, voltage tester

☐ **SKILLS**
Figuring loads on circuits; stripping sheathing and wire insulation; connecting wires to terminals

☐ **PREP**
Install boxes for the new service and run cable from the boxes to the service panel

☐ **MATERIALS**
New circuit breaker and cable

1 **Shut off the main breaker** and remove the panel's cover. Remove a knockout slug from the side of the cover.

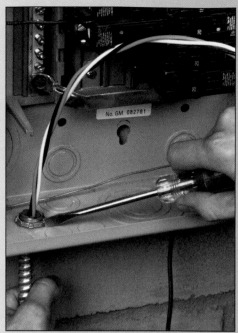

2 Run cable to the box, adding at least 2 feet extra for wiring work within the service panel. Strip enough sheathing from the cable to allow wires to travel most of the way around the panel. Slide the wires through the knockout hole and clamp the cable in place.

REFRESHER COURSE
When do you need a new circuit?

If new electrical service—lights, receptacles, or appliances—use so much wattage that they cannot be added to an existing circuit without overloading it, then a new circuit is called for. See page 25 for the calculations.

Extra protection
Install an arc fault circuit interrupter (AFCI) instead of a standard circuit breaker. It provides extra protection against fire due to frayed or overheated cords. AFCIs are now required for bedroom wiring.

Two for one with a tandem breaker

A tandem circuit breaker makes it possible to install two circuits in the space of one. Unlike double-pole breakers, tandem breakers can be switched off and on individually. Some panels do not accept tandem breakers. Others allow only a certain number of tandems. Get an inspector's OK before you install a tandem.

3 Route the wires so they skirt the perimeter of the panel and stay far away from hot bus bars. Strip ½ inch of insulation from the neutral wire and connect it to the neutral bus bar. Connect the ground wire to the ground bus bar.

4 Bend the hot wire into position along the side of the panel, cut it to length, and strip ½ inch of insulation. Poke it into the breaker and tighten the setscrew.

5 Slide one end of the breaker under the hot bus bar and push the breaker until it snaps in place and aligns with the surrounding breakers. Twist out a knockout slot in the service panel's cover and replace the cover.

WHAT IF...
There is only one neutral/ground bar?

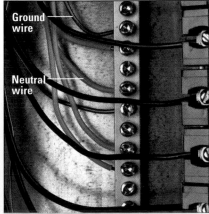

Some service panels have separate bus bars for neutral and ground wires. Others have only one bar that serves both. Connect neutral and ground wires in any order.

STANLEY PRO TIP

Double-pole breakers

A double-pole breaker takes up twice the space of a single-pole breaker. You'll need it for 240-volt circuits and with two-circuit and split receptacles. Connect the ground and neutral wires to bus bars and connect the hot wires to the breaker.

GFCI breaker

A GFCI circuit breaker protects all the receptacles, lights, and appliances on its circuit. Connect both the hot and neutral wires to the breaker. Connect the breaker's white lead to the neutral bus bar.

FINISHING WALLS & CEILINGS

Covering the wall and ceiling framing gives shape to your new rooms. But when it comes to creating the overall decorating scheme that gives your new space style and flair, it's the finished surface that counts.

Drywall is the wall and ceiling covering most often used for remodeling, including basement projects. Hanging drywall sheets and taping the joints provides a smooth surface you can finish to achieve whatever effect you want for the rooms.

Walls and ceilings are more than surfaces that cover the framing; they are opportunities for creative expression and decorative treatment. The finishes you put on walls and ceilings are key elements in your overall design scheme.

When you consider drywall this way, you'll see that raised panels can be part of a character-building program for your remodeled space. With decorative wainscoting, a plain wall becomes a rich-looking room accent. A raised-panel treatment gives a ceiling or wall a sculptural makeover. Even a popcorn finish will give a ceiling texture and add interest. Ceramic tile is one of the best materials for adding color and character to a room. With tile, your design choices are almost endless.

Curved walls can lend any room a sense of vitality. And a curved soffit can define functional areas within an open floor plan, eliminating the need to chop up the space with constricting walls.

You can continue the curved theme with drywall arches. And although it requires more initial effort than a regular rectangular doorway, an arch eliminates the need for time-consuming trimwork, not to mention avoiding mitering hassles, messy staining, and tedious finishing.

Don't forget doors and windows when you're designing your new space. How they're finished and the way you trim them can dramatically alter the look and style of your room.

Trim and moldings are important to the overall look of a room. Select moldings that give the look you want—whether modern or old-world elegant—and use them effectively. Avoid overpowering a room with excessive details.

CHAPTER PREVIEW

You can transform drywall into a medium of expression—not merely a surface that covers the framing.

Hanging drywall
page 120

Finishing drywall
page 124

Decorative finishes
page 128

Drywall panels & wall frames
page 132

Installing wainscoting
page 134

Hanging drywall is the first step in making your new basement rooms look the way you want them to.

Tiling walls
page 136

Creating an arched passageway
page 138

Installing crown molding
page 140

Installing a dropped ceiling
page 142

Installing doors
page 144

Trimming doors and windows
page 148

HANGING DRYWALL

You can attach drywall to wood framing with nails or screws. Many carpenters argue that nailing is faster; others prefer driving screws with a cordless drill. Nails, can pop loose, creating bumps on the wall surface. Screws cost a bit more but they rarely pop loose. In steel framing, screws are the only fastener you can use.

Applying construction adhesive in addition to nails or screws will reduce the number of fasteners needed. It also makes a stiffer wall and reduces nail pops. (See page 122.)

In a basement where moisture could be a problem or on walls that contain plumbing, consider installing paperless drywall as a defense against mold. The nonpaper faces don't give mold a place to grow.

Before you start, decide whether to attach the drywall horizontally or vertically. Horizontal sheets strengthen the wall, especially over steel studs. They also cover the area with fewer seams, leaving a single long joint 4 feet off the floor, a convenient height for finishing. Stagger the vertical seams at the ends of the sheets if you can—doing so makes the wall stronger.

PRESTART CHECKLIST

☐ **TIME**
About 15 to 30 minutes per sheet of drywall, depending on the complexity of the shape

☐ **TOOLS**
Tape measure, chalk line, power drill/driver or hammer, drywall T-square, utility knife, jab saw, Surform plane, dimpler, drywall lifters

☐ **SKILLS**
Measuring and laying out, driving screws or nails, cutting with a utility knife

☐ **PREP**
Framing completed; utilities in place

☐ **MATERIALS**
Drywall sheets, 1⅝-inch drywall nails or screws, construction adhesive

Hanging drywall on a ceiling

Drywall
T square

1 All edges of a drywall sheet must have a nailing surface behind them, so you'll have to add blocking between the joists where a seam edge will fall. Toenail flat 2×4s between the joists.

2 Snap chalk lines or mark the location of the joists on the sheets before you hoist them into position. Install ⅝-inch drywall over steel framing or over wood studs spaced more than 16 inches on center.

Cutting drywall

Front of sheet

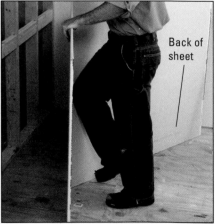

Back of sheet

1 Mark the sheet about ¼ inch smaller than the space it needs to fit. Cut about halfway into the front face of the drywall with a utility knife. Make a couple of passes to deepen the cut; you do not need to cut completely through the sheet.

2 To complete the cut, bump the back of the sheet at the cut line with your knee. This will snap the gypsum along the cut. Fold back the sheet and slice the back paper along the fold line with a utility knife.

Hanging drywall on walls

3 Make a pair of deadman braces from 2×4s to help hold the sheets against the ceiling as you work. The length of the legs should be 1 inch more than the floor-to-ceiling height. This allows the braces to be wedged into position. An alternate method is to rent a drywall lift.

2×2 ledger

1 Screw a 2×2 ledger about 52 inches below the ceiling. Set the drywall on the ledger. Make sure the sheet ends on the middle of a stud; if it doesn't, cut it. Mark the stud locations and snap chalk lines. Then push up the sheet tight against the ceiling and fasten it.

Drywall lifter

2 Cut the lower sheet about 1 inch shorter than the space below the top sheet. With the factory edge up, set the sheet on drywall lifters. Step down on the lifters, lifting the sheet tight to the sheet in place, and fasten it. Baseboard will hide the cut edge and the gap at the floor.

STANLEY PRO TIP

Cutting around an opening

To cut an opening for a window, fasten the drywall over the opening and cut it out. If the sheet extends beyond the opening (as shown above), cut the drywall with a handsaw, guiding the saw against the framing. It doesn't matter if the cuts are ragged or a little uneven because they will be covered by trim or corner bead.

Fastening drywall

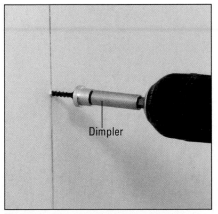

Dimpler

Screws: Use a screw gun with an adjustable clutch or a regular drill with a dimpler attachment. Both the clutch and the dimpler are designed to drive screws so they sink just below the surface without breaking the paper. Space the screws 12 inches apart.

Nails: Double-nail to prevent nail pops. Space ringshank drywall nails 12 inches apart, with a second set about 2 inches from the first. Along the edges use single nails 8 inches apart. When a nail is flush to the surface, hit it one more time to create a slight depression, but don't break the paper.

Back-blocking butt joints

Ordinary butt joints are difficult to conceal because the ends of drywall panels are not tapered like the edges. As a result, the seam surface is already at the finished level of the wall and still must be filled with tape and compound. This increases the likelihood of ending up with a mounded joint.

To avoid that, apply a minimal thickness directly over the seam and feather out the compound away from the joint (see page 126). An easier approach is to install inexpensive back-blocking products that pull the edges of a butt joint back to recess them. You can then tape and mud the joint and make it as flat as a seam with tapered edges. Whether you're a beginner or a pro, back-blocking butt joints give you the best chance of producing a flat wall.

Back-blocking isn't just for walls. The technique works equally well for ceiling panels. But for either application, always use screws to fasten the panels to the back-blocker. The tension produced by bending the drywall against the blocking will quickly pop nails loose.

1 When you use a back-blocker, place the drywall joint in the center of a stud bay and slide the blocker behind the panel. If the bay is 16 inches or wider, you'll be able to position the metal legs perpendicular to the center wood strip. If the stud bay is narrower, angle the metal legs to fit.

2 Mark the location of the metal legs on the face of the sheet. Center the blocker along the end of the drywall, and drive screws 6 inches apart to secure it.

Cutouts for receptacles

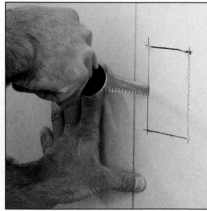

You'll need cutouts to fit drywall around electrical boxes and other obstacles in the wall. Start by measuring and carefully laying out the positions of the cutouts on the face of the sheet. Use a drywall saw or rotary cutout tool to make the cutout.

WHAT IF...
You're using adhesive?

Applying adhesive is an optional step that reduces the number of fasteners, and that means less work in filling and sanding holes. Snap a chalk line across the studs that indicates the width of the top panel. Start the adhesive 6 inches from the ceiling and stop it about 2 inches from the chalk line.

3 Slide the next panel into position, butting it lightly against the first. Drive screws every 6 inches into the center wood strip. Attaching the second sheet puts pressure on the blocker and draws the ends of the panels inward.

Applying corner bead

After all the drywall is up, apply corner bead. The bead protects drywall corners from impacts and provides a guide for your taping knife as you apply joint compound to the corner. You won't need to bead or mud corners on which you plan to install molding—the molding provides protection.

Corner bead comes in two styles: standard, which makes a crisp, square corner; and rounded, which makes a soft, smooth corner. Both are available in white vinyl and galvanized steel. Either material works well, so make your choice based on price and availability.

An arched passageway or other curve calls for flexible bead. It is similar to standard corner bead, but segmented flanges allow it to bend around a curve.

Whichever type of bead you use, it is better to fasten the flanges with drywall nails instead of screws. Screws make the bead pucker. Use nails that penetrate studs or other framing at least ¾ inch.

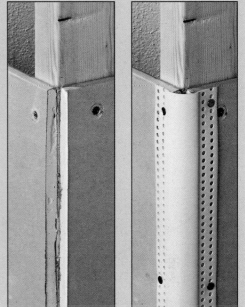

Standard corner bead: Lap one sheet of drywall over the edge of the other (left). Nail the bead in place through the holes in the flanges every 6 to 8 inches. Be careful to keep the flanges flat as you attach them.

Rounded corner bead: This style of corner bead is available in different radii, including some that call for overlapping drywall edges. In most cases, though, you'll need to attach the drywall flush with the edges of the stud (left). Then nail the bead every 6 to 8 inches.

STANLEY PRO TIP

Cut corner bead short

Cut corner bead about ¼ inch short of the floor-to-ceiling height. This makes it easier to put the bead in place. Hold the bead tight to the ceiling as you nail it in place. The baseboard will cover the gap.

WHAT IF...
You have to run drywall up against a different surface?

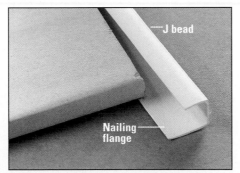

J bead

Nailing flange

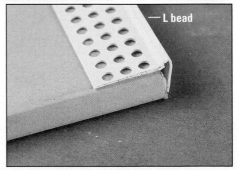

L bead

When a raw drywall edge meets a dissimilar surface, such as wood, it is nearly impossible to get a clean fit. Two products create a crisp edge in this situation: J bead and L bead. J bead is nailed into the wood before the drywall is installed. Prepaint it because it remains visible when the job is finished. (Spray paint works well.) J bead is particularly useful where condensation might wick into the drywall. It encases the drywall, isolating it from the abutting material.

L bead is nailed to the face of the drywall. It is covered with joint compound (as corner bead is) after installation and painted with the rest of the wall. This bead does not extend over the back of the sheet.

FINISHING DRYWALL

Finishing drywall involves taping and filling joints and covering fastener heads with joint compound to create a smooth surface. Taping joints helps keep the joint compound from cracking.

You can tape joints with paper tape or self-adhesive mesh tape. Mesh tape is the best choice because it is easier to use.

Drywall finishing techniques are easy, but creating a smooth surface requires lots of practice. A pro can finish a wall with three coats, but beginners sometimes need more. You'll need three drywall knives: a 6-inch knife for the first coat, a 10-inch for the second coat, and a 12-inch for the final coat. The three knives allow you to feather out the joint—making it gradually thinner toward the edges so it blends level with the wall surface.

Joint compound—commonly called "mud"—comes dry or premixed in 5-gallon buckets. Use the premix compound and keep the bucket covered at all times so the mud won't dry out. Stir in any water that pools on the surface.

PRESTART CHECKLIST

☐ **TIME**
For an 8×8-foot wall, about 1½ hours for the first coat, 45 minutes for each subsequent coat

☐ **TOOLS**
Mud pan; 6-inch, 10-inch, and 12-inch drywall knives; sanding block or sponge

☐ **SKILLS**
Spreading and smoothing joint compound

☐ **PREP**
Check over wall to make sure all fasteners are sunk below surface

☐ **MATERIALS**
Joint compound, fiberglass mesh tape, paper tape (for corners), abrasives

1 Load some joint compound into a mud pan using a 6-inch drywall knife. Start filling the screw or nail dimples with a sweeping motion. Scrape the mud off so the dimple around the screw is filled flush to the surface. Closely spaced dimples can be filled or scraped in one motion.

2 Apply fiberglass mesh tape on joints where two tapered edges come together. This self-adhesive mesh costs a little more than paper tape, but it is easier to use and prevents air bubbles. Start at one end and stick the tape evenly along the length of the joint.

Sponging to smooth a surface

After the final coat of joint compound dries, the final step is to smooth the surface. You can either sand or sponge the joints.

Sanding does the best job of flattening the joint but creates fine dust that can migrate throughout the house. Sponging does not create dust, but smoothing and flattening the compound evenly can be difficult.

To sponge you'll need a bucket of water and a drywall sponge—it has a coarse mesh on one side that removes excess mud and a plain sponge on the opposite side for refining the surface. Wet the sponge and work it across the mudded surfaces. Rinse the sponge frequently to clean out the mud that builds up in it.

Scrape off the ridges and lumps, then sponge the wall smooth. Be careful not to scrub too hard on the paper areas—you can actually wear away the paper and create a rough spot.

3 Cover the tape with a coat of joint compound, using a 6-inch drywall knife. Level this first coat with the surface of the drywall. Resist the temptation to apply a thick coat—thick applications are hard to keep flat and crack as they dry.

4 There is no need to sand between the first and second coats. Just scrape away the ridges and blobs with your knife after each coat has dried.

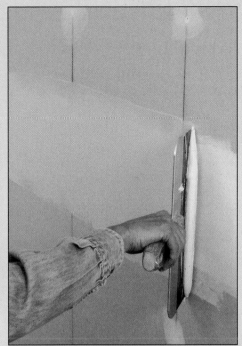

5 Apply the second coat with a 10-inch knife. After the coat dries, scrape the high spots and apply the third coat with a 12-inch knife. Feather out the edges of the mud as thinly and smoothly as possible.

Sanding a wall smooth

For an especially smooth, flat joint, you can't beat hand sanding. This method creates lots of dust, but the results are worth it. Seal off your work area with plastic sheeting and wear a dust mask to avoid breathing the dust. You might be tempted to use a power sander, but don't. Power sanders fray the drywall paper and throw large amounts of dust into the air.

For small jobs a sanding block with regular sandpaper works well. For larger jobs invest in a sanding screen (a screen mesh impregnated with abrasive) and a holder. Some holders attach to a shop-vacuum hose, which helps collect dust during sanding.

Scrape the high spots, then scrub down the wall with a sanding screen. Safety gear is in order, including goggles, dust mask, and ear protectors (because of vacuum noise).

STANLEY PRO TIP

Use a pole sander

The universal pole sander extends your reach and allows you to work efficiently by making long strokes. Its name comes from the universal joint that attaches the pole to a sanding pad. This joint helps you keep the pad flat on the wall at all times. The pad is sized for a half sheet of sandpaper or a standard sanding screen and has clamps to hold the paper or screen in place.

Finishing butt joints

The long edges of drywall sheets are tapered on the finished side. The two tapered edges along a joint form a depression, which makes it possible to create a flat mud joint. The short sides of drywall sheets are not tapered, so they meet at a butt joint.

Butt joints are more challenging to finish because all the drywall compound sits on the surface. That tends to create a slight, but noticeable, high spot over the joint. To make the high spot subtle enough to go unnoticed, you must either back-block the joints (see page 122) or feather the joint compound over a wide area.

Use the same fiberglass mesh tape and similar techniques for applying mud over butt joints as you would for tapered seams.

Mesh tape

1 Cover the butt joint with fiberglass mesh tape. Use your 6-inch knife to spread a thin coat of mud over the tape.

2 When the first coat of mud is dry, apply the second coat along both sides of the joint using a 6-inch drywall knife.

3 Apply the third coat with a 12-inch drywall knife, feathering the edges out 8 to 10 inches on each side of the joint. You may leave a ridge down the center, but it can be scraped away later.

STANLEY PRO TIP: **Check the show coat**

A work light held at an angle to the wall helps reveal ridges, bumps, and depressions as you scrape and sand between coats. But your best—and last—chance to fix finish flaws is after you have applied a primer coat—the show coat—to the walls. At this point the walls are a uniform color and you'll see irregularities you might not have noticed before priming.

The most common beginner's mistake is to make joints too thick. If you find joints like this, add another coat of mud and feather it out farther. Sand again, apply primer to any bare mud, and apply paint once the primer dries.

Another choice is to spray or roll on a textured surface. The texture will hide minor flaws in your taping and adds interest to the wall.

SECOND COAT
Try a drywall trowel

If your project includes several butt joints, consider investing in a drywall trowel. It looks like an ordinary mason's trowel, but the blade has a subtle bow that forms a slight mound over a butt joint. Use the trowel for the second coat only, running it once over the center of the joint.

Finishing corners

Covering corner bead at outside corners is easy because the bead itself guides the drywall knife. Run one side of your knife along the bead to produce a smooth, flat joint as the mud covers the nailing flange. As with other joints, apply at least three coats, sanding in between to feather the joint where it meets the drywall. The bead itself isn't hidden in mud. Scrape excess mud off the bead, then paint it along with the drywall.

Inside corners are more difficult because they require taping and mudding. The hard part is smoothing the mud on one side of the corner without messing up the mud on the other side.

Resist the temptation to try to get these inside joints perfect on the first, or even second, coat. Accept that there will be ridges you'll need to sand or knock off in the first two coats. To avoid ridges on the third coat, think of it as a filler coat; press hard on the knife so you fill imperfections instead of leaving behind a thick layer of joint compound. You can go over the joints a fourth time if necessary for a smooth finish.

Finishing inside corners

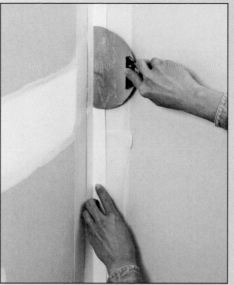

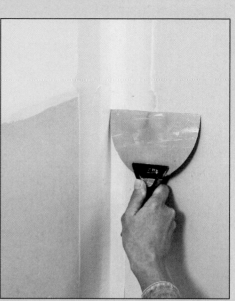

1 Apply mud to both sides of the corner. Fold a length of paper tape in half (it is precreased) and press it into the mud with a 6-inch knife.

2 Bed the tape in the mud by drawing down the knife along both sides of the corner. Repeat this process to apply additional coats of mud. Sand to smooth the final surface.

OUTSIDE CORNERS
Let the bead be your guide

For outside corners, mud the flanges of the corner bead. Apply several coats, sanding the final coat for a smooth surface.

WHAT IF...
There are bubbles under the paper tape?

If there are bubbles under the tape, the tape doesn't stick to the mud, or it wrinkles, peel it off and apply more mud underneath. This is one time when applying a little too much mud is not a problem.

STANLEY PRO TIP

Consider using a corner knife

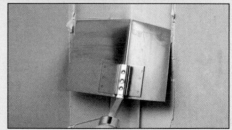

A corner knife will help you achieve straight, smooth inside corners. First embed and cover the tape in mud using a 6-inch knife, but don't attempt to smooth the joint. Next hold the corner knife at the top of the joint, angling it slightly away from the wall, and pull it down to near the floor. Do this in one even stroke. The corner knife leaves ridges on both sides of the joint. When dry, scrape off the ridges before you apply a second coat.

DECORATIVE FINISHES

Textures add interest, variety, and style to walls and ceilings. A soft spray-on texture that's used exclusively on ceilings is sometimes called "popcorn" or "cottage cheese." Contractors love it because it's faster (and therefore less expensive) than carefully taping and sanding a ceiling. Although you can skip the sanding, don't get careless about filling seams and covering the fastener heads. Defects like these will show through the texture—especially under some lighting conditions.

To shoot on popcorn texture, you'll need an air compressor and a hopper. (You can buy or rent them.) Texture material comes in bags. There are several sizes of granules; you should avoid bulky textures in a small room—the texture can become too dominant, making the room seem even smaller.

You can spray thinned-down joint compound through an airless sprayer to create a range of textures on walls and ceilings. But not all applications require fancy equipment. Brooms, sponges, toothed trowels, flat trowels, and other tools yield an unlimited variety of textures. Experiment on scrap pieces of drywall to perfect your technique before tackling an entire room. Closet ceilings are also a good place to practice techniques.

PRESTART CHECKLIST

☐ **TIME**
You can spray the ceiling of an average room (12×15) in 15 minutes or less

☐ **TOOLS**
Compressor and hopper

☐ **SKILLS**
Mixing texture material, operating a spray rig

☐ **PREP**
All ceiling seams are flat and smooth; fastener heads properly covered

☐ **MATERIALS**
Texture material, drinking-grade water, ½-inch drill with mixer

Spraying popcorn ceiling texture

1 Buy a roll of painter's plastic—a thin, translucent sheet—and use masking tape to secure it within 2 inches of the ceiling. Top the plastic with 6-inch-wide masking paper taped along the ceiling/wall joint. A handheld masking machine dispenses half of the tape's width onto the paper. For best results, first paint the ceiling with a primer.

2 Mix the powdered texture with water according to the manufacturer's directions. Pour a small amount into the hopper, and experiment with different spray tips or pressure settings until you get the desired results. Fill the hopper to a comfortable level (half or less until you get the hang of it), and you're ready to start.

Caution: Drywall may sag

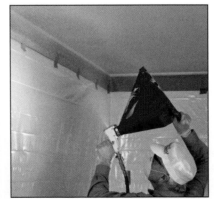

Moisture—plus the added weight of the texture—sometimes causes drywall ceilings to sag noticeably. Before you apply a texture onto a ceiling, verify the thickness of the drywall, the joist spacing, and the application direction of the panels to avoid potential problems.

Paint-on texture

You can purchase a box of texturing additive and mix it with ordinary paint to achieve a variety of looks without the expense of application equipment. Available textures range from slightly sandy to popcorn. With the larger particles, creating a consistent appearance over the entire surface can be difficult. As you work, regularly stir the paint to keep the texture evenly suspended.

Spraying knockdown texture

3 Maintain a consistent distance from the ceiling—most professionals spray from between 2 and 4 feet. Walk sideways to spray the first stripe of texture, then slightly overlap it with the second stripe. Continue until you reach the end of the room. Apply the second coat at right angles to the first.

1 Prime the ceiling to prevent uneven drying of the texture (either water- or solvent-based primer is fine). Thin the all-purpose joint compound with water until it's about the consistency of latex paint. Experiment with an airless paint sprayer on scrap drywall, varying the distance and speed of application until you get the result you want. Spray the ceiling with two coats applied at right angles to each other.

2 Wait until the ceiling has lost the sheen of moisture—about 10 minutes under average conditions. Hold a wide wipedown blade nearly parallel to the ceiling, and very lightly drag it to flatten the tips of the sprayed texture. Vary the direction of the blade on each pass so you don't create a pattern. If you don't have a 24-inch wipedown blade as shown in the photo, use your widest drywall knife.

Protect fixtures and wiring

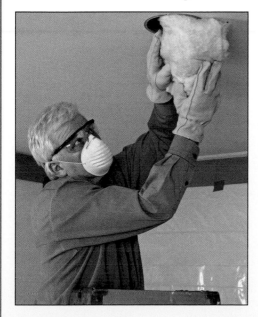

Before applying texture, stuff fiberglass insulation or a wad of newspaper into ceiling canisters. Otherwise, the sprayed material can foul the socket and also make trim rings difficult to install. You can use the same materials to protect wiring in ceiling boxes.

You'll be glad you did this when you get to the electrical work because it's a challenge to wire circuits when all of the wires have been sprayed white. For safety, make sure power is turned off to electrical boxes. The texture is wet and conductive enough to cause the circuit to short out.

STANLEY PRO TIP

Dress the part

Safety glasses are essential when you spray a ceiling, and wearing an inexpensive painter's cap is an excellent idea. Long sleeves and full-length pants make personal cleanup easy. Tossing your clothes into the washer is much easier than scraping oversprayed texture from your skin.

More ways to add texture

Thin the all-purpose joint compound with water and apply it with a textured paint roller. You may like the effect that comes right from the roller, but you can also knock down the texture for a different look. (See page 129 for the knockdown technique.)

Trowel slightly thinned all-purpose joint compound onto a wall, then lightly punch it with a brush on a pole to create a texture. The double crow's foot brush in the photo is specifically made for texturing drywall and stucco, but you can experiment with nearly any type of brush. Poke, punch, or drag for a variety of effects.

Soak a natural sponge in water, then wring it nearly dry. Experiment with the effects you can achieve by daubing, swirling, punching, and rolling. Frequently change your grip on the sponge to avoid too much regularity.

Getting into corners

Use a downscaled brush or a fragment of a sponge to ensure that you continue the texture right into the corner. Otherwise, your eyes will be drawn to the smooth surface.

Putting on texture paint

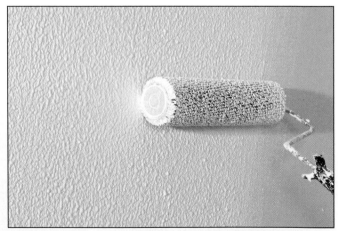

Texture paint isn't a drywall product—you'll find it in the paint aisle of your paint store or home center. You can thin it for application by textured roller or scoop it straight from the tub and handle it like drywall compound to create a wide range of textures. It dries much harder than joint compound.

Virtually any toothed tool can create texture. Choose from tiling tools that have square or V-grooves in varying depths, or choose a paint-graining comb or even a hair comb with widely spaced teeth. If you can't find a design that pleases you, make your own comb from wood, plastic, or metal.

A stucco-type texture usually requires two coats of unthinned all-purpose joint compound. Make the first coat just thick enough to create some tool marks. After it dries, apply the second coat with a flat trowel, placing random irregular dabs of material with a skipping motion. Lightly float the trowel over the dabs to flatten them.

Bold plaster texture

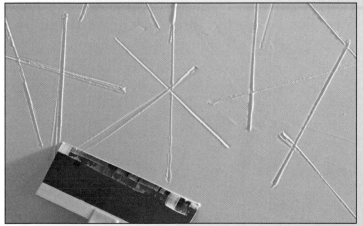

1 Using a 10-inch drywall knife, apply a ⅛-inch coat of all-purpose joint compound with random, sweeping strokes. Then tap the tip in and out of the mud, creating ridges. Overlap your strokes, and work in all directions.

2 Gently float the knife over the surface to flatten the ridges, but do not disturb the low areas. Again, work randomly to avoid a patterned appearance. Apply compound to the next section of wall or ceiling, overlapping into the completed area for a seamless look.

DRYWALL PANELS & WALL FRAMES

Raised panels on walls are usually associated with high-end homes because achieving the look required costly skilled labor. But decorative drywall panels make it easy for do-it-yourselfers to create elegant molded walls without fancy carpentry or plastering skills.

You'll probably have to special-order the panels, which come in a variety of designs that can be applied as wainscoting, an upper-wall design, or even as a ceiling treatment. You don't have to cover your entire wall or ceiling—you can apply the styled panels as an accent and fill in with regular drywall.

Careful layout is essential, so take the time needed to make some careful sketches of your project. Manufacturer's websites offer some helpful design suggestions.

As shown here, the easiest installation method involves using the decorative panels as the overlay in a two-thickness wall. If you're remodeling a room, you probably can skip the demolition phase.

PRESTART CHECKLIST

☐ **TIME**
Installation time depends upon the size and complexity of your project

☐ **TOOLS**
Chalk line, nylon mason's line, line level, caulking gun, hammer or drywall screw gun, measuring tape, countersink pneumatic brad nailer

☐ **SKILLS**
Leveling, accurate measuring and marking, driving fasteners

☐ **PREP**
Framing completed, first layer of drywall installed

☐ **MATERIALS**
Decorative panels and regular drywall, drywall panel adhesive, nails or screws, painter's caulk

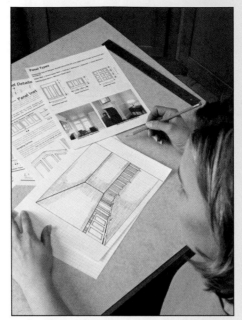

1 Carefully measure your walls and plan your layout. You need not cover the entire wall with decorative panels—you can use ordinary drywall as filler strips and for flat wall surfaces.

2 Transfer layout marks from your drawing to the floor and wall framing. Lines marked on the floor indicate the first panel's position, and nails driven into the sidewalls support a leveled nylon mason's line about ¾ inch away from the installation surface.

WHAT IF...
You want to add wainscoting to an existing wall?

To add wainscoting, you don't necessarily need to start at bare studs. You can overlay an existing wall with decorative wood or drywall panels, then cap the panels with a lip molding that simultaneously conceals the top edge and adds a decorative chair rail. A back band is a molding style that also hides the top edge but has a plain front profile.

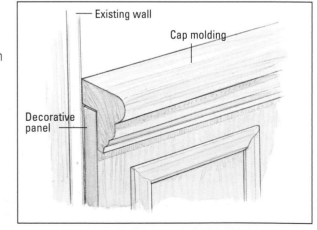

Existing wall

Cap molding

Decorative panel

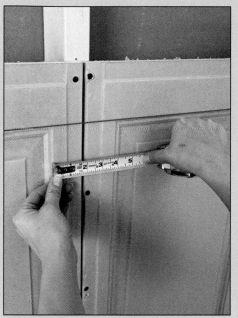

3 Untie one end of the level line so you can apply adhesive to the wall. Press the panel against the wall while a helper resets the level line. Level to the edge of the debossed pattern, not the edge of the panel itself. Drive screws to secure the panel.

4 Repeat the process to install the next panel. This time you'll level again, but you also need to measure between the edges of the pattern to maintain consistent spacing. You cannot simply butt the panels next to each other.

5 Install all of the decorative panels, then fill in with flat wallboard. Tape and finish the joints in the usual manner.

Decorating with wall frames

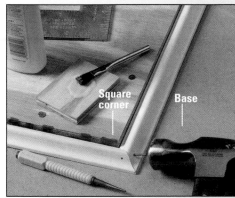

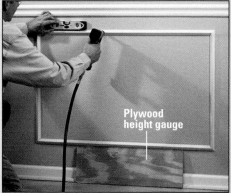

1 Attach simple wooden frames to a wall for a custom look. Make an assembly jig for the frames by fastening a square of plywood to a plywood or MDF base. Check the accuracy of the corner with a framing square. Clamp the jig to your worktable, and assemble the frames with glue and countersunk finishing nails. Place each frame on a flat surface until the glue dries.

2 Apply a bead of construction adhesive to the back of the frame. With the help of a plywood height gauge, position and nail the frame to the wall. Nails driven into studs hold better, but even nails angled into drywall will hold the frame until the adhesive takes over. A pneumatic brad nailer, shown above, makes nailing easier and minimizes the risk of splitting moldings.

3 Fill gaps between the wall and the edges of the frame with painter's caulk. Cut the nozzle at an angle for better control and an accurate bead.

INSTALLING WAINSCOTING

A traditional wall treatment that lends an air of elegance and warmth to a room, wainscot paneling also makes an extremely durable wall because it resists dents and scuffs better than drywall.

Wainscoting includes any type of wooden paneling applied to the bottom portion of a wall. The tongue-and-groove, beaded-board wainscoting in this project is one of the most popular styles. Beaded board is available in various widths and in thicknesses from 1/4 inch to 3/4 inch. This project uses 1/4-inch-thick boards under 1/2-inch-thick baseboard to match the thickness of 3/4-inch-thick door and window casing.

PRESTART CHECKLIST

☐ **TIME**
About 6 hours for an 8-foot section of wainscoting

☐ **TOOLS**
Tape measure, chalk line, chop saw or miter box, hammer, nail set, circular saw, jigsaw, block plane

☐ **SKILLS**
Measuring and laying out, crosscutting, driving finishing nails

☐ **PREP**
Empty room of all furnishings

☐ **MATERIALS**
1/4-inch-thick beaded tongue-and-groove boards, 1/2×4-inch baseboard, cap molding, 8d and 4d finishing nails, construction adhesive, wood glue

1 This project uses a 1/2-inch cap rail. Snap a level chalk line 1/2 inch below the height of the cap rail. Cut 1/4-inch-thick beaded tongue-and-groove boards 1/4 inch shorter than the height. Position the tops of the boards along the chalk line to leave a gap at the floor.

2 Apply a bead of construction adhesive to the back of each board. Insert the tongue of each board into the groove of the adjoining one. To snug the board without damaging the groove, put the tongue of a 1-foot scrap of tongue-and-groove board into the groove of the piece you are installing. Then tap on the groove side of the scrap with your hammer.

WHAT IF...
You have to turn an outside corner?

1 If your wainscoting turns an outside corner, put the last piece in place without adhesive. Trace along the corner on the back of the piece with a sharp pencil. Saw off the piece on the waste side of the pencil line but don't cut away the line. This piece will extend slightly past the corner to make a tight joint with the next piece.

2 Remove the tongue from the first piece around the corner, using a tablesaw or block plane. Put construction adhesive on the piece and attach it with the planed face flush against the edge of the adjacent piece.

3 If there is a switch or receptacle in the way, **turn off power to the room at the service panel.** Disconnect the device. Cut boards to fit around the box. Install a box extender to bring the front of the box out ¼ inch. Reconnect the switch or receptacle and replace the coverplate before turning the power back on.

4 Put the second-to-last piece before an inside corner in place without adhesive. Measure from the base of the tongue to the wall at top and bottom. If the measurements differ, transfer them to the top and bottom of the last piece to lay out a tapered cut. Make the cut with a jigsaw.

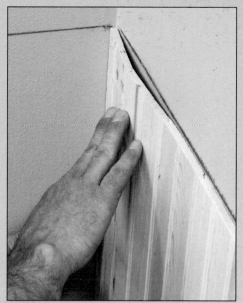

5 Because of the tongue, the last two pieces at a corner must be snapped in place together. Put adhesive on the wall. Fit the last two pieces together. Bend them a bit at the joint and fit the second-to-last tongue into place. Press at the joint to snap the last two pieces into place.

6 Before installing the first piece around an inside corner, shave the tongue off with a block plane. Install the piece with the planed edge toward the corner.

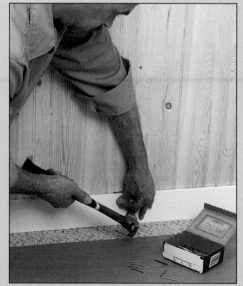

7 Attach ½×4-inch baseboard over the bottom of the wainscoting by driving two 8d finishing nails into each stud.

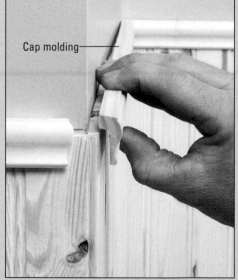

Cap molding

8 Attach a cap molding along the top of the wainscot to cover the top edge of the paneling. At the corner, use yellow carpenter's glue and 4d nails driven at a slight angle toward the wall to ensure they don't come through the face of the top molding.

TILING WALLS

To make installation of wall tile easier, make sure the wall is smooth, level, and free of any substance that would interfere with the action of the adhesive. Once you've prepared the surface, establish vertical and horizontal layout lines.

Wall tiles are affected by gravity and tend to slide down the wall during installation. Organic mastic is one solution—tile sticks to it almost immediately. Mastic is not as strong as thinset mortar, however, and not as water-resistant. You can keep tile that's embedded in thinset in place with spacers, nails, or tape.

If you are tiling a wall and a floor, tile the floor first so you can continue the grout joints up the wall in the same pattern as the floor. Install a cove base, then start wall tile at the cove base. If you are tiling adjacent walls, set the back wall first; tapered edges on a side wall are less visible.

PRESTART CHECKLIST

☐ **TIME**
About 30 to 45 minutes per square yard to prepare and set tile

☐ **TOOLS**
Wide putty knife, 4-foot level, sanding block, small sledge and cold chisel, stud finder, tape measure, chalk line, utility knife, carbide scriber, margin trowel, notched trowel, straightedge, cordless drill/driver, grout knife, snap cutter or wet saw, tile nippers, masonry stone, caulk gun, hammer, grout float

☐ **SKILLS**
Reading level, troweling, laying tile, grouting

☐ **PREP**
Repair structural defects

☐ **MATERIALS**
Deglossing agent, release agent, bucket, thinset, dimensional lumber for battens, backerboard, screws, tape, tile, spacers, caulk, grout, rags, sponge, water, tile base or bullnose, nylon wedges, nails

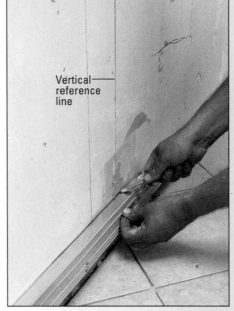

Vertical reference line

1 Set a 4-foot level vertically on the wall about 2 feet from a corner, over a grout joint in the floor if the floor is tiled. If the wall meets at an outside corner, set the level where the inside edge of a bullnose tile will fall. Pencil a line down the level; extend it to the floor and ceiling. Mark a horizontal line at the top of the cove base.

2 Measure up from the horizontal line a distance equal to the size of your tile and mark the wall at this point. Continue marking the wall in the same increments. Using a 4-foot level, mark the wall across from these points and snap layout grids so you can keep each horizontal course straight.

Keeping the tiles on the wall

Batten holds first row level

If you're not using a coved base and your layout results in cut tiles at the floor, tack a level 1× or 2× batten where your first full tiles will be laid. The batten will keep the first row level and prevent it from sliding down the wall. Drive nails partway into the wall at least every third of each tile's length and tape the tiles with masking tape. If your layout calls for a coved-tile base, install it first, leveling it with nylon wedges. Then tile the wall.

WHAT IF...
Tiles are lugged (prespaced)?

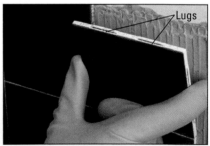

Lugs

Lugged tiles make it easy to space wall installations. They come with small bisque lugs raised on the edges and don't require additional spacers to keep them aligned.

Because the lugs are molded into the tile at the time of manufacture, they don't allow you to make the grout joints narrower. Determine the actual dimensions of the tile when you purchase it so you know how much space each tile actually covers.

3 Mix the adhesive, spread it on the wall, and comb it evenly. Starting at the bottom, press the tile into the mortar with a slight twist. Continue laying the pattern of your choice, using spacers if your tile is not lugged. Inserting spacers with one tab sticking out makes them easy to remove.

4 Use a utility knife or grout knife to remove any adhesive left in the joints and clean any excess off the tile surface. Mix the grout and force it into the joints with a grout float, keeping the float at a 45-degree angle. Work the float in both directions to fill the joints; work diagonally to remove excess grout.

5 Clean the surface and smooth the joints with a damp sponge, then go over the tile with clean water and a clean sponge. When a haze forms, wipe it with a clean rag. You may have to wipe with some pressure to remove the haze.

WHAT IF...
The wall has electrical outlets on it?

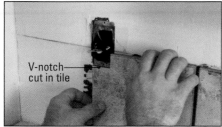

Unless you have removed the wall covering, the finished tile surface will extend beyond the edges of electrical outlet boxes. As a result the mounting screws may be too short to anchor the receptacle. You can simply use longer screws unless local codes require a box extension (page 135).

First **turn off the power to the circuit** and remove the coverplate and receptacle screws. Remove one receptacle screw completely so you can take it to the store to buy a screw

½ inch longer. Push the receptacle into the box and out of your way.

Cut the tiles to fit around the box. Then cut V-shape notches (use tile nippers) that line up with the tabs and screw holes on the top and bottom of the box. Spread adhesive to within ¼ inch of the box and embed the tile. When the mortar cures, pull out the receptacle from the box and fasten it with the longer screws inserted through the notches.

Turning an outside corner

Outside corners can present problems if they are not plumb. You can hide slightly out-of-plumb situations by skim-coating the wall with thinset. Then overlap bullnose tiles or edge tiles on the full tiles on the other wall. As long as the tiles meet crisply, the out-of-plumb wall should not be as noticeable.

CREATING AN ARCHED PASSAGEWAY

Drywall can be bent into a curve to form an arched entryway. Depending on the width and height of the passageway, you can create a complete arch, curved from one end to the other or one with a flat top between curved ends.

First, make a full-sized cardboard mock-up to simulate the arch. This will give you a good idea of how it will look and how much headroom it will provide. The arch itself will be made from plywood ribs with two layers of thin drywall bent over them.

Finishing an arched opening is also quite easy, thanks to flexible archway bead. Once the bead is attached, apply joint compound just as you would for any corner bead.

PRESTART CHECKLIST

☐ **TIME**
About 4 hours to complete a single archway

☐ **TOOLS**
Tape measure, jigsaw, drill/driver, hammer, drywall saw, pencil, string

☐ **SKILLS**
Measuring and laying out, cutting with a circular saw, driving screws, hammering nails

☐ **PREP**
Frame the archway

☐ **MATERIALS**
¾-inch plywood, 1×3, ¼-inch drywall, drywall screws, drywall nails, flexible archway bead

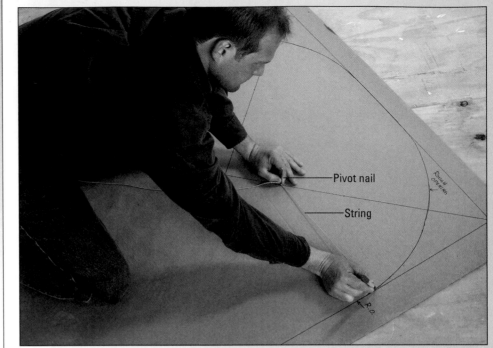

Pivot nail

String

1 Make a full-size drawing of the entry so you can lay out the exact shape and size of the curves. Start with an outline of the rough opening. Draw a line at a 45-degree angle from each corner. The center of the curve will fall along this line. Make a compass using a nail, a string, and a pencil. Draw the curve that represents the finished surface of the drywall. This also will be the curve you cut on the plywood ribs.

STANLEY PRO TIP: **How far will drywall bend?**

Regular ¼-inch drywall can be bent to a curve with a radius of 5 feet. This means the string on your string-and-pencil compass must be at least 5 feet long. For radii of 32 inches or less, purchase ¼-inch drywall that's made specifically for bending. It's usually marked "flexible." If you wet the paper of flexible drywall with a sponge, you can bend it to a radius as small as 20 inches. You don't have to limit yourself to curves governed by a specific radius. If you find a pleasing curve, trace it onto your full-size drawing.

2 Make a pattern by carefully cutting out the curved corner you drew on the cardboard. Use the pattern to lay out the curves on a piece of ¾-inch plywood. Cut four curved ribs with a jigsaw equipped with a fine-tooth blade.

3 Rip-cut four pieces of 1× stock to 2 inches wide to make nailers for the plywood ribs. Make the nailers short enough that the ribs will completely cover them. Place the nailers in the corners of the doorway and center them from side to side using a scrap of ¾-inch plywood as a guide.

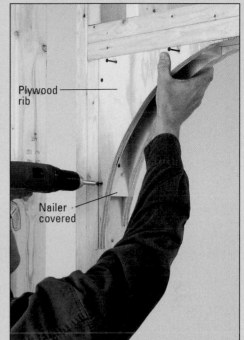

4 Screw the nailers to the corners of the doorway with 1⅝-inch drywall screws. Start the screws in the plywood ribs before you put up the ribs to make them easier to attach to the nailers.

5 Hang the drywall over the arched doorway, just as you would on an ordinary opening (page 121). Use a regular handsaw to cut along the jack studs until you reach the curve. Then use a jab saw to cut the curve.

6 Bend a layer of ¼-inch drywall into the curve and fasten it with screws. Bend a second layer over the first and screw it in place. Attach drywall to the face of the header and the jack studs. Use two layers of the same thickness you used for the arch.

7 Attach flexible archway bead to the arched area with drywall nails driven every 6 to 8 inches. Tape and finish the drywall with joint compound.

INSTALLING CROWN MOLDING

Crown molding is installed at the juncture of the wall and the ceiling. Although it looks like a hefty piece of wood, most crown molding is relatively thin material. The look of depth comes from the way it is installed. Rather than being a solid block nailed into the corner, crown moldings are installed diagonally between the wall and ceiling. Moldings installed this way are said to be sprung into place.

The tricky part about installing crown molding is cutting the joints. Because the molding is installed at an angle, it cannot be cut lying flat in an ordinary miter box. You must hold the molding at the spring angle when you make the cuts. You can cut crown molding that's lying flat if you use a compound mitersaw.

PRESTART CHECKLIST

☐ **TIME**
About 4 hours for a regular room with four straight walls

☐ **TOOLS**
Tape measure, framing square, miter box or mitersaw, hammer, nail set, coping saw, utility knife

☐ **SKILLS**
Measuring and laying out, driving nails, crosscutting moldings, mitering moldings, making coped joints

☐ **PREP**
Walls and ceiling should be finished and painted; molding can be prefinished

☐ **MATERIALS**
Crown molding, 8d finishing nails, wood for blocking

1 First determine how far the edges of the molding will fall from the wall and ceiling. Place a piece of the molding in a framing square to measure it. Mark the distance on the ceiling near the corners and at several points along the length of the wall.

Square-cut both ends of the first piece

2 Start with the wall opposite the door. Cut the molding to length with square cuts on both ends. Hold it in place and nail it first to the wall studs with 8d nails and then to the ceiling joists.

WHAT IF...
You need to end crown molding without running into a wall?

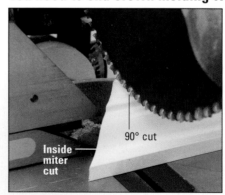

90° cut

Inside miter cut

You may need to end a run of crown molding that doesn't turn a corner or run into a wall. If so, stop the molding with a triangular return piece. To cut this piece, place a scrap of crown upside down in the chop saw or miter box and make an outside miter cut.

Then set the saw to 90 degrees and cut off the triangle, aligning the blade to the point where the miter ends at the back of the molding. Attach the return piece with yellow carpenter's glue. Use masking tape to hold the piece in place until the glue sets.

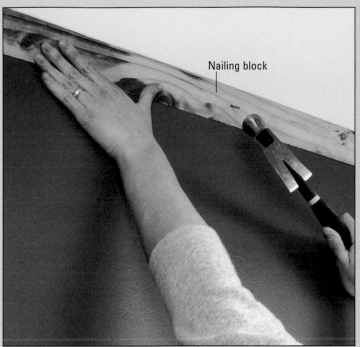

Nailing block

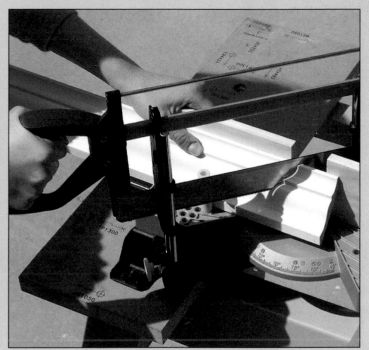

3 If the wall runs parallel to the ceiling joists, there may be no framing members in position to nail the molding to the ceiling. In this situation cut some triangular nailing blocks and attach them to the wall studs. Size the blocks to allow a ¼-inch gap between the front of the block and the back of the crown.

4 The second piece of crown is cut square on one end and coped on the other. To cut the cope, start with an inside miter cut. Hold the crown in your miter box upside down (as if the base of the box were the ceiling and the fence were the wall) and backwards (if the cope is on the right end of the piece, the cut will be on the left as the piece rests in the miter box).

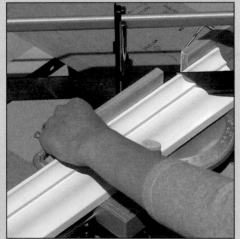

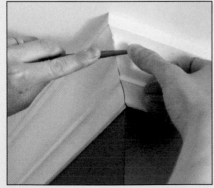

5 Cope the edge by undercutting the joint with a coping saw. Test-fit it against a piece of scrap and fine-tune the edge with a utility knife. Nail the piece in place. Proceed around the room, making square cuts on one end and coped cuts on the other end. Cope both ends of the last piece.

6 For outside miters, the pieces also are held in the saw upside down and backwards, but the cut is angled in the opposite direction. To get a tighter fit in both outside and inside corners, flex and twist the pieces slightly before driving in the nails closest to the joint.

STANLEY PRO TIP

Burnish corners to cure gaps

In spite of careful work, not every joint will fit perfectly. If you find a slight gap in an outside miter, force a little glue into it, then burnish the edges using the side of a nail set. Burnishing the corners folds over the thin wood fibers, bridging the gap.

INSTALLING A DROPPED CEILING

A dropped ceiling (also called a suspended ceiling) consists of acoustical tile panels set in a metal grid. The grid hangs from framing or an existing ceiling. Because the frame can be suspended at any height, a dropped ceiling is ideal for hiding basement pipes and ductwork that hang below the joists. The removable panels allow access to plumbing valves or electrical junction boxes above the ceiling.

The frame consists of wall molding around the perimeter; main runners, which run across the width of the ceiling; and cross tees, which go between the main runners. Depending on the tiles you select, main runners are spaced 24 or 48 inches on center. The cross tees are also placed to fit the tiles.

The space above them makes a handy wiring chase for running low-voltage wires (for telephones, TVs, or stereo speakers) with a minimum of fuss.

PRESTART CHECKLIST

☐ **TIME**
About 6 to 8 hours for a 10×10-foot room

☐ **TOOLS**
Tape measure, chalk line, line level, clamps, 4-foot level, drill/driver, metal snips, utility knife, straightedge

☐ **SKILLS**
Measuring and laying out, snapping chalk lines, driving screws, cutting thin gauge metal, cutting acoustical panels

☐ **PREP**
Walls should be as complete as possible, including paint

☐ **MATERIALS**
Wall molding, main runners, cross tees, hanging wire, screws, hanger screws, acoustical panels

1 Measure the room and draw a floor plan. Then measure the ceiling height. Most grid systems require at least 3 inches of free space above. Place the grid low enough to clear pipes or anything else hanging down, but high enough to clear window and door tops.

2 Slip a line level onto your chalk line and make adjustments. Snap a level line around the perimeter of the room, indicating the top of the wall molding. Double-check the line with a 4-foot level.

Line level

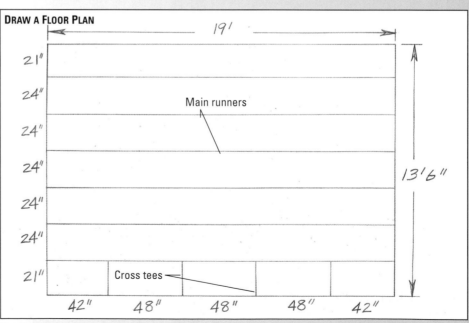

DRAW A FLOOR PLAN

19'

21"
24"
24" Main runners
24"
24"
24"
21" Cross tees

42" 48" 48" 48" 42"

13'6"

For the most symmetrical look, start your layout in the center of each side and work your way toward the edges. If necessary, adjust the layout so spaces at the perimeter are at least half a panel wide.

3 Screw the wall molding to the studs with its top edge even with the snapped lines. Butt the pieces together to make longer runs.

Wall molding

4 Mark the main runner locations on the wall molding. Stretch a string along their path to indicate the level of the bottom of the runners.

Hanger screw

5 Suspend main runners within 2 feet of the end walls and every 4 feet between. Turn hanger screws into the joists or ceiling above the runners. Hang wires from the hanger screws. Cut the runner length so holes align under wires. Twist the wires until the top of the runner aligns with the strings.

Main runner

Cross tee

6 The cross tees clip into slots in the main runners. Install them according to the spacing required by the ceiling panels. At the walls, cut the cross tees so their ends rest on the wall molding.

7 When the grid is complete, drop the panels into place. If you need to make some odd-size pieces, cut the panels with a utility knife guided by a straightedge.

STANLEY Pro Tip

Use a laser level for big jobs

If you are installing a dropped ceiling in a large room, a laser level makes it easy to establish an initial level line around the room.

Be careful not to look directly into the laser while you are working. Don't leave the laser running while you install the wall molding. Instead snap chalk lines along the laser's path. A laser level is also helpful when installing molding, such as a picture frame rail, chair rail, or wainscoting.

INSTALLING DOORS

A prehung door unit takes a lot of the demanding precision out of installing a door. Hinge mortises and holes for the lockset and strike are already cut. But you still need to work carefully for best results. One thing that makes installing doors easier is well-made framing with a rough opening that is plumb and square. Double-check as you build and take the time to fix mistakes as they occur, rather than hoping they will be hidden by the next step (they won't).

When you are hanging a door, keep an eye on the big picture. Before setting the nails, step back and look at your work. When the door is plumb but the floor or wall is off level or plumb, you may want to align the door frame at least a little bit with its surroundings to make sure it looks right. For example, if the wall leans slightly, match the jamb to the wall. It won't be noticeable as long as the door doesn't lean enough to open and close by itself.

PRESTART CHECKLIST

☐ **TIME**
About 2 hours per door

☐ **TOOLS**
4-foot level, circular saw, layout square, hammer, nail set, utility knife

☐ **SKILLS**
Crosscutting, driving nails, checking for plumb

☐ **PREP**
Doorway should be framed and drywall applied to both sides

☐ **MATERIALS**
Prehung door, shims, 16d finishing nails, 8d finishing nails

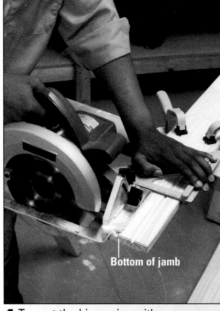

Bottom of jamb

1 Tap out the hinge pins with a screwdriver and hammer. Remove the door. Slip the frame into the doorway and check the head jamb for level. If it isn't, shim under the jamb on the low side. Measure the shimmed space; then remove this amount from the opposite jamb leg.

2 Check that the jack stud on the hinge side of the opening is plumb. Also check to see if the wall leans one way or the other. If the jack stud is plumb, nail the jamb directly to it with 16d finishing nails, two below each hinge and two near the center.

Hanging bypass doors

The most popular choice for closets, bypass doors, need no room to swing open—a plus. But they allow access to only one side of a closet at a time—a minus. Hardware kits are available for opening widths of 4, 5, 6, and 8 feet. To accommodate other size openings, simply cut the standard tracks with a hacksaw.

The kits are designed to work with standard 1⅜-inch-thick interior doors. If you use thicker doors, they may interfere with each other as they open and close. Thinner doors may have a wide gap between them. The combined width of the doors should equal the width of the opening plus at least 1 inch. This provides ½ inch of overlap between the two doors.

Some minor variations exist between bypass door kits from different manufacturers, but they are all easy to install. Just be sure to check the directions carefully before you start.

Track

1 The location of the track depends on how you plan to trim the opening. Consult the manufacturer's instructions. Screw the track to the top of the door opening. Check to make sure the track is level; shim if necessary.

3 If the hinge-side stud is not plumb, nail either the top or bottom, whichever is closer to the center of the opening. Insert shims at the opposite end to make the jamb plumb. Below the shims, drive two 16d finishing nails just far enough to hold the shims and jambs in place. Adjust shims if necessary.

4 Before setting nails, check that the hinge jamb is centered across the wall thickness. A typical jamb is slightly wider than the wall thickness to allow for irregularities in the drywall. If adjustment is necessary, pull the nails, protecting the jamb with a scrap under the hammer.

5 Put the door back on its hinges and swing it closed. Insert shims between the jamb and the stud about halfway between the hinges and adjust them until the gap between the door and jamb is equal from top to bottom. Open the door and drive two 16d finishing nails below the shims.

2 Attach the hangers to the tops of the doors. The hardware kit specifies exact locations. Tip the doors to hook the hangers onto the track. After the doors are hanging, install the center guide on the floor to keep the doors in line.

TRIM THE OPENING

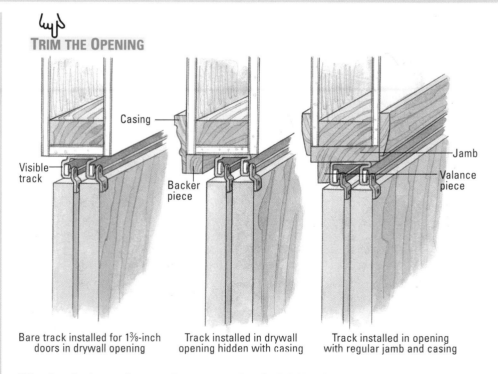

Bare track installed for 1⅜-inch doors in drywall opening

Track installed in drywall opening hidden with casing

Track installed in opening with regular jamb and casing

When hanging bypass doors, you have some options for finishing the opening. For utility applications, simply hang the doors as is (left). For a more finished look, add trim to the header (middle and right).

Installing doors (continued)

Strike plate

Bolt

A playing card provides the right amount of space between a prefinished door and stop.

6 The strike side of the frame is also nailed in three places: top, bottom, and middle. Insert shims and adjust so the gap between the door and the jamb is even, top to bottom. Nail the jamb in place with pairs of 16d finishing nails driven just below the shims.

7 To place the doorstops properly, screw the strikeplate to the jamb and drive or screw the bolt assembly into the door. There is no need to install the entire lockset yet.

8 On many prehung units, the doorstops are temporarily attached. Pry the stops free. Close the door and hold it tightly against the strikeplate. On a prefinished unit, space the stops a playing-card thickness from the door face and nail them to the jambs with 8d nails.

Hanging bifold doors

Bifold doors can be installed easily in almost any opening in your home. They can be used for closet doors, for privacy, or for controlling heat and airflow between rooms. Their chief advantages include ease of installation and a minimum of swing space required. However, they take up more space in the door opening than do swinging doors.

Commonly available with plastic, metal, or wooden doors, bifold door kits come in a variety of styles, including louvered, paneled, and smooth. The kits fit most standard-width openings, although the maximum width of a single door is 24 inches. Units can be combined to cover openings up to 16 feet wide. Wooden doors can be trimmed for a better fit; plastic doors cannot be trimmed. (Keep in mind, if you trim a wooden door kit, each door must be trimmed equally.) Two heights are available—one to fit standard 6-foot 8-inch openings, the other for 8-foot floor-to-ceiling applications.

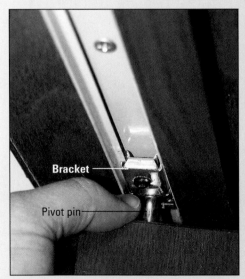

Bracket

Pivot pin

1 Bifold doors require a track similar to that used by bypass doors. Screw the track to the top of the opening. The doors pivot on pins protruding from their top and bottom. These pins engage brackets attached to the floor or jamb and the track.

Roller guide

2 Attach the roller or pin guide to the free end of the doors. This guide rides in the track and keeps the door in alignment.

9 If the door and jamb are to be painted, use a matchbook cover as a spacer between the door and stop as you nail the stop in place. This allows for the thickness of the paint on the various surfaces.

Matchbook cover

10 When you are satisfied with the fit of the door within the jambs and the jambs within the opening, drive 8d finishing nails through the jambs and shims to lock the shims in place. Cut off the shims with a utility knife or handsaw.

11 As a final step, replace two of the screws in each hinge with longer screws that reach into the jack studs. This hangs the door from the jack studs, not just from the thin jamb side.

BIFOLD DOOR TRIM OPTIONS

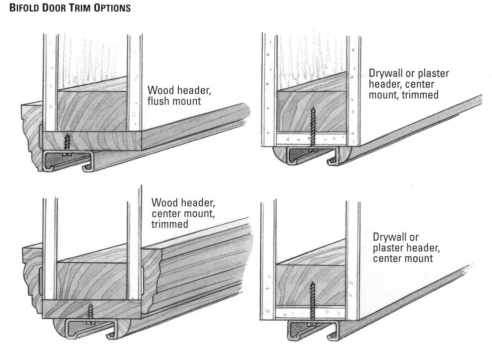

Wood header, flush mount

Wood header, center mount, trimmed

Drywall or plaster header, center mount, trimmed

Drywall or plaster header, center mount

As with bypass doors, you have trim options when installing a bifold door, depending on the look you want.

STANLEY PRO TIP

Check for hidden bumps

When prehung doors are assembled, the hinge screws sometimes poke through the back of the jamb, and these little nubs are enough to throw a jamb out of plumb. File them flat before installing the door frame.

TRIMMING DOORS AND WINDOWS

The molding that frames a door or window opening is called casing. In addition to dressing up the opening, casings cover the gaps between the walls and the jambs and hide the raw edge of the drywall. Before installing casing around a window or exterior door, loosely fill the gaps with shreds of fiberglass insulation poked in place with a drywall knife or similar tool.

The casings usually are the same throughout a room, sometimes throughout a house. But that isn't a rule; creating a hierarchy of casing details can add visual interest and richness to a room or home. Consider making the casings for exterior doors wider than those for interior doors and windows. Or link the casing size to the size of the opening: Larger openings get larger casings. Use your imagination.

PRESTART CHECKLIST

☐ **TIME**
About 45 minutes to an hour per unit

☐ **TOOLS**
Tape measure, chop saw or miter box, hammer, nail set, drill/driver

☐ **SKILLS**
Measuring and laying out, cutting accurate miters, nailing, driving screws

☐ **PREP**
Walls should be finished (and painted, if possible), door should be hung

☐ **MATERIALS**
Molding; 4d, 6d, or 8d finishing nails (depending on molding thickness); 2-inch trim-head screws

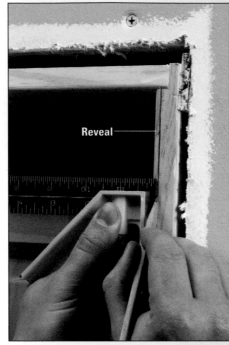

1 Casings are typically positioned to leave ⅛ inch of the jamb's edge visible. This is called the reveal. To lay out the reveal, set a combination square to ⅛ inch, put a pencil point in the notch on the edge, and draw a line along the head jamb and both side jambs.

2 Measure from the floor to the head casing reveal on both sides and miter-cut side casings to length. Attach the side casings with five pairs of nails from top to bottom. Let the nails protrude in case you have to pull them to trim the casing or adjust its position when you fit the head casing.

TRIM OPTIONS
Cutting butt joints

Miter-cut corners make a molding profile continue seamlessly around a door. But if your casings consist of flat boards, it's traditional—and easier—to use butt joints. In a butt joint, the ends of the pieces are cut square and one piece is simply butted up against the other. Most often the head casing sits on top of the side casings, but occasionally the head casing is fitted between the side casings—it's a matter of preference.

Corner blocks came into use during the Victorian era. They introduce a decorative element while allowing butt joints to be used with ornate molded casings. The blocks are slightly wider and thicker than the casing, making them the most forgiving way to put moldings around a window or door.

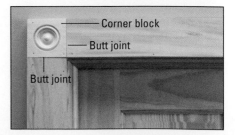

3 Most casings are back cut; that is, they have a shallow channel (or channels) cut in their backs. These channels allow for irregularities in the wall, so the molding can fit tightly against the wall and jamb. When you install casing, drive the nails through the solid edges.

4 Cut the head casing roughly to length. If the molding is mitered as shown here, start with a piece that's long and carefully trim it to fit. For butt-joined head casing, cut one end square and hold it in place to mark for an exact cut on the other side.

5 Nail the head casing to the wall and head jamb with three pairs of nails. As insurance against the miters opening, drill holes in the casing, then drive 2-inch trim-head screws through the head casing into the side casings as shown. Set all the nailheads when you are happy with the fit.

Casing a window

Casing a window is like casing a door, except the casings don't run all the way to the floor. Choose from two options: The traditional style has a sill that protrudes slightly into the room at the bottom of the window. The sill, which is technically called a stool, is the first piece of trim installed. The side casings then butt to the top of the sill. A piece of casing called an apron is applied under the sill as a finishing touch.

In less traditional construction, the sill is eliminated and the casing is wrapped around the window like a picture frame. This technique demands a little more joint-making skill. No clear starting point exists; just pick one of the sides and go from there.

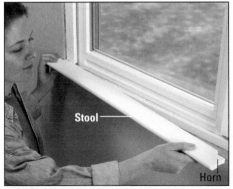

1 Traditional window trim begins with the stool. Use a saber saw to cut the horns on either end so they fit tightly against the drywall and the sides of the jambs.

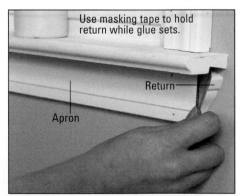

2 The apron is attached under the stool as the final piece of window trim. Measure between the outside of the side casings to determine the apron length. If the apron has a molded profile, miter the ends of the apron toward the wall. Then glue a tiny piece of molding as a return to the wall.

FINISHING FLOORS

Of all the surfaces in a room, floors take the most abuse—a constant parade of feet, sometimes wearing wet or dirty shoes, the occasional sink or tub overflow, misdirected shower sprays, and spilled food and drinks. Fortunately there are plenty of flooring materials that can stand up to the abuse, and do so with style.

Of all the aspects of a remodeling job, you may find nothing more rewarding than installing your new flooring. Floors almost always set the tone for a room, functioning as either the dominant design feature or as a neutral background for the furnishings and the rest of the decorating elements. And they really make the room look finished.

The flooring materials affect the comfort of a room, too, so you'll need to pay attention to more than aesthetics when selecting materials. Tailor your choices to your lifestyle, just as you would when selecting materials for any room in the house. Carpet, for example, is very comfortable underfoot. It makes a great surface for a basement bedroom. But if you have pets and children, a material less prone to staining (tile, resilients, or laminates) might be a better choice for the family room. And of course in the bathroom and kitchen, you'll want a surface that's absolutely watertight—not to keep moisture from wicking up through the slab, but to keep water from getting under the flooring and damaging the adhesive and the surface. While you're at it, consider adding resilient heat before you lay the new flooring. If you have plenty of headroom, you can resurface the slab with hot-water radiant piping, but electric heating mats are less expensive and easy to install (pages 114–115).

Fix the slab first

Whether it be ceramic tile, resilients, laminates, or engineered wood, your basement floor will only be as trouble-free as the slab beneath it. Before installing any finished flooring material, you'll need to inspect the condition of the basement floor and repair it if necessary (page 64). And although you can install finished flooring around an existing toilet and tub, it's better to remove these old fixtures, put down the new floor, and then reinstall them.

Acclimate the materials

Before laying your floor, bring the materials into the room so they can adjust to the ambient temperatures. Unroll resilient sheet flooring and pull tiles out of the box. That way they'll do whatever expanding or contracting they need to before they're on the floor.

Flooring contributes to both the design and comfort of the basement rooms.

CHAPTER PREVIEW

Installing ceramic floor tile
page 152

Installing resilient tile
page 154

Installing sheet vinyl flooring
page 156

Installing laminate flooring
page 158

Ceramic tile is just one of the choices for the new floor in your remodeled basement. Selecting the right flooring and installing it carefully will ensure durability and beauty.

Installing carpet and baseboard
page 162

STANLEY PRO TIP: **Snap a chalk line**

To snap a chalk line accurately, the line must be held tightly on the surface. Pull the line from its housing. Place the metal tab at one end of the surface and the housing at the other. Keeping the line tight, reach out as far from the housing as you can, lift the line about 4 inches off the surface, and let it snap back.

  You may be able to hook the metal tab in the perimeter recess of a slab or wood floor. If you can't, snapping the line is a two-person task: One holds the tab, the other holds the housing.

INSTALLING CERAMIC FLOOR TILE

Before you begin installing a ceramic tile floor, make sure the floor is up to the job required for ceramic substrates. Prepare the surface using the methods described on pages 64–65. Tile installed on basement slab floors won't need cement backerboard as a substrate. You will, however, need a waterproofing membrane—not to keep water from migrating down through the tile and grout, but to keep the slab from wicking moisture up into the floor.

Figure out how many tiles you need in each layout section and stack them around the room. That way you won't have to go back and forth to get more tiles when you start a section.

Sort through all the tile boxes to make sure the dye lots match, and take out any chipped tiles. Use them for cut pieces.

If you are installing saltillo or handmade tile, its color may vary from box to box. Mix some from each box. Doing so spreads the colors evenly in the room.

PRESTART CHECKLIST

☐ **TIME**
About an hour to trowel and set 4 to 6 square feet (varies with tile size)

☐ **TOOLS**
Tape measure, chalk line, mortar mixing paddle, ½-inch electric drill, notched trowel, 4-foot level, utility knife, grout float, sponge, beater block, hammer or rubber mallet

☐ **SKILLS**
Measuring accurately, mixing with power drill, troweling

☐ **PREP**
Install backerboard if necessary, clean surface, snap layout lines

☐ **MATERIALS**
Five-gallon bucket, thinset, spacers, ¾-inch plywood squares, tile

1 Snap layout lines on the floor and dump mortar at the edge of a section. Holding the straight edge of a trowel at about a 30-degree angle, spread the mortar evenly, about as thick as the depth of a trowel notch. Spread the mortar to the layout line; comb it with the notched edge at about a 45- to 75-degree angle.

2 Using the layout pattern you have chosen, lay the tile in place with a twisting motion, keeping the tile aligned on your layout line. Insert spacers between the tiles and adjust the tiles to fit.

LAYING OUT A TILE FLOOR

1. Snap perpendicular lines at the midpoints of the walls and square them .

2. Dry-lay tile in both directions to center the layout and leave tiles of equal width at both edges.

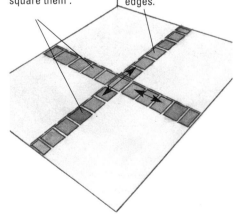

Snap layout lines

Using the dimensions of a tile and grout lines, snap chalk lines to mark out sections that are 3 tiles square. These layout lines will serve as guides to help you keep each course straight and square with the room.

2×4 beater block covered with carpet

3 When you've finished laying a section of tile, use a 4-foot carpenter's level to check for tiles that are higher or lower than the overall surface. Using a beater block, tap high tiles in place with a rubber mallet. Pull up any low tiles, backbutter them with mortar, and reset them.

4 Mix the grout to the consistency recommended by the manufacturer; dump or scoop out a small pile with a margin trowel. Working in 10-square-foot sections, pack the grout into the joints with a grout float. Hold the float at about a 30- to 45-degree angle; work it in both directions.

5 Once you have grouted a section, hold the float almost perpendicular to the tile and scrape the excess off the tile surface. Work the float diagonally to the joints to avoid lifting the grout. If you remove grout, replace it in the joint and reclean the surface. Let the grout set.

Lining up the tile

Periodically check the tile in both directions. Lay a 4-foot level on the edge of the tile— all the edges should line up along the level. Adjust the tiles to straighten the joints, if necessary. Don't kneel or walk on set tiles; support your weight on a 2-foot square of ³⁄₄-inch plywood placed on the set tiles.

Making straight cuts

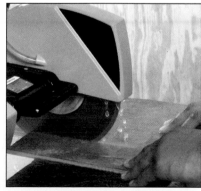

A rented wet saw will cut tiles faster than any other method. Set the tile against the fence with the cut line at the blade. Turn on the saw and feed the tile into the blade with light pressure. Increase the pressure as the saw cuts the tile and ease off as the blade approaches the rear of the cut.

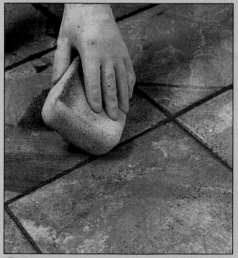

6 When a just-damp sponge won't lift grout from the joint, you can start cleaning. Wring out all excess water from a damp sponge and rub the surface in a circular motion. Rinse and wring out the sponge often. Repeat parallel to the joints to make them neat, and once more to finish cleaning.

INSTALLING RESILIENT TILE

When choosing an adhesive for dry-backed tile, be sure to read labels carefully. Picking an adhesive requires a bit of science—you'll find latex-based solutions, asphalt emulsions, alcohol resins, rubber cements, and epoxies. Ask your supplier to match the qualities of the adhesive to your job site.

Most vinyl adhesives are solvent-based, which means they don't handle like thinset and other cement-based mortars. They tend to grab the trowel and are difficult to spread evenly. If you need to, practice spreading adhesive on a piece of scrap plywood before applying it to the floor. When you work with solvent-based adhesives, you must properly ventilate the room: Open the windows and exhaust the fumes with a window fan. Wear a respirator for full protection.

Work as much as possible from untiled sections of the floor. If you have to kneel on the tile, distribute your weight on 2×2 plywood squares. Cut two pieces so you can move them alternately as you work across the floor.

PRESTART CHECKLIST

☐ **TIME**
About 4 hours for an 8×10-foot floor

☐ **TOOLS**
Trowel, utility knife, hair dryer, chalk line, straightedge, carpenter's pencil, 100-pound floor roller

☐ **SKILLS**
Setting and cutting tile

☐ **PREP**
Repair subfloor and snap layout lines

☐ **MATERIALS**
Tiles, adhesive

Installing resilient tile

1 Starting at an intersection of lines, spread adhesive with the smooth edge of a notched trowel. Lay the adhesive right up to—but not over—the layout lines. Then comb the adhesive with the notched edge of the trowel. Let the adhesive become tacky.

2 Line up the first tile with the intersection of the layout lines and set it on the adhesive. Then set the second tile against the first one and lower it in place. Don't slide the tiles—you'll push mastic up between the joints. Check the grain direction and set the rest of the quadrant.

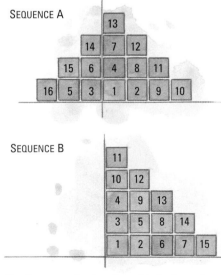

SETTING SEQUENCES
PERPENDICULAR LAYOUTS

SEQUENCE A

SEQUENCE B

Use Sequence A when the adhesive has a long open time, which allows you to work more quickly because you don't have to stop as often to spread mastic. Use Sequence B when using a mastic with a short open time.

Check the grain direction

Most resilient tiles have a grain that results from the manufacturing process. The grain itself is virtually invisible, but it does affect the color and perception of the pattern, depending on the angle of the light falling on the tile. Other tiles, both with and without grain, have a pattern that is directional.

Both grained and patterned tile must be laid in a certain order to achieve the ideal appearance. Look on the back of each tile before you lay it. If it has arrows imprinted on it, use the arrows as a guide. Dry-lay the tile with the arrows going in one direction, then experiment with the pattern, installing the arrows differently. Once you discover a result you like, use it consistently as you set the tile.

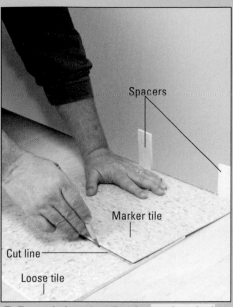

3 To mark the edge tiles for cutting vinyl tile, set a loose tile exactly on top of the last tile in a row. Then set a marker tile on top of that one, positioning it against ¼-inch spacers at the wall (resilient tile won't expand much, but the subfloor will). Run a pencil along the edge of the marker tile to mark the cut line.

4 At outside corners position a loose tile and a marker tile as if you were cutting an edge tile. Mark the loose tile as you did in Step 3, and reposition the loose tile and marker tile to the other corner. Mark the loose tile for the corner cutout.

5 When you have set one quadrant, clean off excess or spilled adhesive with the solvent recommended by the manufacturer (usually detergent and water). Don't wet the floor—excess liquid weakens the adhesive. Set the remaining quadrants. Roll the floor when finished.

Cutting vinyl tile

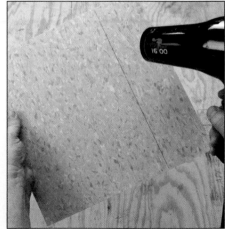

Brittle resilient tiles cut more easily if you warm them slightly with a hair dryer. Use a carpenter's pencil to mark the cut line and a utility knife to make the cut.

Score the surface of the tile with the knife, then make several passes until you have cut through the tile. If the cut edge will not be visible, you can snap the tile after a few passes with the knife.

STANLEY PRO TIP

Mix the lots

Tiles are manufactured in groups called "lots," and the color of the tile may vary from lot to lot. When you're purchasing tile, ask the dealer to supply you with tiles from the same lot. If you can't get the entire order from a single lot, mix the tiles from different cartons as you lay them. Doing so will spread any color variations randomly throughout the floor.

The easiest way to mix the tiles is to open three cartons and intermingle the tiles from each into a single batch.

INSTALLING SHEET VINYL FLOORING

One advantage of sheet vinyl flooring is that it has fewer seams than other materials. That makes it an excellent choice for basement bathrooms. Because it comes in rolls that are 12 feet wide, you can install it in smaller rooms with no seams at all.

Resilient sheet vinyl comes in two types. **Full-spread vinyl** has a felt-paper backing and requires an adhesive spread over the entire floor surface. That makes installation a little more difficult and time-consuming. In return for this extra effort, it rarely comes loose from the floor. It demands, however, an almost flawlessly smooth underlayment—even small particles under the sheet will show up as bumps when the sheet is glued down.

Perimeter-bond sheet vinyl is laid with adhesive only around the edges of the room, making it easier and quicker to lay. It is more forgiving of minor underlayment flaws, but is also more prone to coming loose.

PRESTART CHECKLIST

☐ **TIME**
About 4 hours for full-spread vinyl on a 10×12-foot bathroom floor

☐ **TOOLS**
Utility knife, compass, scissors, floor roller, seam roller, straightedge

☐ **SKILLS**
Measuring and cutting template accurately, lifting and unrolling sheet goods, seaming vinyl

☐ **PREP**
Install or repair underlayment without surface defects, remove all floor trim

☐ **MATERIALS**
Butcher paper or kraft paper, masking tape, duct tape, adhesive, vinyl sheet goods, seaming solvent

1 Cover the perimeter ¼ inch from the walls with butcher paper or kraft paper. Heavier paper will move less. Cut small triangles and tape the sheet to the floor through the holes. Overlap all edges at least 2 inches and fasten with duct tape. Roll up the template and take it to the room where you'll cut the sheet.

2 Unroll the vinyl sheet face up. Overlap seam edges by 3 inches and tape the seam. Unroll the paper template on the sheet, lining up the edges of the template with pattern lines. Tape the template to the sheet and mark its edge on the sheet with a washable marker.

Shopping for quality

Vinyl long ago replaced the mix of linseed oil, cork, and wood that was called linoleum, which graced many midcentury homes. (But special-order linoleum is available.)

All vinyl floor goods, however, are not created equal. The adage "You get what you pay for" applies here with certainty. The quality, and therefore, the durability of the material, varies widely and depends almost entirely on how much vinyl it contains.

Solid vinyl is tough, longest lasting, and most expensive. Its color and pattern are formed by embedded colored vinyl chips in the vinyl base material. Solid vinyl products also boast more choices of colors and patterns. Because the color and pattern go clear through the sheet, you won't find it wearing off easily.

The same goes for **vinyl composition** products whose pattern and color are ingrained but composed of both vinyl and nonvinyl ingredients. The reduced vinyl content makes this product less expensive.

Rotogravure vinyl sheets get their pattern from a printing process, and the printed layer has no vinyl content at all. It is protected by a urethane wear layer, but once this layer wears to expose the printed pattern, you'll find your pretty floor slowly disappearing.

You can tell a lot about the quality of vinyl sheet goods by their thickness. Thicker materials contain more vinyl and will last longer. What kind of material you use may come down to what kind of bathroom it will go in. For example, it might make sense to install a less expensive sheet in an infrequently used guest bath.

3 With a straightedge along the marks on the sheet, cut it with a utility knife. Roll up the sheet with the pattern side in and carry it to the bathroom floor. Unroll the sheet, sliding it under door casings, and tug and shift it into place.

4 For a full-spread floor, lift up one half of the sheet and fold it back. For perimeter-bond, lift up the edges. Spread adhesive from the corners to the center with a ¼-inch notched trowel. Refold the sheet back into place. Adhere the second sheet (or the other half if not seaming the sheet vinyl).

5 Roll the entire surface from the center to the edges with a rented 100-pound floor roller. Use a damp rag to wipe up any adhesive around the edges of the vinyl. Replace the trim, then install baseboards and shoe molding or vinyl cove base. Install thresholds and rehang the doors.

Seaming the sheet vinyl

1 To cut a straight seam, overlap the edges 3 inches and snap a chalk line where you want the seam. Using a straightedge and utility knife, cut through both sheets in one pass. Pull back the edges and apply adhesive under them. Push seam edges down into the adhesive.

2 Roll the seam with a seam roller (called a J-roller). Use moderate pressure to avoid pushing adhesive up through the seam. Wipe off excess adhesive and let it cure. Then apply seaming solvent to fuse the edges.

Easy seams

Place seams on an inconspicuous, low-traffic section of the floor whenever possible. Symmetry is not necessarily your goal— a seam running down the center of the bathroom floor is likely to be distracting. Put it perpendicular to the room and close to a far wall. Find your best seam location before you start cutting the sheet to fit.

After you've laid your floor, protect it until both adhesive and seams have set.
■ If possible, don't walk on the seams for at least eight hours.
■ Keep the room temperature at 65 degrees or above for 48 hours to help the adhesive cure properly.
■ Don't wash the floor for five days.

INSTALLING LAMINATE FLOORING

Laminate flooring comes in two styles—**locking laminate,** which snaps together, and **glued laminate,** which has snap-together joints that are strengthened by applying a thin coat of glue. Both types float on a plastic foam underlayment. The flooring can then expand and contract as a unit, and the foam makes the floor feel more resilient.

Assembly of the planks varies among manufacturers. Some styles use tongue-and-groove edges, while others employ metal locking strips. Some brands require that you angle the units as you engage the planks. Others snap together flat with the aid of a tapping block and hammer.

The "tilt-and-engage" style is the most common. Installing the first three rows of planks works best if you pull them toward you. That means you will assemble the first three rows about 3 feet from the wall, then slide them to the wall as a unit. You can work on top of the flooring you've installed.

Acclimate the planks for 48 hours in the room where you'll install them. If you will be using laminate baseboards in the room, extend the underlayment about 2 inches up each wall.

PRESTART CHECKLIST

☐ **TIME**
About 5 to 6 hours for an 8×10-foot floor, not including subfloor preparation

☐ **TOOLS**
Tape measure, metal straightedge, jigsaw, circular saw or table saw, trim saw, utility knife, hammer, tapping block, pull bar, pencil, compass

☐ **SKILLS**
Measuring, setting, and cutting laminate

☐ **PREP**
Repair, replace subfloor

☐ **MATERIALS**
Underlayment, laminate planks, caulk

A. Preparing the layout

1 Roll out the underlayment, butting or overlapping the joints as instructed by the manufacturer. Tape the joints as instructed. Measure the room and divide the result by the width of the planks. Add the remainder to the width of a plank and divide by 2. This is the width of your first and last border row.

2 Open three cartons and mix the planks so color variations spread throughout the room. Use your computations from Step 1 to mark the width of the tile plank for the border row. Rip enough border planks for your starting wall. When using a circular saw, place the finish side down.

How much do you need?

The amount of laminated flooring to buy depends on the coverage in a carton. Some tiles are 15½ inches square; others are a foot square. Some planks are just under 4 feet long and a foot wide; others are larger.

Find out the carton coverage from the manufacturer or retailer—most large companies now maintain thorough websites, complete with colors, patterns, and specifications.

When you order tiles, add 5 percent to the amount you think you need. When ordering tiled planks, add 15 percent. The extra accounts for mistakes and any damaged units.

Generally you can expect one roll of underlayment to cover about 100 square feet of floor. For a room of this size, you'll need two bottles of glue.

Choosing single laminate tiles

Laminate flooring is also available in individual square tiles, which offer more design options than planks. However, you may have a hard time finding them. And because production costs are higher for individual pieces, these tiles are slightly more expensive than their plank equivalents. On the other hand, there can be more waste with planked products because they require more end cuts to fit. So the cost difference may even out in the long run.

Clamp plank
face down on
work surface.

3 Starting in the center of the wall, snap the border planks together. When you no longer have space for a full plank, center the row, leaving an equal space at each end. Measure from the edge of the plank face (not the tongue) to the wall and subtract ¼ inch (to allow for spacers).

4 Mark the top of a full border plank, using the length from Step 3 and measuring from the edge of the face. Transfer the mark to the back of the plank with a combination square; cut the plank with a circular saw. Cut the left and right ends from separate planks to maintain the pattern.

5 Lock the left and right ends of the border row in place. Then push the border row against the wall, inserting ¼-inch spacers every foot or so. Number the order of the planks on small pieces of masking tape.

Laying out the grout lines

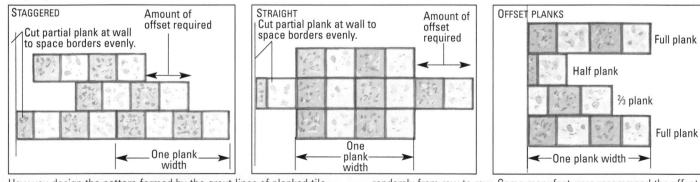

STAGGERED
Cut partial plank at wall to space borders evenly.
Amount of offset required
One plank width

STRAIGHT
Cut partial plank at wall to space borders evenly.
Amount of offset required
One plank width

OFFSET PLANKS
Full plank
Half plank
⅔ plank
Full plank
One plank width

How you design the pattern formed by the grout lines of planked tile depends on the plank pattern and how much the manufacturer requires the joints between the planks to be offset. Some planks can only be laid in a straight grout pattern. Others have a pattern that may permit more flexibility. Each will require some experimentation in planning the borders.

Both staggered and straight layouts will produce evenly spaced tiles at the walls but require cutting partial planks and result in more waste than an offset plank layout. An offset plank layout produces grout joints spaced randomly from row to row. Some manufacturers recommend the offset shown here. Others specify different lengths for each starting plank.

Because different grout patterns create dramatic differences in the appearance of a room, decide on the pattern in the planning stage and purchase a product that will produce the look you want. Bring your design to a tile retailer to get help in choosing the style that will meet your needs, and be sure to get detailed instructions on how to lay the tile for the look you want.

B. Marking and cutting contours

1 Variations in the wall can affect the layout, so the first row must follow the contour of the wall. Draw a compass along the planks, skipping the spacers. (Read the instructions; some recommend doing this after laying three rows.) Snap the second row together and cut the end planks.

2 Disassemble the border planks and use a jigsaw with a fine-tooth blade to cut the scribed line. With a reverse cutting blade, set the good side up to avoid chipping the plank. If using a regular blade, keep the good side down.

C. Installing the planks

1 Working away from the starting wall, reassemble the border row planks in their original order. Maintain the offset directed by the manufacturer and snap the end plank of the second row to the first row. Tilt the plank and pull the tongue into the groove. Prop the plank on a piece of scrap.

The larger the floor, the wider the gap

All laminate flooring requires a gap around the edges of the room to give the flooring space to expand and contract with changes in the humidity. Manufacturer's instructions generally call for about ¼ inch; this measurement is the minimum gap required.

Because wood fibers expand in relation to the amount of wood in the floor, the larger the floor area, the wider the gap has to be. In fact, the ¼-inch standard holds true for floors only from 100 to 1,000 square feet. From 1,000 to 1,800 square feet, you'll need to expand the gap to ⅜ inch, and for a 3,000 square-foot area, to as much as ⅝ inch. Large installations, generally over 40 linear feet in either direction, require a T-molding between sections.

Using a pull bar

When you reach the end of a row, you won't be able to lift the tile to snap it in place. In this case use a pull bar to assemble the units. Slide one end of the bar over the far end of the tile and tap the other end until the tile snaps into place.

Closing up the gaps

From time to time, even your best efforts will leave a gap between tiles that don't fit just exactly right. Close up these gaps as you go, using a tapping block and a hammer.

2 Tilt the second plank and push the tongue into the groove of the first one. Depending on the instructions, you can either pull each plank toward you and into the first row as you go or wait until you have assembled the entire row. Regardless of the method, lower the plank until it snaps into place.

3 Continue using the same methods to fit the planks together. When you have completed the first three rows, slide the assembly toward the starting wall, stopping short by a little more than the thickness of the spacers. Insert the spacers against the wall and snug the rows against them.

4 Continue snapping the planks together, working toward the other wall, closing up gaps as necessary with a tapping block and trimming the final row to fit. Tilt the final row and pull it into place, using a pull bar to snug the planks together. Trim underlayment flush with the planks as necessary.

Installing glued laminates

Set the first end plank in the corner, and using the method recommended by the manufacturer, apply glue to the second plank—either the tongue, the groove, or both. Engage the planks with the method recommended by the manufacturer and pull them together. Properly applied glue seeps from the joint in a thin line. Wipe it up immediately with a damp rag, then wipe the residue again.

Trimming the final row

Despite your best efforts to make the last row of tiles come out exactly the same width as the beginning row, it won't—and that is why you don't cut all the edge tiles at once. Cut each tile in the last row separately, setting in the spacers first and marking loose tiles with a guide tile. Set the cut tiles in place, snapping them to each other and to the field tiles with the pull bar and tapping block.

INSTALLING CARPET AND BASEBOARD

Cushion-backed carpet is easy to install on a basement floor. It has its own bonded foam backing, so you don't have to install separate underlayment. Order carpet slightly larger than the dimensions of the floor so you can cut it to fit. To install conventional carpet, you will have to fasten tack strips around the perimeter of the floor with concrete nails.

If your room is so large that you must seam the carpet, snap a chalk line on the floor where a seam will fall. When seaming, carefully align the edge of one piece on the chalk line. Set the second piece of carpet with its edge overlapping the first one by ¼ inch. Then fold back the edge, apply mastic or tape and a bead of seaming fluid, and press the edges together.

If you're using double-faced tape, buy the thickest you can find. The thicker the tape, the better the hold. You can apply the tape to the floor before rolling out the carpet (but don't pull off the protective backing), or apply the tape after you've cut the carpet to fit.

PRESTART CHECKLIST

☐ **TIME**
From 3 to 4 hours to carpet an 8×8 floor

☐ **TOOLS**
Wide putty knife, utility knife, hammer, nail set

☐ **SKILLS**
Lifting and moving carpet, installing tape or mastic, cutting and seaming

☐ **PREP**
Repair and clean floor

☐ **MATERIALS**
Carpet, dole-faced carpet tape or mastic, seaming fluid, baseboard, finishing nails

Installing carpet

1 Roll out the carpet across the floor and jockey it into position so it's square with the room. Push or pull the carpet into place so you have about 2 inches of excess on each wall. Slice the corners with a utility knife to make them fit.

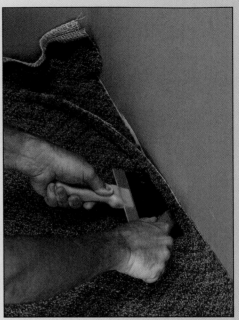

2 Starting in a corner and using a wide, stiff putty knife, push the carpet firmly into the corner where the wall meets the floor. Cut the carpet along this joint with a utility knife. Take care not to push on the corners of the putty knife—they will pierce the carpet.

Installing baseboard

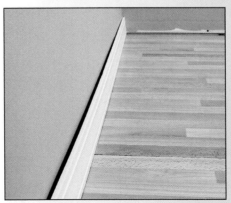

1 Start installation on the wall opposite the door. Cut baseboard to reach from corner to corner. For runs longer than 5 feet, cut the pieces about ¹⁄₁₆ inch longer than the measurement. The molding will bow slightly so it will press tightly into the corners when nailed in place.

2 Fasten the baseboard with 8d nails driven into the studs and along the bottom plate. Use as many nails as needed to close any gaps between the molding and the wall. Cope the end of the next piece of molding (page 141), leaving the other end long for now.

3 Pull up the carpet carefully without altering its position on the floor, and apply carpet tape along the edges of the wall. Do not pull off the protective liner from the tape until you have taped the entire perimeter. If you're using mastic, apply it in sections and smooth the carpet into it toward the wall.

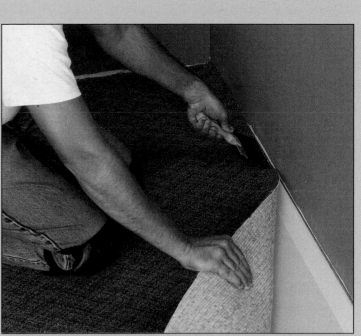

4 Make sure the carpet is still square to the room and pull it back from the wall. Remove the protective liner from the tape and press the carpet on the tape. Then install the baseboard.

3 After coping the end of the second piece, measure and cut it to length. Again, cut about $\frac{1}{16}$ inch long for a tight fit. If the piece runs into a door casing, use a notched piece of plywood to help mark it for length.

4 Outside corners are mitered. Fit the coped end of the molding first, then mark the miter location with the piece in place. Keep in mind that corners are rarely perfectly square. You may need to adjust the miter angles slightly for a good fit. Make test cuts in scrap.

STANLEY PRO TIP

Nail to a solid base

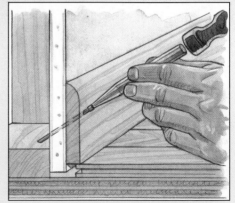

There may be times when you need to drive a nail into a baseboard to eliminate a gap, but a stud isn't where you need it. Drill a hole and drive a 16d finishing nail at a downward angle through the molding to catch the bottom plate.

Installing A New Bathroom

Installing a new bathroom might be the most challenging part of your basement remodeling project. You'll need a thorough understanding of plumbing systems and techniques, a good helper, and the patience to keep at it until you get everything right.

Getting a handle on the plumbing

The following pages show how to install major bathroom improvements (plus some variations of a few) using conventional techniques. Remember that you must always make alterations to fit your specific situation. Your plan may require pipe runs that differ from those shown, so you may need to develop a custom plan that suits your home.

If you're new to making plumbing improvements on this scale, practice some of the rudiments of working with pipe before you start. Develop a general plan for hooking the new plumbing to the old. Pay special attention to the drain vents and make sure you use pipe types and sizes that conform to code. If possible, hire a professional plumber to spend an hour or two giving you advice. This modest investment could save you time and money later on.

A look at the entire project

You will also need some proficiency in basic carpentry skills. Framing walls correctly can make plumbing work easier. Plan and install the plumbing to require minimal drilling and notching of joists and studs and reinforce any framing members that have been compromised. It's usually best to run electrical lines after the plumbing has been installed.

Working safely

Working with bathroom fixtures can be heavy and tiring work. Safe working habits should be just that—habits— and should not require you to pay special attention to them. Wear gloves and safety equipment as appropriate, masks or a respirator when doing anything that raises dust, and take frequent breaks to keep your mind and body fresh.

A complete bath installation calls for thorough planning, advanced plumbing skills, and patience.

Chapter Preview

Installing a tub
page 166

Installing a prefab tub surround
page 168

Building a shower enclosure
page 170

Hooking up a shower or tub faucet
page 174

**Installing
a toilet**
page 176

**Installing an
upflush toilet**
page 177

**Installing a
wall-mounted
sink**
page 180

**Installing a
vanity and sink**
page 182

Tiling a vanity
page 184

**Laminating
a vanity**
page 186

**Installing a
bath vent fan**
page 188

INSTALLING A TUB

When you're shopping for a tub for your basement bath, select one that's wide enough to be comfortable. Most tubs fit into a 60-inch opening, but if you buy an antique tub, it may be longer. Measure the tub to make sure it will fit.

Home centers carry spa (or whirlpool) tubs that can fit into a standard tub opening. Installing one of these models is not much more work than installing a standard tub. The difference is that a spa or whirlpool needs an electrical supply, usually a GFCI (ground fault circuit interrupter) electrical receptacle.

It is usually easiest to lay the finished flooring material before you install the tub. Caulk well at the base of a tub; even a small gap can allow water that puddles on the bathroom floor to seep underneath the tub, damaging the floor beneath the tub and providing a habitat for mold.

PRESTART CHECKLIST

☐ **TIME**
About a day to install a replacement tub where there is an existing drain

☐ **TOOLS**
Groove-joint pliers, pry bar, level, drill, screwdriver, strainer wrench, putty knife

☐ **SKILLS**
Making drain connections in a tight spot, basic carpentry skills

☐ **PREP**
Clear the area; cover the floor with plywood and a drop cloth

☐ **MATERIALS**
Tub, waste-and-overflow unit, plumber's putty, caulk, cement board and tiles, or other wall-finishing material

Ledger supports tub flange

1 Consult the manufacturer's literature and measure to make sure the drain is in the correct location. Purchase a waste-and-overflow unit and determine how you will connect it to the drain line. Screw ledger boards to the studs at the height recommended by the manufacturer. These ledgers support the tub flange.

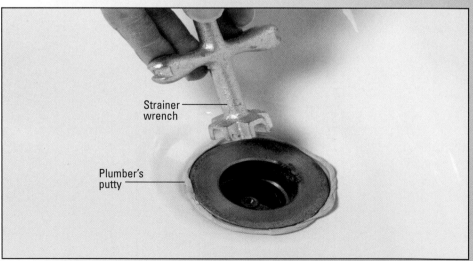

Strainer wrench

Plumber's putty

5 Inside the tube place a rope of plumber's putty under the strainer or drain flange. Hold the shoe with one hand while you screw in the flange. Finish tightening with a strainer wrench. Clean away the squeezed-out putty with a plastic putty knife.

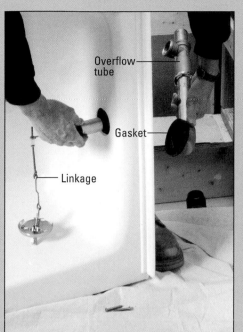

Overflow tube

Gasket

Linkage

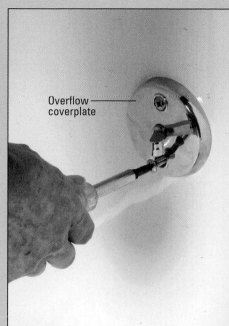

Overflow coverplate

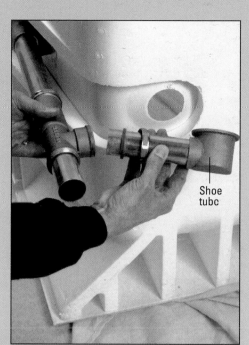

Shoe tube

2 Working with the tub turned on its side, dry-fit the overflow tube and the shoe. Make any necessary cuts, then make permanent connections. Place the gasket on the overflow flange, position it behind the overflow hole, and insert the linkage.

3 Inside the tub slip the screws into the overflow trim. Hold the overflow flange in place and hand-tighten one of the screws. Start the second screw and tighten both with a screwdriver.

4 Insert the shoe tube into the opening in the overflow tube, and slip the other end up into the drain hole.

Torpedo level

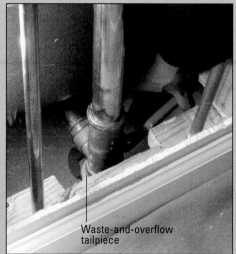

Waste-and-overflow tailpiece

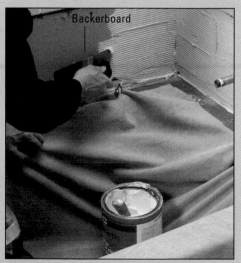

Backerboard

6 Slide the tub in place against the ledgers and check it for level; an out-of-level tub may not drain completely. Attach the tub to the studs according to the manufacturer's directions. You will probably nail or screw through an acrylic flange (shown). For a metal tub, drive nails just above the flange.

7 Working from behind or below, connect the waste-and-overflow tailpiece to the drain line. To test for leaks, close the stopper and fill the tub. Open the stopper; watch and feel for any sign of wetness.

8 To cover the wall, cut and install strips of cement backerboard, which is more moisture-resistant than green drywall. Install tiles, allow the adhesive to set for a day, and apply grout. Apply silicone or tub and tile caulk where the tiles meet the tub.

INSTALLING A PREFAB TUB SURROUND

A prefab tub surround is an inexpensive way to finish a tub and shower area. High-quality units have colorful, durable finishes as well as convenient niches and towel bars.

Make sure the unit you buy has panels with flanges that overlap each other so you don't have to cut the panels to fit precisely. With a standard 60-inch opening, you probably won't have to cut at all, other than making holes for the spout and the faucet control or handles.

Preparing the wall surface

The walls should be smooth and even. If you're covering existing shower walls, scrape away any peeling paint and patch cracks. Prime the walls to give the adhesive a finish to which it can bond securely. Installing a prefab panel over tile will result in gaps at the front edges. Cover these gaps with tile or an acrylic strip.

PRESTART CHECKLIST

☐ **TIME**
Several hours to install a solid-surface tub surround

☐ **TOOLS**
Level, drill, caulk gun (or tube), notched trowel, tape measure, utility knife

☐ **SKILLS**
Measuring and drilling holes

☐ **PREP**
Clean and prime the walls, close the drain and place a drop cloth in the tub, remove the spout and the faucet control or handles

☐ **MATERIALS**
Shower surround kit, manufacturer's recommended adhesive, masking tape, cardboard for a template

Notched trowel

1 Press a corner piece into position and mark the sides and top with a pencil. Using a notched trowel or a caulk gun (depending on the manufacturer), apply adhesive to the center area inside the pencil lines. Apply evenly so the panel will not be wavy.

Center panel

2 Press the center panel in place and smooth it with your palm. Install other pieces in the same way, following the manufacturer's installation procedures.

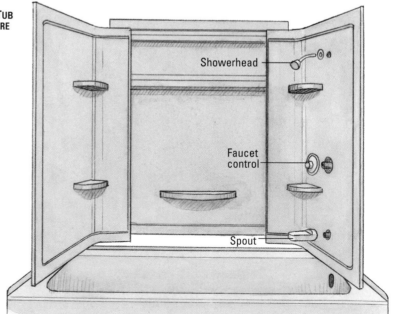

PREFAB TUB ENCLOSURE

Showerhead

Faucet control

Spout

Available acrylic or polystyrene tub surrounds may have a modern, decorative, or retro look and come in various colors. While these units are less permanent than tile, they install quickly, are relatively inexpensive, and will last for many years.

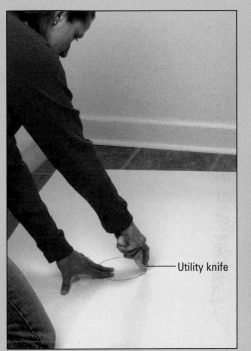

Utility knife

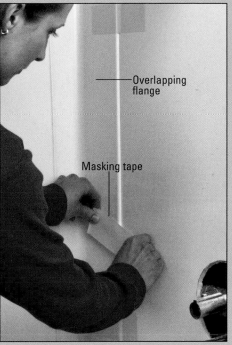

Overlapping flange

Masking tape

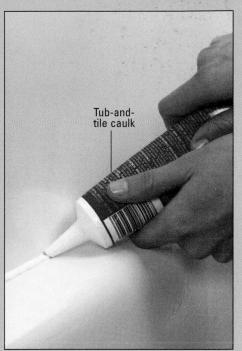

Tub-and-tile caulk

3 Place the piece that will cover the faucet wall on a scrap piece of plywood. Make a template and cut holes using a utility knife or a drill bit and a hole saw of the correct size. Install the end pieces in the same way as the back pieces.

4 The panels can be adjusted before the adhesive hardens, which usually occurs about a half hour after application. Apply pieces of masking tape to ensure that their top edges form a straight line. (The bottom edges will be caulked, so they can be slightly uneven.)

5 Apply caulk to the space between the strips and a bead where the panels meet the tub. Practice applying even pressure to the tube while drawing smoothly along the joint. After applying the caulk, smooth it with your finger. Clean up any mistakes with a damp sponge.

Make a template

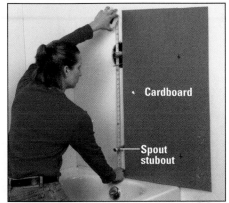

Cardboard

Spout stubout

To prevent mistakes in cutting holes, cut a piece of cardboard the same width as the panel to be installed. For each hole, measure up from the tub and over from the corner panel and mark the center of each hole. (If the panel will overlap the corner panel, take that into account.)

Cut holes with a utility knife. Then hold the template up against the wall for a trial run. Once you are certain the holes line up with the plumbing, place the template on the panel, mark the panel, and cut the holes.

WHAT IF...
You're installing a shower faucet?

If you need to replace an existing shower faucet, remove the old wall surface material. Follow the installation instruction provided by the manufacturer. Cover the wall with water-resistant drywall (greenboard) or cement backerboard if you're finishing it with tile.

BUILDING A SHOWER ENCLOSURE

Where you locate a shower enclosure in the new bathroom determines how many walls you'll have to frame for it. A corner shower on framed walls will require only one wall. In the middle of a framed wall, two new walls are required, and against a block wall, you'll have to frame three new walls. The opening can have a door or you can install a curtain rod.

Buy a shower base that is at least 34 inches square; a smaller one will feel cramped. Some bases must be set in thinset mortar or in a bed of sand, while others can be simply placed on the floor.

For a corner installation, a one-piece base unit is much simpler to install, though your choice of colors will be limited.

For details on how to run drain and supply lines, see pages 82–99.

PRESTART CHECKLIST

☐ **TIME**
Two or three days to install a base, plumbing, tiled walls, and a shower door

☐ **TOOLS**
Carpentry tools, groove-joint pliers, drill, tools for plastic and copper pipe (see pages 39–40), tiling tools, steel rod, stapler, hair dryer

☐ **SKILLS**
Working with plastic and copper pipe, framing a wall, installing tile

☐ **PREP**
Install a drainpipe with trap in the center of the base, as well as supply pipes, faucet, and shower riser

☐ **MATERIALS**
Shower base, roofing felt, PVC primer and cement, 2×4 studs, cement backerboard, backerboard screws, tiles, tile adhesive, grout, caulk, shower door

BUILDING A TILED SHOWER ENCLOSURE

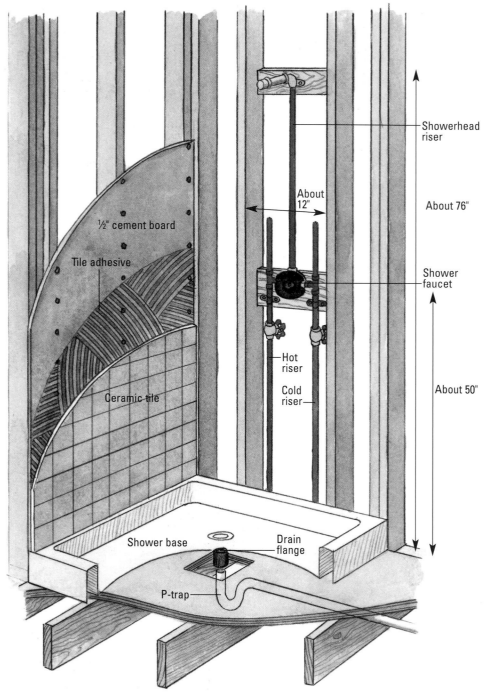

½" cement board

Tile adhesive

Ceramic tile

Showerhead riser

About 12"

About 76"

Shower faucet

Hot riser

Cold riser

About 50"

Shower base

Drain flange

P-trap

A shower drain should be installed at the center of the shower base. The flange should be level with the floor. Run the supply pipes after the framing is installed.

A. Framing the shower

2×4 stud wall

Doubled 2×4 stud at outside corners

Protect base with drop cloth.

1 Install the base and frame the side walls with studs on 16-inch centers. On the plumbing wall, space at least one pair of studs about a foot apart to accommodate the shower faucet. Install horizontal blocking to support the faucet and showerhead. Install the supply pipes and faucet (pages 174–175).

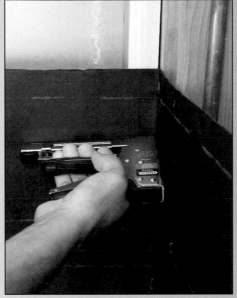

2 Cut a piece of felt paper long enough to turn all corners and cover the surface in a single run. Apply asphalt mastic to the studs, then staple the paper, warming it with a hair dryer before pressing it into the corners. Overlap top pieces on lower ones, and seal overlaps with asphalt mastic.

3 Cut backerboard so its edges will be centered on the studs and fasten it to the studs with backerboard screws. When fitting backerboard above a tub, set the sheet on ¼-inch spacers to leave a gap (for caulking) between the bottom of the board and the tub rim.

WHAT IF...
I'm tiling a tub surround?

1 Apply asphalt roofing cement to the tub flange. This is the place where most tub and shower surrounds fail; water that gets into this joint will migrate upwards, and down into the floor. The asphalt cement seals the tub to the waterproofing felt or 4-mil poly sheet.

2 After you've hung the backerboard, caulk the gap at the bottom with clear or white silicone caulk. The caulk seals the joint between the tub and backerboard and allows for some expansion and contraction of the different materials without breaking the seal.

STANLEY PRO TIP

One-piece shower units

Corner and rectangular shower stalls made of acrylic fiberglass or polystyrene are easier to install than a framed shower enclosure.

One-piece units are designed for new construction or a basement location with wide or double doors—they are too large to fit through a standard door. Three-piece units can be quickly assembled and are ideal for any remodeling.

Two or three walls of these units must be installed against solid walls. A corner unit can be installed in any corner that is reasonably square. A rectangular or square unit requires an opening of the correct width and height.

B. Installing the tiles

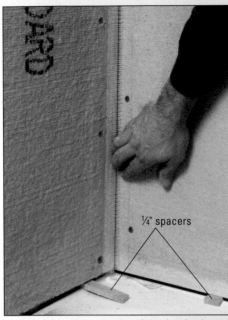

¼" spacers

1× batten

1 Reinforce the corners of the backerboard with fiberglass mesh tape. Skim-coat the tape with thinset, let it dry, and sand it smooth. Repeat the process, feathering the edge of the thinset. The spacers create a ¼-inch gap for the bead of caulk.

2 Using a dimensional layout drawing, locate the point on which a horizontal and vertical grout line will fall. Hold a 4-foot level on both planes and mark reference lines. Then snap layout grids whose dimensions equal the width of the tiles and grout joints.

3 To keep the first and subsequent rows of tile level, tack a 1× batten to the backerboard one full tile width above the tub. Spread and comb thinset on the back wall first and tile the wall.

Installing a custom shower pan

A custom mortared shower pan allows you to fit a shower enclosure in the desired space, rather than being limited to the sizes of a prefab unit. The key to a successful installation lies in the use of a tough plastic membrane that makes the floor waterproof.

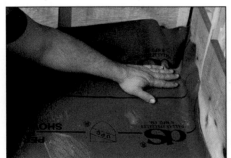

1 Frame the walls of the unit and install 15-pound felt paper and metal lath on the floor. Then spread mortar on the floor in an even layer. Unroll the membrane on the floor and smooth it. Then staple the top 1-inch blocking between the studs and solvent-weld the corners.

2 Install the drain plate and staple waterproofing membrane to the studs. Spread a sloped coat of mortar, keeping the slope about one-third of a bubble on a level.

3 When the floor has dried, scrape off any remaining imperfections with a steel trowel, then spread and comb latex-modified thinset. Press the tiles firmly into the mortar to make sure they conform to the slope of the floor. Line up all the edges with a 2-foot straightedge and let the mortar cure overnight. Grout the tiles with latex-modified grout.

4 When the back wall is done, set the tile on the side walls. Start from the front, leaving cut tiles for the back edge at the corner of the adjoining wall. Tape the tiles if necessary to hold them in place (page 136). Remove excess adhesive from the joints and let it cure.

5 When the adhesive is dry, clean the surface and joints of any remaining excess. Mix latex-modified grout and apply it with a grout float, forcing it into the joints in both planes. Let the grout cure until a damp sponge won't lift it out of the joints.

6 To scrape excess grout off the surface, hold the float almost perpendicular to the tile and work diagonally to avoid pulling the grout from the joints. Dampen a sponge, wring it out thoroughly, and clean the surface twice, smoothing the joints. Scrub off the haze with a clean rag.

WHAT IF...
I'm tiling around faucets?

When cutting tile around faucets, mark the cut line and chip the profile out with tile nippers. Cut the tile about ¼ inch larger than the outside edge of the fixtures and fill that recess with silicone caulk. Let the adhesive cure.

LOCATING GRAB BARS

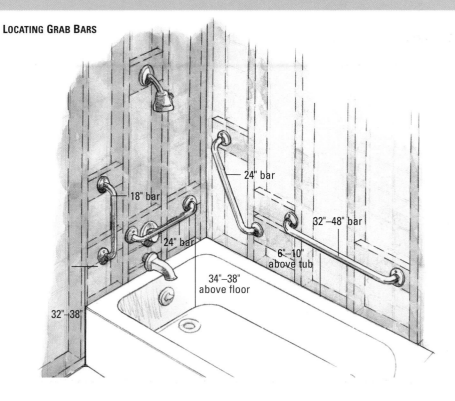

24" bar

18" bar

32"–48" bar

24" bar

6"–10" above tub

34"–38" above floor

32"–38"

HOOKING UP A SHOWER OR TUB FAUCET

In most cases you should install separate ¾-inch lines to supply hot and cold water to the shower in your new basement bathroom. This ensures good water pressure and protects anyone in the shower from a sudden change of temperature when a faucet is turned on or the toilet tank refills. Connect the supply lines as close to the water heater as possible.

Choose the tub or shower faucet before you start installing pipes. Read the manufacturer's directions carefully so you know exactly where the pipes should go.

If your faucet does not have integrated shutoff valves, install shutoff valves on the lines leading to the shower so you can turn off the water if repairs are needed.

Assuming an 18-inch-tall tub, position the faucet about 28 inches above the floor for a tub, about 48 inches for a shower. You may want to compromise and position it about 38 inches above the floor.

PRESTART CHECKLIST

☐ **TIME**
About half a day to run supply lines and install a tub/shower faucet

☐ **TOOLS**
Drill, propane torch, tubing cutter, multiuse wire brush, flame guard, damp rag, groove-joint pliers, flux brush

☐ **SKILLS**
Accurate measuring and drilling, working with copper pipe

☐ **PREP**
Tap into the hot and cold water lines and run ¾-inch pipe up into the room; if needed, move a stud to make room for the plumbing behind the tub

☐ **MATERIALS**
Tub/shower faucet, copper pipe and fittings, flux, solder, pipe-thread tape

Crossbrace

1× scrap stands for ½" backerboard plus ¼" tile

1 Most faucets come with a plastic cover that protects the faucet and serves as a guide for the depth at which it must be set. To determine where to place the braces, consider the total thickness of the finished wall—often ½-inch-thick backerboard plus ¼-inch-thick tiles.

2×6 crossbrace

2 Determine how high you want to locate the spout (make sure it will clear the tub), the faucet handles, and the showerhead. Install a 2×6 brace for each. Anchor the braces with screws rather than nails so you can move them more easily if they need adjustment.

TUB/SHOWER INSTALLATION

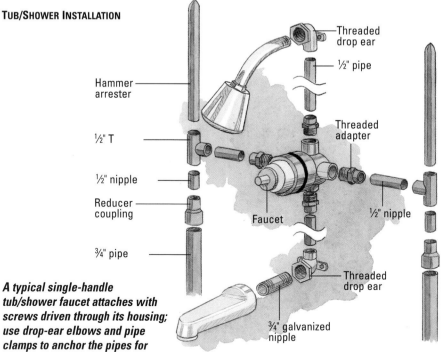

Threaded drop ear

½" pipe

Hammer arrester

½" T

Threaded adapter

½" nipple

Reducer coupling

Faucet

½" nipple

¾" pipe

Threaded drop ear

A typical single-handle tub/shower faucet attaches with screws driven through its housing; use drop-ear elbows and pipe clamps to anchor the pipes for the shower arm and the spout.

¾" galvanized nipple

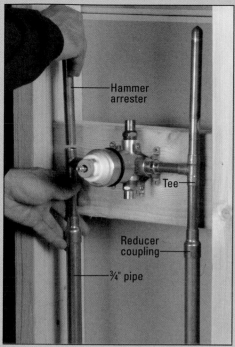

Hammer arrester

Tee

Reducer coupling

¾" pipe

3 Assemble all the pipes in a dry run. Install ¾-inch pipe up to the height of the faucet, add reducer couplings or elbows, and run short lengths of ½-inch pipe to the threaded adapters on the faucet. Add hammer arresters. Anchor the faucet according to the manufacturer's directions.

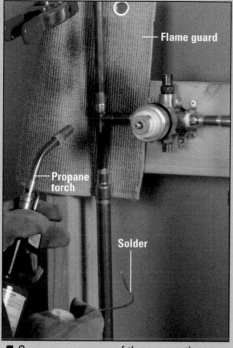

Flame guard

Propane torch

Solder

4 Once you are sure of the connections, sweat all the fittings (pages 88–89). Start at the faucet, then move on to the shower arm and spout connections. Run ½-inch pipe up to the shower arm and down to the spout; attach drop-ear elbows at both spots.

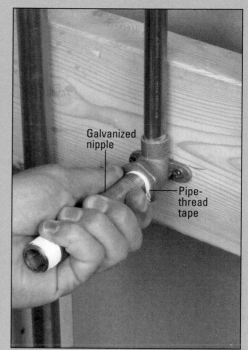

Galvanized nipple

Pipe-thread tape

5 Finger-tighten a threaded nipple—either brass or galvanized—into both drop-ear elbows. Once the wallcovering is in place, remove them and install the shower arm and the tub spout.

STANLEY PRO TIP

Add reinforcement to shower-arm drop ears

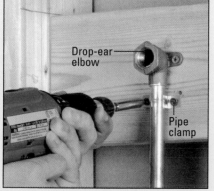

Drop-ear elbow

Pipe clamp

Whacking the showerhead with your elbow can bend or crack a drop-ear elbow. As an extra safeguard, screw a pipe clamp just below the drop ear.

WHAT IF...
You have other faucet setups?

Three-handle faucet setup

Adapter

Integral shutoff

A three-handle faucet may require supply pipes that are farther apart than for a single-handle faucet. Threaded adapters screw in for the supplies, spout, or shower arm.

A faucet with integral shutoffs comes with a large escutcheon (coverplate), so you can more easily reach the shutoff valves.

INSTALLING A TOILET

Installing a toilet is one of the last things you will accomplish in your bathroom remodeling project. Before the toilet is installed, complete the rough plumbing, run electrical lines, and install the lights, switches, receptacles, and ceiling fan. Lay the finish flooring if you haven't already done so. Install cement backerboard on the walls that surround the tub/shower and moisture-resistant drywall (also called greenboard) on the other walls. Tile or apply prefab sheets to the tub/shower surround. Tape, prime, and paint the walls and the ceiling. You may want to install baseboard and trim, but often it's best to wait until the sink and toilet are installed to avoid bumps and nicks on the trim.

To install a stop valve for the toilet, follow the instructions on pages 98–99. Measure the length of the supply tube needed and confirm the connection dimensions.

PRESTART CHECKLIST

☐ **TIME**
Half a day to install a toilet

☐ **TOOLS**
Adjustable wrench, screwdriver, drill

☐ **SKILLS**
Assembling plumbing parts, cementing PVC fittings

☐ **PREP**
Finish all the wiring, carpentry, and wall preparation; remove the drop cloth from the floor

☐ **MATERIALS**
Toilet, wax ring, toilet flange with bolts, supply tubes and decorative flanges, toilet, PVC primer and glue

Installing a toilet

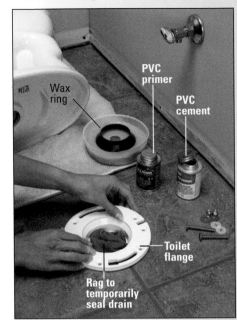

Wax ring · PVC primer · PVC cement · Toilet flange · Rag to temporarily seal drain

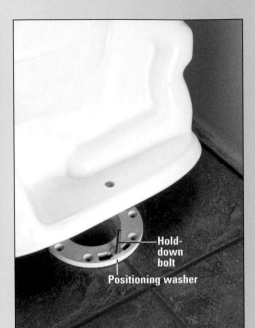

Hold-down bolt · Positioning washer

1 Install finish flooring to within an inch of the drain hole. The toilet flange can rest on top of the finished floor or on top of the subflooring. Test-fit the flange, then prime and glue it so that you will be able to place the hold-down bolts on either side of the opening (Step 2). Remove the rag.

2 Press a wax ring onto the bottom of the toilet. Place the hold-down bolts in the flange and slip plastic positioning washers over them. Lower the bowl, threading the bolts through the holes in the bowl. Press down to seat the bowl firmly. Slip on washers and nuts and gently tighten.

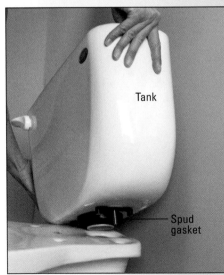

Tank · Spud gasket

Toilet supply tube · Adjustable wrench

3 Assemble the tank and the bowl of a new toilet following the manufacturer's instructions. A large spud gasket seals the opening below the flush-valve seat. Place a rubber washer under the head of each mounting bolt. Don't overtighten the nuts.

4 Attach a toilet supply tube by hand-tightening the nuts at the underside of the tank and the stop valve. Tighten a half turn or more with a wrench and open the stop valve. You may need to tighten the connection a bit farther.

INSTALLING AN UPFLUSH TOILET

Installing a new toilet, shower, or tub in a basement can be a major undertaking. If you don't want to break into the concrete, install new drain lines, and repour the floor (page 94), install an upflush toilet.

An upflushing unit makes installation much easier. Instead of using gravity to drain, it has an electric pump that efficiently discharges waste up and away. A GFCI receptacle must be installed nearby.

Upflushing units usually are installed under or near the toilet. Most can serve a sink and a tub as well.

Some upflushing units, especially those installed in the 1970s and 1980s, were unreliable and needed frequent repairs. Newer units are more dependable. Ask a plumbing supplier about the track record of the model you are considering. Make sure the unit's pump is powerful enough to send wastewater the required distance to the house's drain.

PRESTART CHECKLIST

☐ **TIME**
A day to install an upflushing unit and a toilet

☐ **TOOLS**
Groove-joint pliers, screwdriver, level, drill, PVC saw, deburring tool

☐ **SKILLS**
Planning and running drain and vent lines, basic carpentry skills

☐ **PREP**
Purchase a unit, draw a plan, consult with a plumbing inspector to make sure the plumbing will meet code, install GFCI outlet

☐ **MATERIALS**
Upflushing unit, toilet, PVC pipe and fittings, primer, cement, wax ring

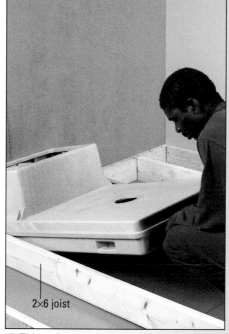

2×6 joist

1 This unit is designed to fit between 2×6 joists. It must rest on a stable, fairly level surface. If necessary, build a simple 2×2 frame, mix and pour sand-mix hydraulic concrete, and set the unit in the concrete. Level in both directions. Allow the concrete to cure before proceeding.

Adjustable wrench

2 Prepare the unit for the toilet: Install the iron support flange. Make sure that the toilet mounting bolts are in the correct positions and are long enough for mounting the toilet.

UPFLUSH TANK AND PUMP

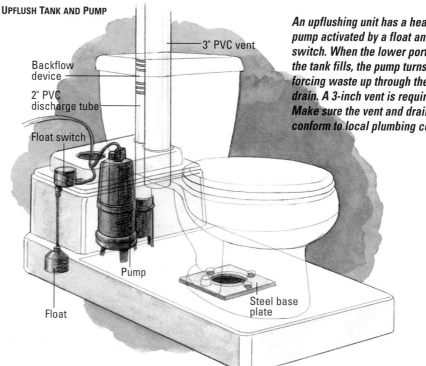

3" PVC vent

Backflow device

2" PVC discharge tube

Float switch

Pump

Float

Steel base plate

An upflushing unit has a heavy-duty pump activated by a float and switch. When the lower portion of the tank fills, the pump turns on, forcing waste up through the 2-inch drain. A 3-inch vent is required. Make sure the vent and drain conform to local plumbing codes.

Installing an upflush toilet (continued)

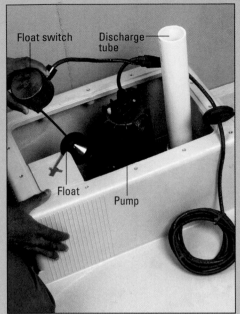

Float switch

Discharge tube

Float

Pump

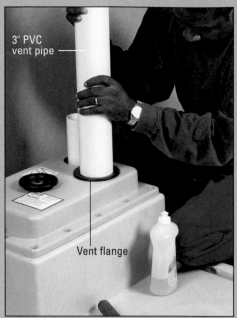

3" PVC vent pipe

Vent flange

3 Assemble the float switch. Install the discharge pipe. Place the pump in the tank, and mount the float switch. Before sealing the unit, make sure the pump works. Attach a garden hose to a water supply and run it into the flange hole.

4 Connect the discharge to a drainpipe leading to a bucket or floor drain. Tape the temporary drainpipe joints—the pump is forceful. Plug the unit into a GFCI receptacle. Slowly fill the tank with water. The pump should come on and discharge water once water reaches the correct level.

5 Insert the rubber flange provided and insert 3-inch PVC vent pipe to the unit. (It's a tight fit; liquid soap helps.) Run the vent to the main stack. See page 85 for recommendations on proper venting. Be sure to configure the vent and drain in a code-approved manner.

WHAT IF...
A toilet must be placed well below the sewer line?

A macerating toilet is useful if a bathroom will be well below the sewer line (as much as 12 feet below), or if pipes must travel a long distance (up to 150 feet away) before connecting with the main sewer line. A macerating toilet has a rotating blade that grinds waste before pumping it away. Macerating units have smaller discharge and drain pipes. The flush cycle normally takes 15 to 18 seconds.

A macerating unit must be connected to a horizontal outlet toilet. Some manufacturers combine a toilet and pump. You can choose between stand-alone macerating toilets and units with connections for a tub/shower and a sink. (With either type, the tub/shower must be raised to facilitate drainage.)

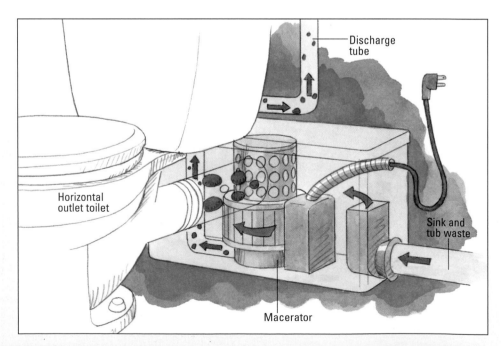

Discharge tube

Horizontal outlet toilet

Sink and tub waste

Macerator

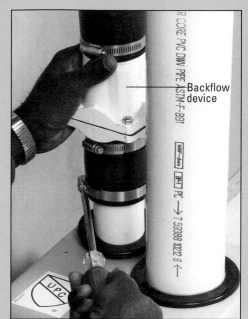

Backflow device

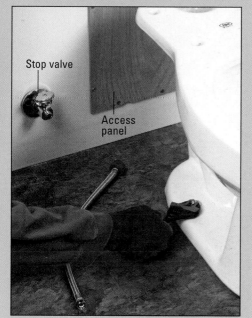

Stop valve

Access panel

6 The discharge pipe connects to a backflow preventer to ensure that wastewater will not flow back into the unit. (Be sure to install it correct-end up.) Connect a 2-inch PVC drainpipe to the discharge unit and run it toward the house's drain in a code-approved manner.

7 Connect the drain and vent pipes to the house's system. (See pages 96–97 for ways to tie new pipes to old.) Plug the unit into a GFCI receptacle within reach from the access panel. Install the supply line. Install the subfloor and walls, being careful not to puncture the tank with any fasteners.

8 Finish the floor and walls and install the access panel. Install the toilet onto a wax ring where the bowl rests on the upflush unit (page 176). Connect the toilet to a cold-water supply line with a stop valve.

WHAT IF…
Other fixtures will be connected?

Additional plumbing fixtures such as a tub/shower and a sink can be connected to an upflush unit. Drainpipes for these fixtures must flow downhill to the upflush unit.

This does not pose a problem for the sink, since its drain is usually 16 inches above the floor. The tub, however, usually must be raised so the drain line can flow downward to the upflush unit. One solution is to rest the tub on a platform made of 2×4s and plywood. Vent pipes must be run in the standard manner.

Most manufacturers supply an extra flange for hooking up a tub/shower and sink drain to the tank. Follow the manufacturer's specs exactly for cutting the access hole for the drain.

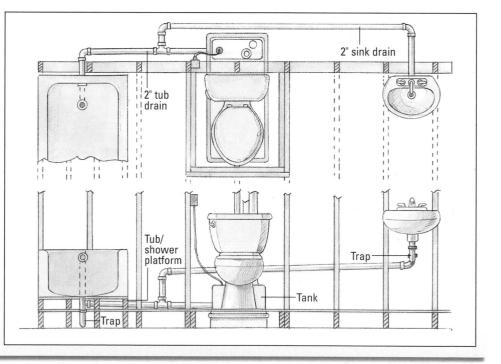

2" sink drain

2" tub drain

Tub/ shower platform

Trap

Tank

Trap

Trap

INSTALLING A WALL-MOUNTED SINK

A wall-mounted sink saves space in a bathroom compared to a vanity-mounted model but requires blocking between the studs to provide support. Once you have framed the walls for your new basement bathroom, measure up from the floor the distance recommended by the manufacturer and fasten 2×6 or 2×8 blocking by nailing through the studs. Install the bracket after hanging the finished wall material. If you're tiling the wall, drill through the tile with a masonry drill. Then install the bracket.

An inexpensive pedestal sink is actually a wall-mounted sink with the addition of a pedestal. The pedestal is for looks only.

If your supply lines are close together, you may be able to hide them behind the pedestal. Otherwise let the plumbing show.

PRESTART CHECKLIST

☐ **TIME**
From 2 to 3 hours

☐ **TOOLS**
Drill, hammer, screwdriver, adjustable wrench, groove-joint pliers, basin wrench

☐ **SKILLS**
Installing a bathroom faucet with pop-up drain, connecting a trap, cutting drywall

☐ **PREP**
Frame and finish wall

☐ **MATERIALS**
Wall-mounted sink, bathroom faucet, supply tubes that fit the stop valves, plumber's putty, 2×6 or 2×8 piece, screws, drywall, joint compound

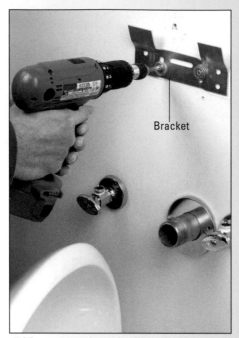

Bracket

Rope of putty

1 Measure up from the floor the distance recommended by the manufacturer and mark the location of the bracket on the wall. Hold the bracket in place and mark the position of the bracket. Install the bracket by driving screws through the wall into the 2× blocking behind it.

2 You can install the faucet and supply tubes before or after mounting it. Whenever you install the faucet, seal the bottom of the unit with the manufacturer's gasket (if supplied) or a rope of putty pressed on the sink deck.

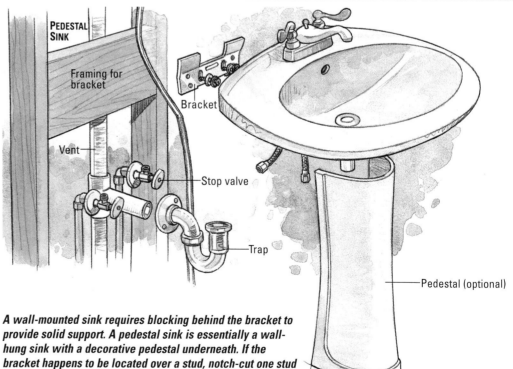

PEDESTAL SINK

Framing for bracket

Bracket

Vent

Stop valve

Trap

Pedestal (optional)

A wall-mounted sink requires blocking behind the bracket to provide solid support. A pedestal sink is essentially a wall-hung sink with a decorative pedestal underneath. If the bracket happens to be located over a stud, notch-cut one stud in order to install the brace.

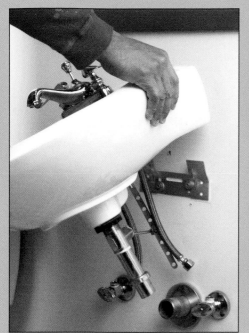

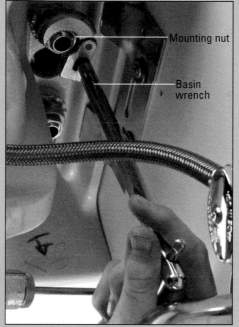

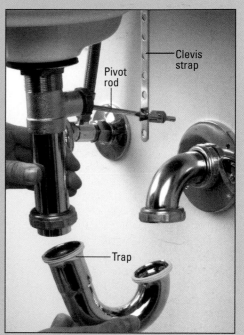

3 Install the drain body on the sink, then lift the sink and lower it onto the bracket, making sure the tabs on the bracket slide firmly into any recesses on the back of the sink. If you have mounted the faucet and supply tubes, hook them to the stop valves.

4 If you have not already mounted the faucet, have a helper hold the faucet straight while you tighten the mounting nuts from below with a basin wrench. Then attach the supply tubes to the faucet and the stop valves.

5 With the stopper closed all the way, slide the clevis strap onto the lift rod and the pivot rod, using the spring clip to hold it in place. Tighten the setscrew that holds the strap to the lift rod. Then install the trap.

WHAT IF...
You want a freestanding bowl sink?

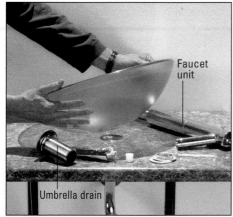

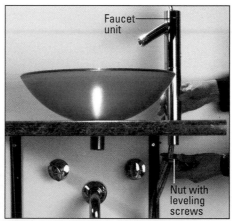

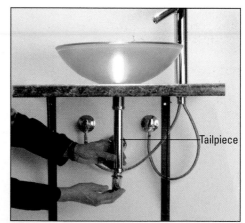

1 Install the countertop of your choice, then drill two holes in the countertop, one for the drain and one for the faucet. There is no overflow, so use an umbrella drain (shown), which covers the drain but does not close it. Apply silicone sealant and anchor by tightening the nut from below.

2 The faucet unit comes with flexible supply tubes already attached. Apply silicone sealant to the bottom of the faucet and drop the lines through the hole in the countertop. Anchor the faucet from below by tightening the nut and leveling screws.

3 Wrap the threads of the stop valves with pipe-thread tape and attach the supply tubes. Make a tailpiece from a section of trap and attach it with a rubber washer and trap nut.

INSTALLING A VANITY AND SINK

Installing a bathroom sink in a vanity is easier than other installations because the supply lines and the drain are all hidden within a cabinet. If the cabinet has no back, attach it to the wall and it will hide the plumbing. However, if the cabinet has a back, measure and cut three holes for the two supply lines and the drain.

Choosing a cabinet and top
A high-quality vanity cabinet is made of hardwood to resist water damage. A less expensive cabinet made of laminated particleboard will quickly disintegrate if it gets wet.

A vanity top typically is a single piece comprised of the bowl, countertop, and backsplash. Acrylic or plastic vanity tops are inexpensive, but they scratch and stain more easily than other materials.

PRESTART CHECKLIST

☐ **TIME**
Two to three hours to install a basic cabinet and vanity top with faucet

☐ **TOOLS**
Drill, hammer, screwdriver, level, adjustable wrench, groove-joint pliers, basin wrench, jigsaw

☐ **SKILLS**
Installing a faucet, attaching a P trap, connecting supply tubes, simple carpentry

☐ **PREP**
Shut off the water and remove the old sink

☐ **MATERIALS**
Vanity cabinet and top, faucet, P trap, supply tubes that fit the stop valves, plumber's putty, wood shims, screws, silicone caulk

Stop valve

Drain

1 The stop valves and drainpipe should be in place and close enough together to be enclosed by the cabinet. If your vanity cabinet has a back (many do not), remove the handles from the stop valves. Then measure and cut holes for the drain and the two supply pipes.

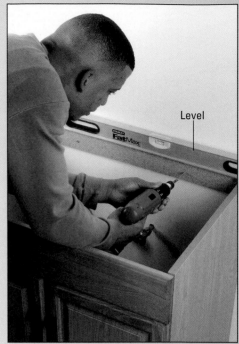

Level

2 Slide the cabinet into place and check it for level in both directions. If necessary slip shims under the bottom or behind the back of the cabinet. Drive screws through the cabinet framing into wall studs to secure the cabinet.

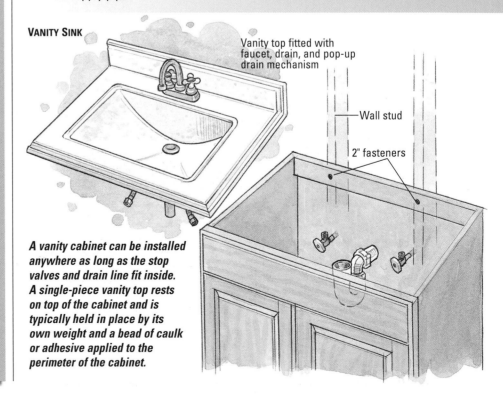

VANITY SINK

Vanity top fitted with faucet, drain, and pop-up drain mechanism

Wall stud

2" fasteners

A vanity cabinet can be installed anywhere as long as the stop valves and drain line fit inside. A single-piece vanity top rests on top of the cabinet and is typically held in place by its own weight and a bead of caulk or adhesive applied to the perimeter of the cabinet.

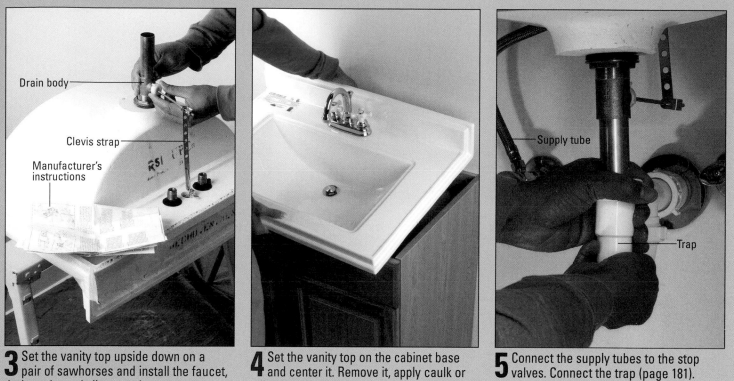

Drain body

Clevis strap

Manufacturer's instructions

Supply tube

Trap

3 Set the vanity top upside down on a pair of sawhorses and install the faucet, drain and supply lines, and pop-up assembly. Check the manufacturer's instructions for details.

4 Set the vanity top on the cabinet base and center it. Remove it, apply caulk or adhesive along the top edge of the vanity, and reinstall the top.

5 Connect the supply tubes to the stop valves. Connect the trap (page 181).

Installing a drop-in sink

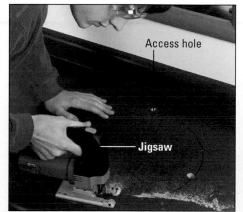

Access hole

Jigsaw

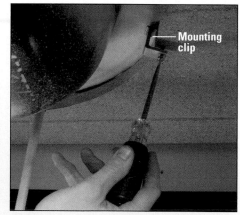

Mounting clip

1 To install a drop-in, self-rimming sink, install a laminate countertop or plywood and concrete backerboard for a tile top. Use the template if provided, or turn the sink upside down on the counter and trace its outline. Draw another line the specified distance inside the first one. Cut the inner line with a jigsaw.

2 Plumb the sink (Step 3 above). Apply a bead of bathtub caulk or a rope of plumber's putty around the hole and set the sink. If the sink doesn't have mounting clips, apply a bead of silicone caulk instead of putty. Set the sink in, wipe away the excess caulk, and wait several hours before attaching the plumbing.

3 If your sink has mounting clips, slip several of them in place and turn them sideways so they grab the underside of the counter. Tighten the screws. Attach the supply lines and the drain trap.

TILING A VANITY

Atiled vanity gives your bathroom a designer look without completely redesigning the whole room. If you plan to tile a bathroom wall, tiling the vanity will make the vanity and sink an integral part of the space.

Even if your existing base cabinet is in good condition, you'll have to build up the top. Commercial vanity countertops are not made to support the weight of ceramic tile. Remove the top and add bracing, a ¾-inch plywood base, and a polyethylene waterproofing membrane.

Buy the tile for all the surfaces you'll be tiling—vanity tile, wall tile, and bullnose trim. That way you can be more certain of getting tiles of a consistent color throughout the entire project. Make sure the cartons have the same lot number.

Select the right tile to use on your vanity. Use glazed tile ⅜ to ½ inch thick. Purchase a sink whose texture matches the glaze— vitreous china and enameled cast iron are good choices. Self-rimming sinks are easy to install, and the rim will cover the rough edges of the cut tile.

PRESTART CHECKLIST

☐ **TIME**
Eight to nine hours to build the substrate and lay the tiles; an hour more the next day to grout them

☐ **TOOLS**
Circular saw, cordless drill, jigsaw, level, stapler, notched trowel, beater block, straightedge, caulking gun, grout float, tile nippers

☐ **SKILLS**
Basic carpentry skills, setting tile, cutting tile, grouting

☐ **PREP**
Remove existing vanity top or install a new prefab or custom unit

☐ **MATERIALS**
Drywall screws, ¾-inch exterior-grade plywood, cement backerboard, backerboard screws, tile, thinset mortar, 4-mil polyethylene or 15-pound felt, grout

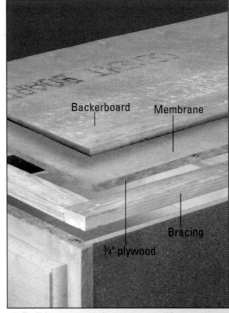

Backerboard Membrane
¾" plywood Bracing

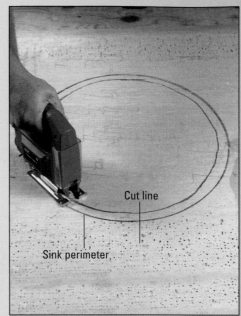

Cut line
Sink perimeter

1 Build your own base or modify a commercial unit. Glue and screw bracing inside the cabinet, then install ¾-inch exterior-grade plywood with a 1-inch overhang, according to your design. Staple waterproofing membrane to the plywood and install ½-inch backerboard.

2 Mark the sink outline and cut line using the manufacturer's template. If a template isn't available, place the sink upside down on the surface and mark its shape. Draw a second line 1 inch inside the first line and drill a starter hole. Cut the second line with a jigsaw.

Removing a flush-mounted or recessed sink

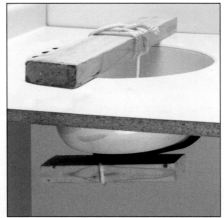

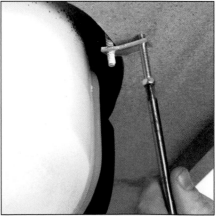

Most flush-mounted and recessed sinks are supported with clips under the cabinet. If you remove the clips without some sort of bracing, the sink will fall into the cabinet.

First unhook the plumbing, then support the sink with 2×4 braces tied with nylon rope. Thread one end of the rope through the drain and tie it to the bottom brace. Soak any rusted clips with penetrating oil, then remove them. Lift the sink or let it down with the braces.

3 Lay out the tiles in a dry run using spacers. Try to minimize cutting as much as possible. Mark the edges of your dry run and snap chalk lines to guide the installation. Then comb thinset onto the backerboard.

4 Set the tiles in place and level them with a beater block (page 153). Cut tiles don't have to fit exactly to the edge of the sink hole but must not extend beyond the edge. Keep the tiles in line using a metal straightedge. Let the mortar cure, then grout the tiles.

5 When the grout has cured, run a bead of silicone caulk around the edge of the hole and set in the sink. To avoid pinched fingers, ask a helper to support the bottom of the sink. Install and tighten any mounting clips and hook up the plumbing lines. Run another bead of caulk around the edge of the sink.

WHAT IF...
You're tiling an alcove?

If you plan to tile a sink enclosed in an alcove, design the layout carefully. First decide whether you want the grout joints on the wall to line up with those on the vanity. Draw a scaled plan to avoid ending up with small slivers of tile at the edges—you'll want the same-size tile on both ends of the installation.

Tile the walls first, then the countertop, then the ledge. Finish with V-cap edging.

Other sink installations

Both flush-mounted and underhung sinks make for easier cleaning, but they require special countertop treatments.

Install a flush-mounted sink with its rim resting on plywood substrate. Install concrete backerboard around the sink and top it with tiles that partially rest on top of the sink flange.

Install and plumb an underhung sink after the substrate is installed. Then install tiles, as shown, with thin vertical pieces around the perimeter and bullnose trim overlapping them.

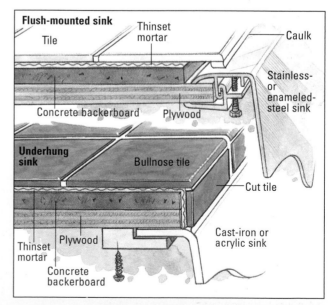

Flush-mounted sink — Thinset mortar — Caulk — Tile — Concrete backerboard — Plywood — Stainless- or enameled-steel sink — Underhung sink — Bullnose tile — Cut tile — Thinset mortar — Plywood — Cast-iron or acrylic sink — Concrete backerboard

LAMINATING A VANITY

Laminating a vanity countertop requires some careful planning. Your primary defense against mistakes is cutting the laminate slightly oversize to provide a little margin of error.

You can apply laminate over an existing laminated countertop or put it onto a new base as shown here. Build a new base from ¾-inch exterior grade plywood. Laminate will stick securely to an existing laminate countertop as long as it is clean and in good repair.

Preparation steps

Bring the laminate into the room at least 48 hours before you work with it so it can acclimate to the conditions.

Make sure the countertop surface is clean of anything that would hinder the adhesive bond—grease, cooking residues, or dust. Cut the sink hole in the base (page 184) before you laminate the top. You will cut out the sink area in the laminate as the final step.

PRESTART CHECKLIST

☐ **TIME**
Between 8 to 10 hours to build the base and cut and install the laminate

☐ **TOOLS**
Metal straightedge, laminate scribing tool, tablesaw with laminate cutting guide (optional), router or laminate trimmer with flush-cutting bit, brushes for adhesive application (in lieu of spray application), 3-inch rubber roller, venetian blind slats or dowels, fine-toothed file, cordless drill

☐ **SKILLS**
Measuring and marking, gluing, cutting and trimming laminate

☐ **PREP**
Prepare clean, smooth, and level surface

☐ **MATERIALS**
Exterior plywood, laminate, adhesive

1 Mark the sheet for the top an inch larger than the base. Mark the edge laminate ¼ to ½ inch wider than the thickness of the plywood. Lay the sheet face up on a work surface and clamp a straightedge on the line. Score the line in several passes with a laminate scribing tool. Lift one side of the sheet to snap it along the line.

2 Two pieces that butt together must have perfectly straight edges. Clamp two pieces between 1× guides, overlapping them about an inch. Make sure the sheets are square with each other. Trim the pieces using a router with a flush-cutting bit.

STANLEY PRO TIP

Cut laminate

You can cut laminate sheets with a variety of tools. One of the easiest and least expensive is the laminate scriber shown on these pages. Used correctly and with a little patience, it will produce clean, straight cuts.

If you own a tablesaw with a wide table, you can cut laminate faster. If the rip fence does not fit tightly against the table, install a laminate cutting guide to keep the laminate edge from creeping under the fence as you saw. Cut the sheet with its good side up to prevent chipping the surface. A variety of hand and electric shears are also available, some from rental outlets.

Getting the right adhesive

Contact adhesive for laminates comes in spray cans or as solvent- or water-base liquids applied with a brush. Use natural bristles for solvent-based products. Synthetic bristles are fine for water-base brands. Plan on throwing the brushes away.

You may find water-base adhesives easier to apply, and they change color as they cure, a feature which lets you know when the pieces are ready to install.

If you choose a spray-on product, practice spraying on scrap until you are able to apply it evenly. Once you start spraying the adhesive, don't stop until the surface is covered completely. Setting the spray can down in the middle of the job can cause the spray head to clog.

3 Spray or brush contact adhesive on both the edge of the base and the back of the laminate edge strip. Let the adhesive set up. Tack one end of the strip and, coiling it in one hand, work your way down to the other end. Keep an even amount of overhang on top and bottom.

4 Use a laminate trimmer or a router with a flush-cutting bit to trim the laminate even with the top and bottom of the plywood base. To save time you can trim one piece while the adhesive on another edge is setting up, working your way around the top until all edges are trimmed.

5 Lay the top sheet upside down on the countertop or other work surface. Spray or brush on the adhesive. Make sure to cover 100 percent of the surface (even if the manufacturer recommends only 80 percent). Remove the sheet and set it aside to dry. Apply adhesive to the plywood base.

6 Lay venetian blind strips or dowels on the base and carefully set the laminate on them so the laminate will not touch the base until you are ready. Start at one end and pull out the spacers, pressing down on the sheet as you go. Roll the surface with a 3-inch rubber roller and trim the overhangs.

7 When the adhesive has cured, file the outside corners of the trimmed edges, holding a fine file almost flat. File with a forward motion only. Then file the top edges, filing forward and down. Use light pressure.

8 Go under the countertop and drill a starter hole at the corner of the sink outline. Working from above, trim the laminate to the opening using a router with a flush-cutting bit.

INSTALLING A BATH VENT FAN

Many bathroom fans do little more than make noise, either because they are too weak or because their ductwork does not permit free movement of air. Usually venting is the culprit. Plan for a vent duct that is as short as possible and that makes as few turns as possible.

In addition to a vent fan, a bathroom unit may have a light, night-light, or heater unit. Because a heater uses much more power than a light and fan, it may need to be on its own circuit.

A fan-only unit or a light and fan that come on at the same time require only two-cable wiring. The more features you want to control separately, the more complicated the wiring becomes. To replace an existing fan, check the wiring; you may need to replace two-wire cable with three-wire cable or even two cables.

PRESTART CHECKLIST

☐ **TIME**
About seven hours to install ducting, a fan, and a switch

☐ **TOOLS**
Voltage tester, drill, drywall saw, jigsaw, hammer, nonconductive ladder, fish tape, screwdriver, wire stripper, long-nose pliers, lineman's pliers

☐ **SKILLS**
Cutting through siding, stripping, splicing, and connecting wires; installing boxes, running cable

☐ **PREP**
Find the shortest path for the ductwork; find power source and make sure the new lights will not overload the circuit

☐ **MATERIALS**
Vent fan, switch, ductwork, duct tape, sheet metal screws, cable, clamps, switch box, wire nuts, electrician's tape

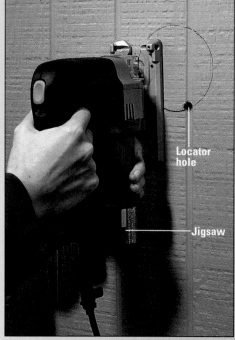

1 Follow the manufacturer's instructions carefully to locate and mark the position of the fan housing between the joists.

2 For the wall vent, drill a locator hole from the inside through the outside wall. Outside, cut a hole for the duct.

WALL AND SOFFIT VENTING OPTIONS

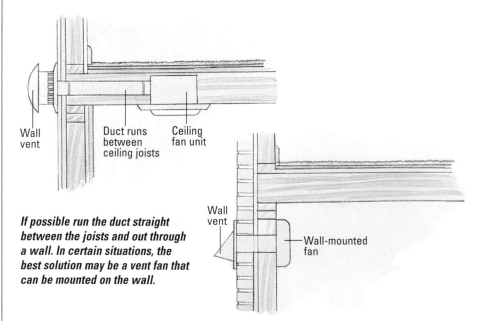

Wall vent

Duct runs between ceiling joists

Ceiling fan unit

Wall vent

Wall-mounted fan

If possible run the duct straight between the joists and out through a wall. In certain situations, the best solution may be a vent fan that can be mounted on the wall.

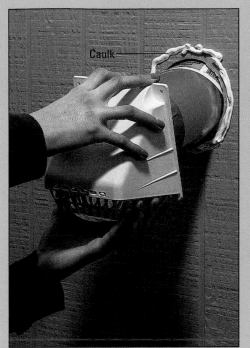

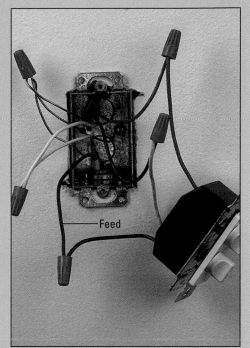

3 Run a bead of caulk around the exterior hole. Slide the vent through the hole and fasten the wall cap to the wall with screws. Fit the remaining sections of ductwork between the outside vent and the fan housing if you have not already done so.

4 If necessary run the correct cable or cables to the switch box. As shown above, power enters the switch box. If power enters the fan, consult the manufacturer's instructions.

5 To wire a fan/light switch, connect the grounds and splice the white wires. Connect the red and black wires from the fan to the fan and light terminals. Connect the feed wire to the remaining terminal.

STANLEY PRO TIP

Make ducts short, wide, and smooth

The shorter, smoother, and wider the ductwork, the more freely air can move through it. Most ductwork for bathroom fans is 4 inches in diameter; don't use anything smaller. Solid ducting is the smoothest and most efficient, but it may be difficult to install in tight places. All-metal flexible duct is bendable and fairly smooth. Plastic-and-wire ducting is the easiest to install but is the least efficient.

At every joint use sheet metal screws or clamps to make tight connections; then cover the joint completely with professional-quality duct tape.

WIRING A MULTIPURPOSE UNIT

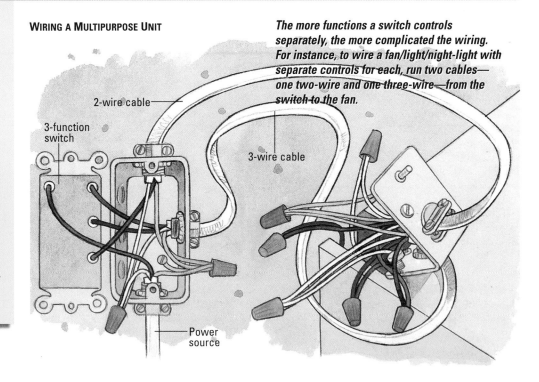

The more functions a switch controls separately, the more complicated the wiring. For instance, to wire a fan/light/night-light with separate controls for each, run two cables—one two-wire and one three-wire—from the switch to the fan.

INSTALLING A KITCHEN & LAUNDRY ROOM

Rough plumbing for a typical kitchen and laundry room is simpler than for a bathroom. Assuming there will be one sink and one dishwasher in your kitchen, you'll need only one drain line and one pair of supply pipes. All other connections—the drain and supply for the dishwasher, a supply line for an icemaker, and even a hot-water dispenser or a water filter—are made with flexible rubber or copper tubing that does not run through walls. For a laundry room, you'll only need to extend the hot- and cold-water supply lines and install one drain line for the washer, and perhaps new wiring for the dryer.

Wiring in a kitchen or laundry room can be complex. You will need receptacles for appliances and convenience outlets as well as circuits for ambient and room lighting. Receptacles should be protected by GFCIs for safety. You may also need 220-volt wiring for a range, oven, or dryer.

The master plan

Remodeling a kitchen involves most aspects of construction and involves many different operations. As with all building projects, you'll save yourself a lot of frustration by establishing a sensible work schedule. Usually, the most efficient order of work is organized along these lines:

■ Install the rough plumbing—the drain, vent, and supply lines.
■ Install electrical wiring and boxes and cut a hole for an exhaust fan, if included.
■ Apply new drywall and patch any damaged walls. Prime and paint.
■ Install the flooring, then cover it with a protective drop cloth.
■ Install the wall and base cabinets, as well as the countertops.
■ Do the finish electrical work— lights, receptacles, and switches.
■ Install the sink, faucet, garbage disposer, dishwasher, and any other plumbing appliances.

Remodeling or adding a kitchen calls for skills in carpentry, plumbing, and wiring.

CHAPTER PREVIEW

Installing supply and drain lines
page 192

Preparing the cabinets
page 194

Hooking up the sink
page 196

Setting up a laundry room
page 198

You can plan to tile a countertop and backsplash together as a single project or as separate projects. Because backsplashes are hard to reach, the work goes slowly; work in small sections to avoid the grout setting up before you're finished.

INSTALLING SUPPLY AND DRAIN LINES

In a typical kitchen, hot and cold supply lines run through the walls and emerge from the wall in the cabinet just below the sink, where they are connected to stop valves. If you have more than one base cabinet, run the supply piping inside walls rather than through cabinets to keep them safe from harm.

Because kitchens require only a 2-inch drain/vent pipe, you usually won't need the extra-thick wet wall required for a bathroom. But if your pipes run through an exterior wall, insulate them. Half-inch rigid copper pipe is large enough for most kitchen installations. (See pages 82–91 for installation instructions.)

These pages show separate stop valves for the hot and cold faucet lines, the dishwasher, and an icemaker. If you want to add a water filter, hot-water dispenser, or other appliance, you may need additional stop valves. Saddle T valves, which simply tap into a pipe, are easy to install but are prone to clogging.

PRESTART CHECKLIST

☐ **TIME**
Several hours to run copper supply lines through a floor or wall

☐ **TOOLS**
Drill, level, combination square, propane torch, groove-joint pliers, C-clamps

☐ **SKILLS**
Cutting and joining copper pipe, running pipe through walls or floors

☐ **PREP**
Install the drain line and carefully plan the location of the supply lines; **shut off the water** before beginning work

☐ **MATERIALS**
Copper pipe and fittings, galvanized nipples, stop valves, flux, solder, nailing plates, shims

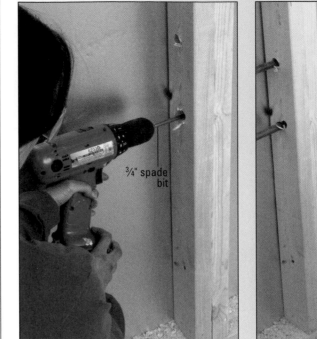

¾" spade bit

1 Where possible, run pipes through the centers of studs. Use a level or other long straightedge to mark for straight runs from stud to stud and use a combination square to mark the center of studs. Drill ¾-inch holes to accommodate ½-inch pipe.

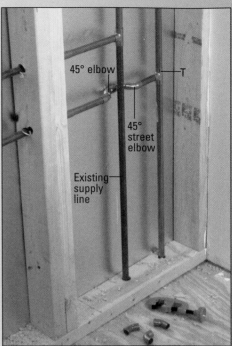

45° elbow — T
45° street elbow
Existing supply line

2 **Shut off water** and drain the lines you will tap into. Cut the existing pipes and install new T fittings (page 98). If you must run around a pipe or other obstruction, use 45-degree elbows and street elbows.

INSTALLING A KITCHEN DRAIN-WASTE-VENT SYSTEM

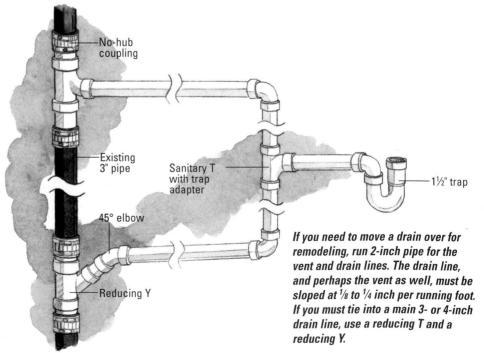

No-hub coupling

Existing 3" pipe

Sanitary T with trap adapter

1½" trap

45° elbow

Reducing Y

If you need to move a drain over for remodeling, run 2-inch pipe for the vent and drain lines. The drain line, and perhaps the vent as well, must be sloped at ⅛ to ¼ inch per running foot. If you must tie into a main 3- or 4-inch drain line, use a reducing T and a reducing Y.

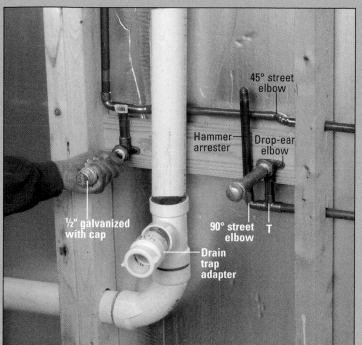

3 Usually, the most convenient location for stubouts is on each side of the drain trap adapter, as shown. However, feel free to place them wherever they will be within easy reach but within 18 inches of the faucet inlets. At each stubout, install a hammer arrester and a drop-ear elbow. Do a dry run (shown), then sweat the fittings and reattach the drop-ears to the braces. Add nipples with caps; turn on the water and check for leaks.

4 Install the wall covering, prime and paint the walls, and install the flooring. Install the kitchen base cabinets. Plumb and level them and attach them to each other (shown) and to the walls. If the sink base has a back, you'll need to drill holes for the stubouts.

STANLEY PRO TIP

Choosing the right stop valve

Make sure each stop valve is the right size and type for both the pipe and the supply tube. A kitchen stop valve should have a ½-inch outlet. If you will be joining to rigid copper pipe (rather than a galvanized nipple), buy a valve that sweats onto the pipe or one that joins with compression fittings.

Stop valves with compression fittings are easy to install.

ELECTRICAL CONNECTION FOR GARBAGE DISPOSER AND HOT-WATER DISPENSER

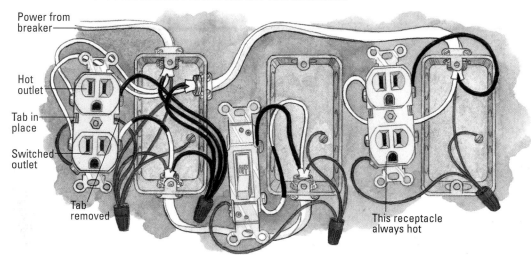

A garbage disposer should be plugged into a receptacle that is controlled by a switch. In the circuit illustrated above, a separate receptacle is always *hot, so you can plug in an appliance such as a hot-water dispenser. Shut off power before running wires and make sure that the new appliances will* *not overload the circuit. Consult with a professional electrician if you are not completely sure of doing the job yourself.*

PREPARING THE CABINETS

Once you have installed the drain and supply pipes and tested them for leaks, run any electrical lines for receptacles and lights. Cover the walls with drywall, and apply the finish coats of your choice. Install the finish flooring, then protect it with cardboard or heavy paper and a drop cloth.

Unpack the sink, garbage disposer, dishwasher, and any other appliances, and check the manufacturer's literature for the installation requirements. In particular, be sure about the dimensions of the opening for the dishwasher, as well as the size and location of the hole for its drain and supply lines.

A sink base cabinet has no drawers or shelves, so there will be room for all the appliances, tubes, and pipes that must fit inside it. Some sink bases are actual completed cabinets, while others consist of only the face and the floor.

PRESTART CHECKLIST

☐ **TIME**
A full day to install kitchen cabinets, plus several hours to run the electrical line for the dishwasher

☐ **TOOLS**
Hammer, drill, level, groove-joint pliers, adjustable wrench, hole saw, saber saw, measuring tape

☐ **SKILLS**
Measuring, drilling, and sawing accurately to install cabinets that are level and properly spaced

☐ **PREP**
Run and test all the rough plumbing

☐ **MATERIALS**
Cabinets, shims, screws, Ts, nipples, pipe-thread tape, stop valves, 14/2 armored cable

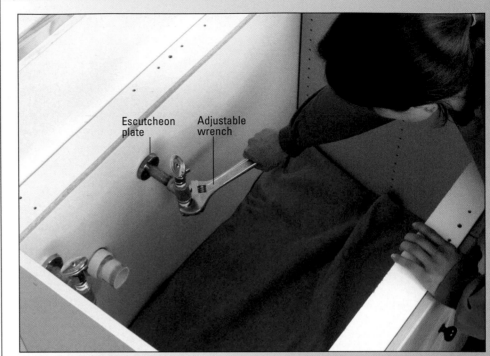

Escutcheon plate   Adjustable wrench

1 Remove the caps from the nipples on both the hot and cold water supplies and slide on the escutcheon plate to cover the hole at the wall. Wrap the nipple threads with pipe-thread tape, and install a T fitting. Wrap pipe-thread tape around the threads of two short nipples, and screw them into the T fitting. Screw stop valves onto the nipples. Turn the valve handles off and turn the water on to test for leaks.

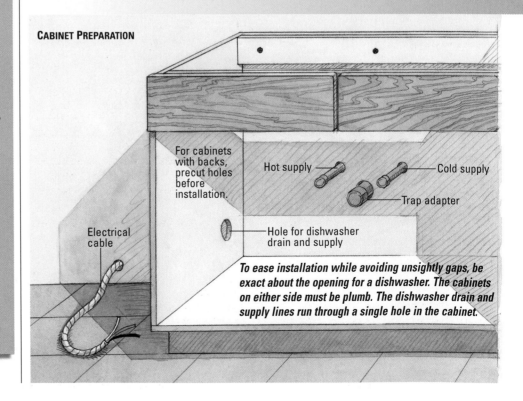

CABINET PREPARATION

For cabinets with backs, precut holes before installation.

Hot supply

Cold supply

Trap adapter

Electrical cable

Hole for dishwasher drain and supply

To ease installation while avoiding unsightly gaps, be exact about the opening for a dishwasher. The cabinets on either side must be plumb. The dishwasher drain and supply lines run through a single hole in the cabinet.

2 The dishwasher opening should be 24¼ inches wide for most models; check manufacturer's instructions. If installing a cabinet to the other side of the dishwasher (shown above), level from the sink base cabinet, plumb, and fasten it in place.

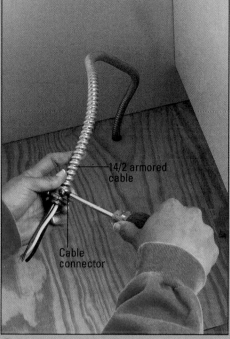

14/2 armored cable

Cable connector

3 Run an electrical line for the dishwasher. Usually a 14/2 armored cable connected to a 15-amp circuit is sufficient, but check codes and the manufacturer's literature. Be certain that the dishwasher will not overload the circuit. **Hire an electrician if you are not sure of your wiring abilities.**

1½" hole saw

4 The dishwasher instructions will tell you the best place to drill a hole for running the drain and supply lines. Usually a single 1½-inch hole is sufficient.

STANLEY PRO TIP

Cutting a countertop for a sink

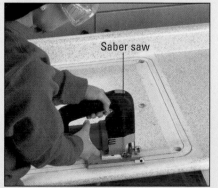

Saber saw

To cut a laminate countertop for a sink, place the new sink upside down on top of the countertop, centered over the base cabinet. Trace around the sink, then draw another line ¾ inch inside the first line. Cut along the second line using a saber saw equipped with a fine-cutting blade.

Choosing a sink

When it comes to sinks, price and quality are often closely related. An inexpensive stainless-steel sink flexes when you push on it, scratches easily, and is difficult to keep clean. A higher-quality heavy-gauge (6- or 8-gauge) stainless-steel sink, such as one with a burnished finish, is a better choice. When choosing a stainless-steel sink, make sure the underside is well coated with sound-deadening insulation.

An enameled cast-iron sink comes in a variety of colors. It lasts much longer than an enameled steel sink. Acrylic sinks (like the one shown) have the look of enameled cast iron, and the higher-end models are nearly as durable. Both cast-iron and acrylic sinks have insulating properties so that water stays warm in them longer than it does in a stainless-steel sink.

Stainless steel

Heavy-gauge stainless steel

Cast iron

Acrylic

HOOKING UP THE SINK

Once you have cut the hole in the countertop (page 184), set in the sink to make sure it will fit.

It is possible to install the sink first and then attach the faucet, garbage disposer, and drain from below. However, you'll save yourself hassle and time if you connect most of the components to the sink before installing it. Spread a drop cloth on the countertop nearby and set the sink upside down on the cloth. The faucet holes should overhang the counter so you can install the faucet. Even better is to set the sink on two sawhorses, padded with rags or towels.

Enameled-steel (shown) and stainless-steel sinks clamp to the countertop with special clips that are usually included with the sink. Test to make sure that the clips will work on your countertop before you install the plumbing. A cast-iron sink is heavy enough that it needs no clips.

PRESTART CHECKLIST

☐ **TIME**
About half a day to install a sink with disposer and dishwasher connections

☐ **TOOLS**
Drill, screwdriver, groove-joint pliers, adjustable wrench, strainer wrench or spud wrench, hacksaw

☐ **SKILLS**
Connecting a trap, installing a faucet and garbage disposer

☐ **PREP**
Install the rough plumbing, a switched receptacle, and the cabinets

☐ **MATERIALS**
Sink, faucet, garbage disposer, appliance extension cord, wire nuts, trap assembly, supply tubes, flexible copper line for dishwasher and icemaker supplies, drain hose (usually included with the dishwasher), air gap, plumber's putty, drop cloth

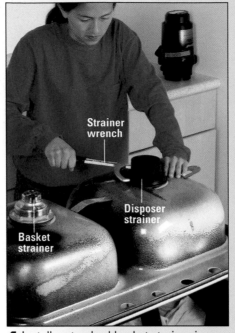

1 Install a standard basket strainer in one sink hole, and the garbage disposer strainer in the other hole. Make sure you know which strainer goes to which hole. Place a rope of putty under the lip of the strainer body and hold it in place as you slip on the washers and tighten the nut.

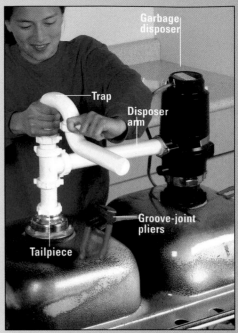

2 Following the manufacturer's instructions, install the garbage disposer, including the appliance extension cord. Install the tailpiece, disposer arm, and trap. Set the sink in the hole to see whether the trap lines up with the trap adapter in the wall; you may need to trim a piece or add an extension.

SINK ASSEMBLY

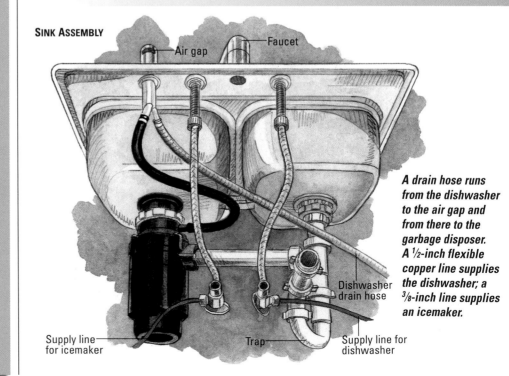

A drain hose runs from the dishwasher to the air gap and from there to the garbage disposer. A ½-inch flexible copper line supplies the dishwasher; a ⅜-inch line supplies an icemaker.

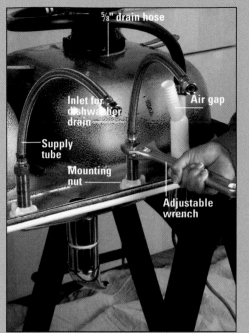

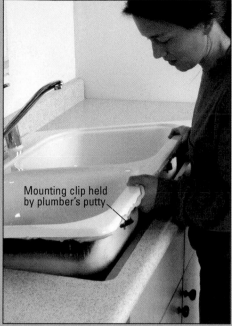

3 Attach the air gap and ⅝-inch hose to the disposer. Then install the faucet with its plastic or rubber gasket. Screw flexible supply tubes onto the faucet inlets. If the faucet has flexible copper inlets, use two adjustable wrenches to avoid kinking the inlets.

4 Hook up as much plumbing as possible in the cabinet—for example, supply lines for the dishwasher and icemaker. Position some of the mounting clips in the channels and hold them upright, using dabs of putty. With a rope of plumber's putty on the lip, carefully lower the sink into the hole.

5 Attach the trap to the trap adapter in the wall. Tighten all the connections with groove-joint pliers. To test, fill each bowl with water, then remove the stopper and watch for drips. Run the disposer with the water on and check for drips.

ALTERNATE TRAP CONFIGURATIONS

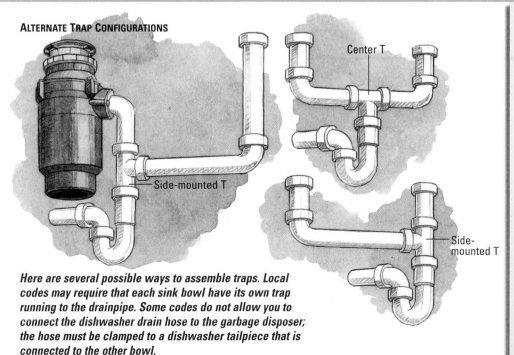

Here are several possible ways to assemble traps. Local codes may require that each sink bowl have its own trap running to the drainpipe. Some codes do not allow you to connect the dishwasher drain hose to the garbage disposer; the hose must be clamped to a dishwasher tailpiece that is connected to the other bowl.

Assembling a trap

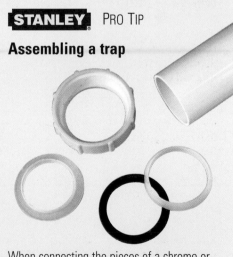

When connecting the pieces of a chrome or PVC trap, don't forget the slip nut and washer for each joint. Where a tailpiece attaches to a strainer, a special type of washer may be used. You'll probably need to cut at least one pipe; use a hacksaw or a fine-toothed saw (for PVC only) and a miter box.

SETTING UP A LAUNDRY ROOM

A washing machine needs hot and cold water and a place for the water to drain. Hot and cold water must be brought to within a couple of feet of a washing machine. Install washing machine valves, which look like outdoor hose bibs but point straight down.

The washer drain hose hooks to a sink or a standpipe. The drain for either of these must slope downward at a rate of ¼ inch per running foot.

Many washing machines are self-leveling. Grab the machine by its control panel at the top rear, pull forward to slightly tilt the machine, and let it drop back solidly on all four feet. Adjust the front legs to make sure the machine is level in both directions.

PRESTART CHECKLIST

☐ **TIME**
About half a day

☐ **TOOLS**
Screwdriver, groove-joint pliers, propane torch, hacksaw, tubing cutter

☐ **SKILLS**
Working with copper and PVC pipe

☐ **PREP**
Locate the nearest supply and drain lines

☐ **MATERIALS**
Utility sink, washing machine with drain hose, solder, flux, PVC primer and glue, 1½-inch trap, pipes and fittings, masonry screws

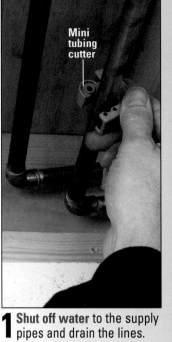

1 **Shut off water** to the supply pipes and drain the lines. To tap into a copper supply pipe, cut the pipe with a tubing cutter where you plan to install a T fitting.

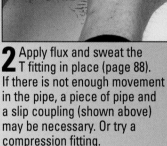

2 Apply flux and sweat the T fitting in place (page 88). If there is not enough movement in the pipe, a piece of pipe and a slip coupling (shown above) may be necessary. Or try a compression fitting.

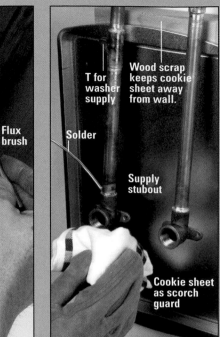

3 Add lengths of pipe to reach the utility sink, including Ts to run pipes to the washer. At the end of each supply pipe, sweat on a brass supply stubout. Anchor the stubouts to the wall with masonry screws.

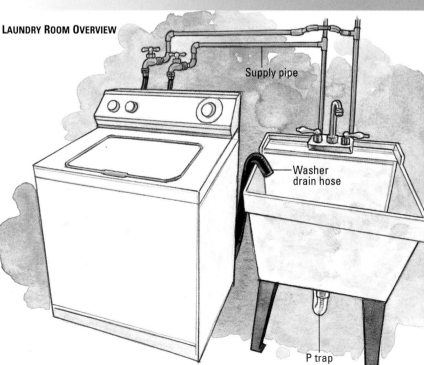

LAUNDRY ROOM OVERVIEW

Supply pipes branch off to provide both the utility sink and the washing machine with hot and cold water. The machine's drain hose clips to the side of the utility sink, which has a P trap that connects to a house drain line.

Elbow

Hose bib

Supply stubout

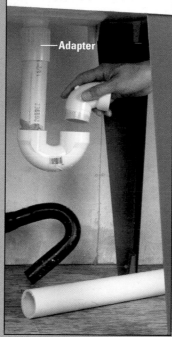

Adapter

Washing machine supply line

Washing machine drain hose

4 Run copper lines to the washer. Add supply stubouts and anchor them to the wall with masonry screws. Apply pipe-thread tape and hand-twist each hose bib into its stubout; then tighten it with a wrench.

5 Install stop valves (page 193) on the sink stubouts. A plastic utility sink is inexpensive and easy to assemble. Install a faucet onto the sink and connect supply tubes to the stop valves.

6 To work with PVC drainpipe, see pages 90–91. Tap into a drain line with a T fitting, and run a drainpipe (sloped at ¼ inch per running foot) to the sink. Glue an adapter to the pipe end and attach the trap.

7 Set the washing machine in place and level it. Screw the machine's supply lines to the valves and tighten with pliers. Drape the drain hose over the side of the utility sink and clamp it firmly in place.

WHAT IF…
You extend steel pipe?

To tap into galvanized steel lines, cut and remove a section of pipe. Replace the section with a combination of lengths of threaded pipe, nipples, a T fitting, and a union to suit your situation. Extend the supply line from the T and attach a stop valve.

T

Nipple

Union

Making a direct drain connection

Where there is no room for a utility sink, install a standpipe for the drain. The pipe must be large enough to insert the washing machine's drain hose into it, and it must rise above the top of the machine's water level.

Washing machine supply box

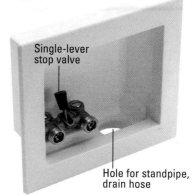

Single-lever stop valve

Hole for standpipe, drain hose

A washing machine supply box, which attaches to the sides of a stud, is recessed into the wall for a neater look. Many styles are outfitted with a single valve that controls both hot and cold water and provide an outlet for a drain hose.

CABINETS & STORAGE

Creating ample storage space can often present itself as a problem with a major contradiction. On the one hand, more storage is almost always a useful addition to a room. On the other, storage units can gobble up needed open space. The answer—construct built-in storage benches, shelves, and cabinets. They'll increase your storage space without getting in the way and will add an attractive design element to boot.

The projects in this chapter lend themselves to custom touches so you can make them an integral part of your new basement design. Optional trim styles, the right color paint, or matching wood species are all details that will blend in your built-in with the overall character of the room.

You'll find that building custom storage units is a straightforward venture. Most require skills only a few grades above the basics. In all cases, careful measuring and attention to detail will ensure a pleasing final result. Above all, the key to an enjoyable construction experience is to take every project one step at a time.

Don't overlook the possibility of combining one storage unit with another to meet both your storage and design needs. For example, combine a built-in window seat with bookcases to make a cozy, stylish retreat in a family room.

These projects offer a lot of flexibility in where you put them. Recessed shelves are ideal for a den, living room, or dining room. But you also could build them into a hallway or any other wall to create an attractive and unusual accent. The contemporary cubic storage units on page 206 can be conceived as a stand-alone design or will put that unused space under the basement stairs to use in style.

You can alter and combine individual parts of projects too. To make a medicine cabinet or a laundry room utility cabinet, you could build recessed shelves with doors that fit the style of the room.

Think of each project plan as simply a starting point for your own custom design. Choose any wood and finish you like, alter the size to meet different needs, change the style of trim, add or remove shelves, and make any other changes that will adapt the unit to your needs and the characteristics of your remodeled space.

Built-ins increase your storage space and enhance the looks of your new basement rooms.

CHAPTER PREVIEW

Built-in window seat
page 202

Contemporary cubes
page 206

Corner linen cabinet
page 212

With a few basic shop tools and some moderate carpentry skills (plus some patience and time), there's no end to the storage wizardry you can create for your remodeled basement space.

Recessed built-in shelves
page 218

BUILT-IN WINDOW SEAT

This handsome window seat doubles as a built-in storage bench. It's a place to enjoy the sun or a great view. You can easily customize the seat to fit under any location just by adjusting the lengths of the top, side, front, and back pieces.

Because it's a built-in unit, the chest doesn't need a bottom. You can add a bottom to make the bench a freestanding chest that's ideal as a blanket chest for the foot of a bed or even as a child's toy chest. Install rollers on the bottom to make the chest easy to move when cleaning or when the room needs a design makeover.

Although the lid is supported with a sturdy piano hinge, you may want to consider adding lid supports to your design (page 205). Lid supports are spring-loaded mechanisms that hold the lid open, then make it close gently so it won't slam down on your head or fingers. If children are around, it's important to install a lid support on a low bench like this one.

Customizing to fit your décor. The chest shown here is painted to match the room. The box itself is made of birch plywood that's painted the main wall color. The trim is made of ¼-inch pine that's painted to match the room trim. The chest would also look very elegant made of oak plywood and solid oak trim with a clear finish.

PRESTART CHECKLIST

☐ **TIME**
About four hours to build plus two hours to finish

☐ **TOOLS**
Tape measure, clamps, electric drill/driver, screwdriver, hammer, nail set, tablesaw or circular saw with straightedge jig, router with piloted ⅜-inch rabbeting bit

☐ **SKILLS**
Sawing, gluing, clamping, routing

☐ **PREP**
Prepare a work area

MATERIALS NEEDED

Part	Finished size			Mat.	Qty.	Part	Finished size			Mat.	Qty.
	T	W	L				T	W	L		
A lid	¾"	19⅜"	50"	BP	1	H cross support	1¼"	1½"	46½"	pine	1
B hinge rail	¾"	2"	50"	BP	1	I front horizontal trim	¼"	1½"	48½"	pine	2
C sides	¾"	16"	19"	BP	2	J side horizontal trim	¼"	1½"	19"	pine	2
D front	¾"	16"	48"	BP	1	K side horizontal trim	¼"	1½"	16¼"	pine	2
E back	¾"	16"	48"	BP	1	L vertical trim	¼"	1½"	13"	pine	9
F upper supports	¾"	3½"	19"	BP	3	M angled trim	¼"	1½"	13¾"	pine	2
G lower supports	¾"	3½"	16⅞"	BP	3	N bottom*	½"	17¾"	46½"	BP	1
						O bottom cleats*	¾"	3½"	23⅝"	BP	4

Material key: BP—birch plywood
Hardware: 48-inch piano hinge, lid support, 1¼-inch coarse-thread drywall screws, ¾-inch brads
Supplies: Glue, wood putty, 120-grit sandpaper
*optional

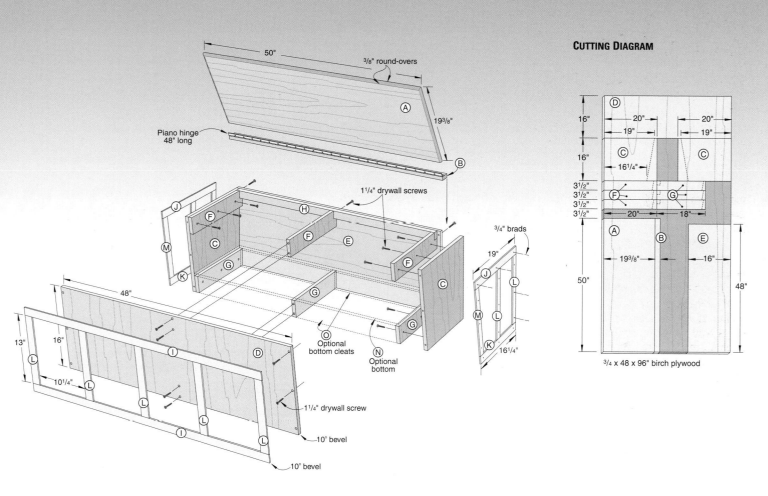

CUTTING DIAGRAM

3/4 x 48 x 96" birch plywood

TRIM LAYOUT

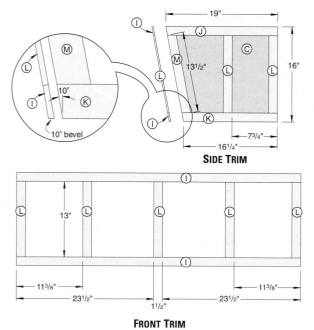

SIDE TRIM

FRONT TRIM

WHAT IF...
You want a clear finish?

If you want to give your bench a clear finish, start out with a piece of plywood 20⅝×48½ inches for the lid and hinge rail. Glue and clamp a ¾×¾-inch hardwood edge to both ends and one long side of the piece, using miter joints at the front corners. You can use 4d finishing nails instead of clamps, but be sure to center them top to bottom and set them deeply.

Rout the bullnose, then rip the hinge rail from the lid. Routing a bullnose on plywood also works fine if you intend to paint the lid. Just fill the voids in the edge of the plywood with wood putty before you paint.

A. Cutting the bench parts

1 Guide a circular saw with a straightedge jig to crosscut two 16-inch-wide pieces and one 50-inch-wide piece from a sheet of ¾-inch birch plywood as shown in the cutting diagram on page 203. Then cut two 20-inch-long pieces (C) from one of the 16-inch-wide pieces.

2 On each side piece (C), mark one edge at 19 inches and the other at 16¼ inches as shown on the cutting diagram. Draw a line between these points. Starting at the 16¼-inch mark, cut to these lines with the circular saw guided by the straightedge jig.

3 To make the lid (A) and hinge rail (B), use a tablesaw or a circular saw with straightedge jig to rip a 21½-inch-wide piece from the 50-inch-long section of plywood. Working counterclockwise, rout a bullnose on one long side and both ends of this piece.

B. Assembling the bench

U sing the exploded view on page 203, attach top and bottom supports to the sides, glue and screw the back and front to the sides, and cut and fasten the cross support (H). As you assemble the pieces, make sure everything is square and the edges flush.

C. Preparing the lid

1 Apply glue to the top of the cross support. Put the hinge rail in place and make sure it is flush with the front of the cross support and overhangs equally on both sides. Clamp the hinge rail to the cross support.

2 Set the lid in place flush with both ends of the hinge rail. Use a quarter to space the hinge rail and the lid, checking the space at the middle and both ends. Center the piano hinge over the space and predrill holes for the hinge screws.

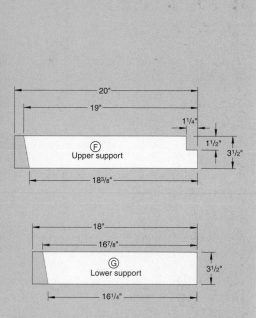

4 Set the tablesaw fence at 19⅜ inches. Rip the hinge rail from the lid by running the 21⅜-inch-wide piece through the saw with the long bullnose against the fence. Make sure the remaining piece is 2 inches wide for the hinge rail.

5 Rip 16 inches from the remaining 50-inch-long piece. Crosscut this piece to 48 inches to make the back (E). Rip-cut three 3½-inch-wide pieces from the remaining piece, then crosscut these into three 20-inch pieces and three 18-inch pieces for the supports (F and G).

6 Lay out the cuts for the upper and lower supports as shown in these diagrams. Clamp the stock to a workbench and make the angled cuts with a circular saw. Then cut the notches in the upper supports with a jigsaw or handsaw.

Upper support diagram: 20", 19", 1¼", 1½", 3½", 18⅜" — (F) Upper support

Lower support diagram: 18", 16⅞", 3½", 16¼" — (G) Lower support

D. Finishing Up

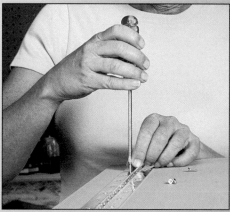

1 Cut trim pieces J and K and hold them in place to mark the angled cuts at the front. Then cut and install all the horizontal trim (I, J, and K). Mark the 11 vertical trim pieces (L, M) for a snug fit. Glue and nail them in place, spacing them as shown.

2 Fill and sand any exposed plywood edges. Prime and paint the bench and lid inside and out. When the paint dries, set the lid in place and fasten the piano hinge. Use a screwdriver (not an electric drill) to avoid stripping the small brass screws.

3 Install the lid support on either side of the upper support (F). Put the lid support in place on the upper support (F) and predrill holes for the screws. Attach the lid support, then predrill holes for the screws into the underside of the lid. Install the screws.

CONTEMPORARY CUBES

Modular construction makes it easy and efficient to customize your built-in cabinets and shelves. You just build a simple standard box, shelf, and door. On this design there's a simple base made of 2×4s below and plywood countertops above. These cubic storage units are easily adaptable for under-the-stairs installation.

Once you set up to build any of these components, the main variable is the time it'll take to build however many you want. The completed project shown here has 10 boxes, four open shelves, and four doors. Mix these components in whatever way suits your needs and your space. The materials list includes what you need to build one cabinet with a door and a shelf. The instructions explain how to adapt the unit to your needs.

PRESTART CHECKLIST

☐ TIME
About four hours for the first cabinet, door, and shelf. Add about one hour for each additional cabinet or door and 30 minutes for each additional shelf. Allow additional time for finishing.

☐ TOOLS
Tape measure, hammer, nail set, combination square, 4-foot level, tablesaw or circular saw with straightedge guide, electric drill with stop, ¼-inch bit, ⅜-inch bit, 1⅜-inch Forstner bit, #6 counterbore bit, drill press, jigsaw, straightedge or chalk line, clamps, studfinder

☐ SKILLS
Measuring, sawing, gluing

☐ PREP
Measure installation space, configure built-ins, prepare workspace

MATERIALS NEEDED

Part	Finished size			Mat.	Qty.	Part	Finished size			Mat.	Qty.
	T	W	L				T	W	L		
A top and bottom	¾"	15¾"	23½"	BP	2	G base rails	1½"	3½"	to fit*	CL	**
B sides	¾"	15¾"	28½"	BP	2	H base crosspieces	1½"	3½"	10"	CL	**
C back	¼"	23½"	30"	BP	1	I countertops	¾"	17½"	to fit*	BP	**
D door	¾"	23¼"	29¾"	BP	1	J toe-kick covers	¼"	3 ½"	to fit*	BP	**
E shelf	¾"	15⅝"	21⅞"	BP	1	K filler panels	¾"	to fit*	to fit*	BP	**
F back supports	¾"	3½"	23½"	pine	3						

*See instructions.
** as needed
Material key: BP—birch plywood, CL— construction lumber (Douglas fir or spruce)
Hardware: 1¼-inch, 1½-inch, 2½-inch, and 3½-inch drywall screws (all coarse thread), 1-inch brads, European-style self-closing concealed hinges, doorknobs or pulls
Supplies: Birch edge-banding veneer, glue, construction adhesive, 120-grit sandpaper, clear finish

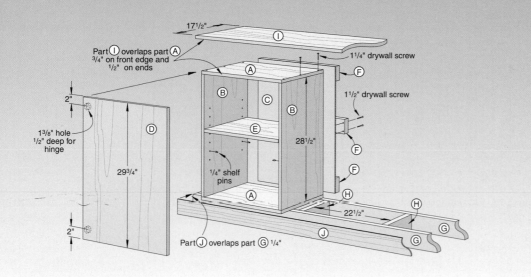

Part Ⓘ overlaps part Ⓐ
3/4" on front edge and
1/2" on ends

17 1/2"

1 1/4" drywall screw

1 1/2" drywall screw

2"

1 3/8" hole
1/2" deep for
hinge

29 3/4"

1/4" shelf
pins

28 1/2"

2"

22 1/2"

Part Ⓙ overlaps part Ⓖ 1/4"

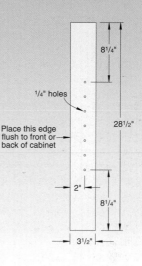

SHELF-PIN DRILLING TEMPLATE

8 1/4"

1/4" holes

28 1/2"

Place this edge
flush to front or
back of cabinet

2"

8 1/4"

3 1/2"

Materials and finishing

The units shown here are built with birch plywood, edged with veneer banding tape, and given a clear finish. Birch plywood also takes paint very well. You might also check the price of medium density overlay (MDO) plywood that has face veneers that are designed to be painted. Oak or cherry plywood with a clear finish is another option.

CONFIGURING YOUR BUILT-INS
Size up the location first

The cabinets shown here are installed between two walls. Of course, your cabinets can be flanked by one wall or by none. In any case, the length of the bottom run of cabinets will have to be divisible by 23½ inches—the width of each cabinet. With walls on both sides, you'll center the bottom run and install filler panels on each side. With one flanking wall, you might be able to butt the cabinets against the wall and install a piece of molding where the cabinet meets the wall. But if the wall is much out of plumb, you'll need a 2-inch-wide, custom-tapered filler panel.

The cabinets sit on a base made of 2×4s. For built-ins flanked by two walls, measure between the walls at the floor. Make the base to fit minus about ½ inch on each end. Make the toe-kick cover to fit exactly.

Each level of your built-in will have a countertop. Cut the countertops to length after you install the cabinets, adding an overhang of ½ inch on any side that doesn't abut a wall.

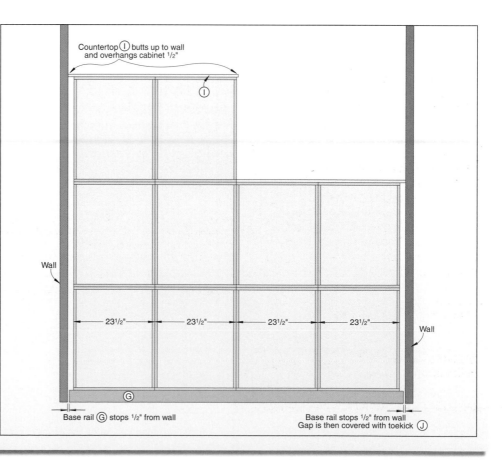

Countertop Ⓘ butts up to wall
and overhangs cabinet 1/2"

Wall

Wall

23 1/2"   23 1/2"   23 1/2"   23 1/2"

Base rail Ⓖ stops 1/2" from wall

Base rail stops 1/2" from wall
Gap is then covered with toekick Ⓙ

A. Cutting the cabinet parts

1 To rip stock for the top and bottom (A) and the sides (B) of the cabinet, set the tablesaw's fence to rip 15¾ inches wide. Have a helper hold up the unsupported end of the plywood while you rip 15¾ inches from a full sheet. Or use a circular saw with a straightedge guide.

2 Crosscut the 15¾-inch-wide piece into two pieces for the top and bottom (A) and two sides (B). If you will make a number of cabinets, you'll save time if you set up a stop block on the tablesaw.

3 Rip and crosscut ¾-inch plywood to make the door (D). Then rip and crosscut ¼-inch plywood to make the back (C). Crosscut 1×4 stock to make three back supports (F). You can crosscut to a layout line with a circular saw or tablesaw or use a stop block on the tablesaw.

STANLEY PRO TIP

Pay attention to grain direction

When planning how you will cut parts from a sheet of plywood, consider how the wood grain will be oriented in the finished piece. Generally, the grain should run in the same direction as solid boards—vertically for sides, backs, and doors; and from side to side on top and bottom pieces and shelves. This is especially important for the doors and the cabinet sides with visible outside surfaces. It won't be as noticeable if horizontal grain is inside the cabinets.

OPTIONS TO CONSIDER
Add a dramatic hardwood edge

If you'd like to add a strong horizontal visual element to your built-ins, consider covering the exposed countertop edges with ¾-inch-by-¾-inch edging made from a contrasting wood instead of matching veneer tape. The rich, dark brown of walnut or the deep red of cherry would both have a dramatic look. (Remember that cherry gets darker with age.) Attach the wood with glue and clamps or glue and 4d nails in predrilled holes. Make miter joints at the corners.

4 Make a template for drilling the shelf pins (page 207) and set a stop on a ¼-inch drill bit to ⅞ inch so you'll drill ⅝-inch-deep holes. Clamp the template on a side piece (B), flush with the front, and drill the holes. Then turn the template over, clamp it flush with the back of the side piece, and drill again.

B. Assembling the cabinets

1 Apply glue to the top edges of the side pieces. Put the top piece in place, make sure it is flush with the sides, then attach with 1¼-inch drywall screws. Attach the bottom piece the same way. Check the cabinet for square before the glue dries.

2 Apply glue to the back edges of the cabinet, then put the back in place. Check that the back is flush with the outside of the cabinet all around. Secure the back with 1-inch brads.

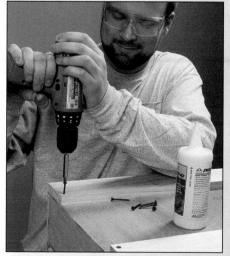

3 Attach the back support pieces (F) with glue and 1½-inch screws into the back edges of the sides. Center one crosspiece and attach the others flush with the top and bottom. If there is baseboard on the wall, raise the bottom crosspiece to clear it.

4 Use edge-banding veneer to cover the front edges of the cabinets and shelves. Cover all edges of the doors. Slightly round veneered edges with 120-grit sandpaper.

C. Installing hardware

1 To drill the holes for the self-closing hinges, use a drill press with a 1⅜-inch-diameter Forstner bit. Bore holes 2 inches from the top and bottom of the door, ½ inch deep and 3/32 inch from the door edge. Check manufacturer's instructions.

2 Place each hinge in its hole. With the flange parallel to the inside edge, mark and drill holes (usually 3/32-inch) for the hinge-plate fasteners.

D. Installing the cabinet

1 Cut 2×4s for the base rails (G) to length. Cut enough base crosspieces (H) to place them 24 inches on center. Lay out the crosspiece spacing on the rails and assemble the base with 2½-inch drywall screws or 10d nails.

2 Rip ¼-inch plywood to 3½ inches wide and cut it to the lengths you need to cover the front of the base and fit exactly between the walls. Attach these toe-kick covers (J) with 1-inch brads.

3 Set the base in position and level it front to back and side to side, shimming it if necessary. Set in the lowest row of cabinets, predrill countersinks, then attach the cabinets to each other with two 1¼-inch drywall screws. Attach each cabinet to the base with two screws.

4 Find the studs behind the first row with a stud finder. Drive 3½-inch drywall screws through the back of the cabinets into each stud. Drive the screws just under the cabinet tops where they will be inconspicuous.

E. Installing filler panels

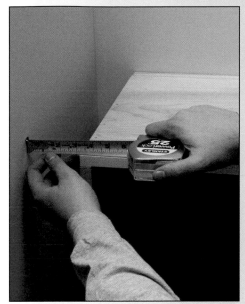

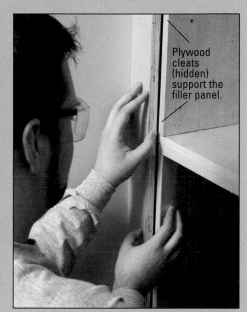

Plywood cleats (hidden) support the filler panel.

1 The walls on either side of the cabinets may not be perfectly plumb, so the filler panels (K) may need to be tapered to fit. To find out, measure the distance from the top of the cabinet to the wall and from the bottom of the cabinet to the wall.

2 Snap a line between the points you marked on the ends of the filler panel. Cut along the line with a circular saw.

3 Fasten plywood cleats to the front edge of the cubes and check the fit of your filler panels. Spread a bead of construction adhesive on the back of the panels and press them onto the cleats. Install the hinges and adjust them according to the manufacturer's instructions.

EUROPEAN-STYLE HINGES:
Make sure you get what you need

The streamlined look of doors that fully overlap the face of a cabinet built without face frames first became popular in Europe. European-style hinges were designed for this type of cabinet.

All European-style hinges close into a cup fitted into a hole on the inside of the door, so they are completely hidden when the door is closed. Usually, the hole is 1⅜ inches in diameter; European-made versions usually state this size as 35 millimeters. They are self-closing, so there's no need for a latch. They are all adjustable up and down and side to side after installation. More expensive ones can also be adjusted in and out.

Some European-style hinges have a separate piece that mounts inside the cabinet; others are one piece. Check the hinges before you buy them; some hinges sold as European style are designed to fit on the front or side of a face frame and won't work on frameless cabinets.

FORSTNER BIT
A special bit for flat-bottomed holes

Forstner bits are specially designed to drill larger holes with a very cleanly cut circumference and a flat bottom—just what you need to drill cup holes for European-style hinges. The bits have a short pointed spur in the center to allow you to exactly locate the center of the hole and to keep the bit on track as it starts cutting.

CONSTRUCTING A CORNER LINEN CABINET

Corner cupboards put unused space to work. This compact closet is designed to hold linens or towels. It's small enough to tuck into a hallway by the bathroom, the bathroom itself, or a corner of a bedroom. Don't be put off by those handsome doors; there's no fancy joinery involved in building them.

Materials and finishing

The face frame and doors of this cabinet are made of birch plywood and solid poplar that looks great when painted. You might choose to make these parts of oak and matching plywood or of another hardwood with a clear finish. The sides and shelves, which won't be visible with the doors closed, are made of lauan plywood, which doesn't take paint quite as smoothly as birch but still looks fine and is a bit less expensive.

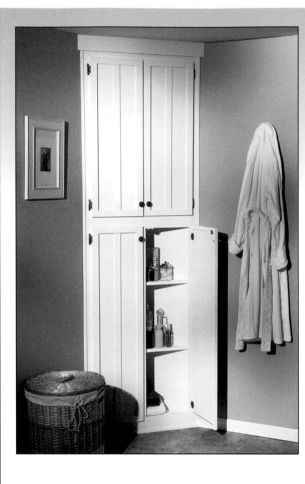

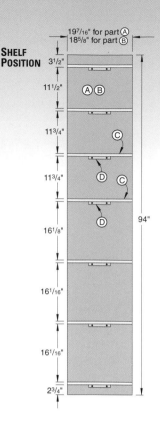

PRESTART CHECKLIST

☐ **TIME**
About 16 hours to construct, plus finishing time

☐ **TOOLS**
Hammer, nail set, combination square, bar clamps, tape measure, chisel, stepladder, tablesaw, circular saw with ripping guide, power drill/driver with #6 adjustable counterbore bit and 1/16-inch bit (for predrilling nail holes), router with 1/2-inch piloted rabbeting bit, doweling jig, pocket-hole jig, straightedge

☐ **SKILLS**
Accurate measuring, sawing, routing, drilling

☐ **PREP**
Assemble tools and materials, prepare a large work area, prepare installation site

MATERIALS NEEDED

Part	Finished size			Mat.	Qty.	Part	Finished size			Mat.	Qty.
	T	W	L				T	W	L		
CABINET						**UPPER DOORS**					
A side	3/4"	19 7/16"	94"	LP	1	J rails	3/4"	1 1/2"	12 3/4"	PL	4
B side	3/4"	18 5/8"	94"	LP	1	K stiles	3/4"	1 1/2"	34 1/2"	PL	4
C shelf blanks	3/4"	12 5/8"	25 3/8"	LP	7	L panels	1/4"	10 3/4"	35 1/2"	BP	2
D side cleats	3/4"	3/4"	6"	Pine	14	M center stile	1/4"	1 1/2"	34 1/2"	PL	2
FACE FRAME						**LOWER DOORS**					
E side stiles	3/4"	2 1/2"	87"	PL	2	N rails	3/4"	1 1/2"	12 3/4"	PL	4
F upper center stile	3/4"	1 1/2"	36 1/2"	PL	1	O stiles	3/4"	1 1/2"	45"	PL	4
G lower center stile	3/4"	1 1/2"	47"	PL	1	P panels	1/4"	10 3/4"	46"	BP	2
H rails	3/4"	3 1/2"	30"	PL	2	Q center stile	1/4"	1 1/2"	45"	PL	2
I center rail	3/4"	3 1/2"	25"	PL	1	**TRIM**					
						R top trim	1/4"	3 1/2"	31 1/2"	PL	1
						S shoe molding	3/4"	3/4"	31 1/2"	Pine	1

Material key: LP—lauan plywood, BP—birch plywood, PL—poplar
Hardware: Eight semiconcealed hinges, four magnetic catches, four handles or knobs, 1 1/4-inch coarse-thread drywall screws, 1 1/2-inch coarse-thread drywall screws, 4d finishing nails, 1 1/2-inch brads, pocket-hole screws
Supplies: Edge-banding veneer, glue, 80-grit sandpaper, paint, 1/4-inch dowels

CORNER LINEN CABINET

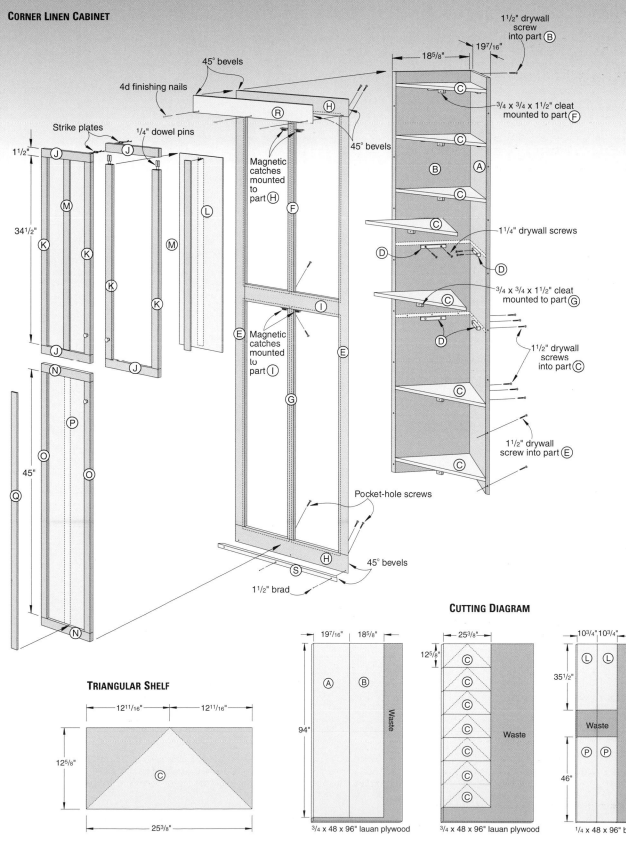

1½" drywall screw into part B

19⁷⁄₁₆"

18⁵⁄₈"

45° bevels

4d finishing nails

¾ x ¾ x 1½" cleat mounted to part F

Strike plates

¼" dowel pins

1½"

45° bevels

Magnetic catches mounted to part H

1¼" drywall screws

34½"

¾ x ¾ x 1½" cleat mounted to part G

Magnetic catches mounted to part I

1½" drywall screws into part C

45"

1½" drywall screw into part E

Pocket-hole screws

45° bevels

1½" brad

CUTTING DIAGRAM

TRIANGULAR SHELF

12¹¹⁄₁₆" — 12¹¹⁄₁₆"

19⁷⁄₁₆" — 18⁵⁄₈"

25³⁄₈"

10³⁄₄" 10³⁄₄"

12⁵⁄₈"

12⁵⁄₈"

35½"

94"

Waste

Waste

Waste

46"

Waste

C

A   B

25³⁄₈"

¾ x 48 x 96" lauan plywood

¾ x 48 x 96" lauan plywood

¼ x 48 x 96" birch plywood

A. Make the cabinet

1 Set the rip guide on the circular saw to cut 2 inches wide, including the kerf—the wood cut away by the blade. Cut off one end of a sheet of ¾-inch lauan plywood, leaving a 94-inch sheet for the sides (A and B).

2 Set your tablesaw fence to 19⁷⁄₁₆ inches and tilt the blade 45 degrees. With someone to help support the plywood, rip the sheet to make side A. You could make the cut with a circular saw set to 45 degrees and guided by a straightedge.

3 Set the blade to 90 degrees and set the fence to 18⅝ inches. Put the beveled side of the remaining piece against the fence with the bevel's point on top, then rip side B. With a circular saw and straightedge, it's better to leave the factory edge square and recut the beveled side.

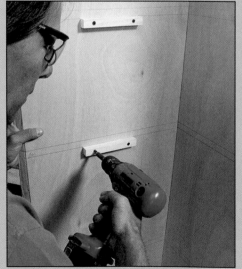

7 Reset your miter gauge to the 45-degree mark on the right side of 90 degrees. Put the gauge in the slot to the left of the blade and make the second cut to complete the shelf triangles.

8 Cover the front edges of the shelves with self-stick edge-banding veneer. Lay out the shelves on the sides. Extend the lines around the outside of the cabinet to help locate screws later when you install the shelves.

9 Rip and crosscut side cleats (D) to the dimensions listed. Predrill and countersink two holes in each cleat. With glue and 1¼-inch drywall screws, attach a side cleat under each shelf location, 6 inches from the back of the cabinet.

4 Have a helper hold side B upright while you stand on a stepladder to apply glue to the long square edge. Put side A in place and make sure its edge is flush with the back of B as you join the pieces with 1½-inch drywall screws spaced about 12 inches apart.

5 Check the inside dimensions of the cabinet. Plywood thickness can vary, so you might have to modify the triangular shelf dimensions shown on page 213. Rip a sheet of ¾-inch lauan plywood to 25⅜ inches for the shelf blanks (C). Then set the fence to 12⅝ inches to rip the blanks to width.

6 Lay out the triangular shelves on the blanks as shown on page 213. Set the miter gauge on your tablesaw to the 45-degree mark to the left of 90 degrees. Put the gauge in the slot to the right of the blade and make one cut on each blank.

10 Apply glue to the top of a pair of cleats and install a shelf. Drive three 1½-inch drywall screws through each cabinet side into the shelf. Install the remaining shelves the same way.

STANLEY PRO TIP: **Label parts with sticky notes**

You should always label parts as you cut them. You can mark the parts in pencil, but the marks can be hard to find and you'll have to sand them off for finishing. Use sticky notes instead to label the parts. They come off easily and don't leave adhesive residue on the wood.

B. Assemble the face frame

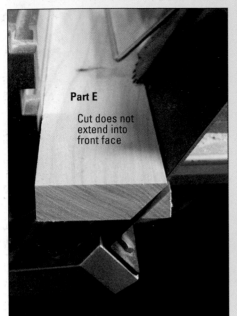

Part E

Cut does not extend into front face

1 Rip and crosscut poplar to make the face frame parts E through I. Set the tablesaw blade to 45 degrees and bevel one back edge of each side stile (E) and the ends of the rails (H). Be careful not to reduce the front face dimensions of the pieces.

2 Use glue and pocket-hole joinery to join the parts. Use two pocket-hole screws for each joint to attach the rails (H and I) to stiles and one screw at each joint to attach the center stiles (F and G) to rails.

3 Lay the frame face down. Apply glue to the edges of the cabinet sides, top, bottom, and middle shelf. With someone to help, place the cabinet on the face frame. Make sure the stiles extend equally past both cabinet sides. Drive 1¼-inch screws every 12 inches straight into countersunk holes through the back and into the stiles.

4 Turn the cabinet on one side. Add a pocket-hole screw through the bottom of each shelf into the center stile. Drive screws into the middle of the rail for the top, bottom, and middle shelf.

C. Install the doors

1 Rip and crosscut poplar to make the door rails and stiles (J, K, M, N, O, and Q). Use glue and two ¼-inch-diameter dowels at each joint to join the stiles to the rails. Clamp the joints with bar clamps.

4 When the glue has cured, mark each rail at the center of the door panel. Mark center points on the ends of the ¼-inch-thick center stiles (M and Q). Align the marks and glue the stiles to the panels.

D. Finish and install

2 Put a ½-inch piloted rabbeting bit in the router and set the depth to ¼ inch. Rout clockwise around the inside of all the rails and stiles. Square the rounded corners of the rabbets with a chisel.

3 Rip and crosscut ¼-inch birch plywood to make four door panels (L and P). Apply glue in the rabbets and press the panels in place. Turn the doors over and wipe off any glue squeeze-out.

1 Measure across the top of the cabinet and cut 45-degree angles on the top trim to fit. Remember, your measurement is for the back of the miters—the front will be 1½ inches longer. Cut the shoe molding to fit the same way.

5 To locate the hinges on the doors, lay out lines across the back of each left stile 2 inches from each end. Position semiconcealed hinges on the lines and screw them to the backs of the doors.

6 The doors will overlap the face frame by ½ inch on all sides. To locate the doors, set a combination square to ½ inch and draw guidelines around the opening, ½ inch from it. Have someone help align the door on the lines while you predrill hinge holes in the stiles.

2 Put the trim piece against the ceiling. Predrill holes and attach the trim piece to the face frame with 4d finishing nails. Attach the shoe molding with 1½-inch brads. Replace the doors and touch up the paint.

RECESSED BUILT-IN SHELVES

This handsome shelf unit is designed to be recessed into the wall between two studs. It works great as display space in the living room or dining room or as handy extra shelving in a bathroom.

Materials and finishing

It's easy to adapt this versatile design to fit your space and home style. This unit is made of clear-finished solid oak with a lauan plywood back. The peaked top rail has a triangular cutout flanked by small diamond cutouts. You might instead want to match the window and door trim in the room—casing the unit just as you would a window. You can make the unit from any hardwood you like, or use pine with a painted or clear finish.

MATERIALS NEEDED

Part		Finished size			Mat.	Qty.
		T	W	L		
A	sides	¾"	3"	32"	Oak	2
B	supports	¾"	3"	14½"	Oak	2
C	back	¼"	14½"	33½"	LP	1
D	shelves	¾"	3"	13"	Oak	3
E	side trim	¾"	3½"	32¼"	Oak	2
F	top trim	¾"	5½"	20¼"	Oak	1
G	bottom trim	¾"	3½"	20¼"	Oak	1

Material key: LP—lauan plywood
Hardware: 1½-inch coarse-thread drywall screws, 4d finishing nails, 1-inch brads, pocket-hole screws or #20 joinery biscuits
Supplies: Glue; 80-, 150- and 220-grit sandpaper; wood filler, polyurethane clear finish

PRESTART CHECKLIST

☐ **TIME**
About four hours

☐ **TOOLS**
Tape measure, combination square, hammer, nail set, drywall saw, 4-foot level, pocket-hole jig or biscuit joiner, tablesaw or circular saw with straightedge guide, drill/driver with #6 counterbore bit and ¹⁄₁₆-inch-diameter bit, jigsaw, drywall saw

☐ **SKILLS**
Accurate measuring, sawing, joining

☐ **PREP**
Wall surface should be painted; apply finish to all components of the cabinet

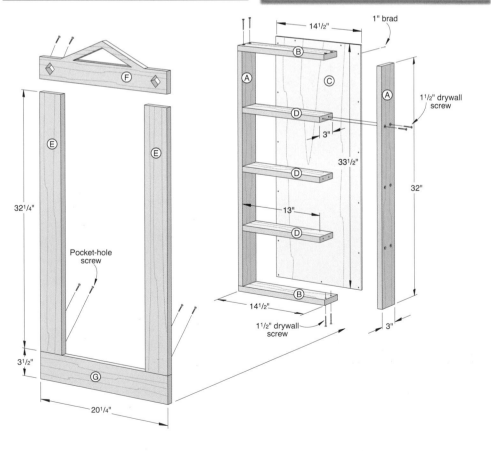

Assembling the cabinet

1 Attach the back with 1-inch brads and glue, making sure it is flush to all edges. Predrill with a ¹⁄₁₆-inch bit if you have trouble driving the brads.

2 Transfer the shelf layout lines around to the outside and back of the unit. Put the shelf in place and predrill two countersunk holes into each side. Apply glue to the back and ends of a shelf. Secure the shelf with 1½-inch drywall screws and three brads through the back. Install the other shelves.

3 Sand the trim faces and slightly round all edges. Apply finish. Predrill the sides for 4d finishing nails, position the shelf unit in the wall, then drive and set the nails. Align the trim frame and secure it with 4d nails in predrilled holes into the studs and front edges of the unit.

Constructing a cabinet frame between studs

1 A standard medicine cabinet fits between existing studs. Lay out the opening on the wall. Drill holes at the corners to help start the cuts. Saw along the lines with a drywall saw.

2 Using 2-inch drywall screws, fasten 6-inch 2×4 blocks to the studs to provide support for a header and sill. Use four screws per block and position the blocks 1½ inches from the top and bottom of the opening.

3 Attach the header and sill at each end with one toenailed fastener into the stud and one driven into the support block. Install the cabinet with 1¾-inch woodscrews.

LIGHTS & HEATERS

Lighting contributes dramatically to the beauty and comfort of your remodeled basement space. In fact, lighting is so important to the appearance and safety of room designs that you should make a separate lighting plan for your remodeled basement, showing the location and type of all the fixtures. Shop several stores before you make your final decisions. Lighting options are almost endless.

In addition, if you're building a new basement bathroom, you should include a vent fan. (Your local building codes may require one.) Fans not only make the bathroom more comfortable, they remove moisture from the air that can otherwise condense on basement surfaces and cause damage.

Fans require only basic wiring; it's the installation of the fan itself and ductwork that requires the most time.

Lighting hardware
Mounting hardware has changed little over the years, and new fixtures usually come with all the parts you need. Simply attach a strap to the ceiling box, and perhaps a center stud as well. Splice the wires, screw the fixture to the strap or the stud, and you are done. Dress up the whole installation by installing a medallion between the ceiling and the canopy (the part that fits against the ceiling).

Wiring a light or fan
Installing most new fixtures starts right after you've framed new walls. Install the fan housing between the open joists, following the manufacturer's instructions for placement of the electrical box. Turn the power off and run cable to the box. Leave the power to this circuit off until you're ready to install the fixture. If, however, you need the power to operate tools, cap the bare ends of the wire with wire nuts. Then make sure to turn the power off again when you install the light.

Wiring a light or fan is straightforward: Splice white lead to white wire, black to black, and connect the grounds.

Choosing the right fan
When you shop for a bathroom fan, you'll see many sizes and styles. Before you choose a fan for its looks, find out how much air it moves. The packaging on most fans will make it easy for you to determine which size to install for the size of your bathroom. If you're in doubt, do a little Internet research or ask the home center staff.

Make your basement more comfortable with the right lighting and electric heating.

CHAPTER PREVIEW

Recessed cans
page 222

Wall-mounted lighting
page 224

Installing flush-mounted lights
page 226

Installing track lights
page 228

A wall fixture like this should be mounted between wall studs. A hole is cut into the wall to house the electrical box. After the wires are connected they are pushed into the electrical box and the mounting plate and fixture are attached. The power is turned off during this process and is not turned back on until the fixture and lightbulb are fully installed.

Installing electric heaters
page 230

RECESSED CANS

The most inconspicuous way to illuminate a new room is with a series of recessed canister lights, also called "cans" or "pot lights."

Install them in pairs about 6 feet apart. Use eyeball-type can lights to highlight wall features, task lights to brighten a vanity, and a watertight recessed fixture above a tub or shower.

The best time to install them, of course, is right after you've framed the new walls. But if you decide to put them in after the drywall is up, you can use "remodel" lights. Even running cable is not too difficult, because cans are usually spaced only two or three joists apart. Trim styles vary considerably, so shop around for the style that best fits your design theme. Most inexpensive recessed cans are rated to use only 60-watt bulbs.

PRESTART CHECKLIST

☐ **TIME**
About a day to cut holes, run cable, and install six to eight lights with a switch

☐ **TOOLS**
Voltage tester, drill, spade bit or fishing drill bit, stud finder, ladder, drywall saw, level, hammer, fish tape, screwdriver, wire stripper, long-nose pliers, lineman's pliers

☐ **SKILLS**
Precision cutting of drywall or plaster; stripping, splicing, and connecting wires to terminals; installing boxes; running cable through walls and ceilings

☐ **PREP**
Find power source and make sure the new lights will not overload the circuit; clear the room of all obstructions and lay a drop cloth on the floor

☐ **MATERIALS**
Recessed canister lights, cable, switch box and clamps, wire nuts, electrician's tape

1 Install a new-work can-light housing. Position the fixture to accommodate the thickness of the drywall you'll put up later. Slide the mounting bars out and hammer each tab into a joist. Slide the housing to position it precisely.

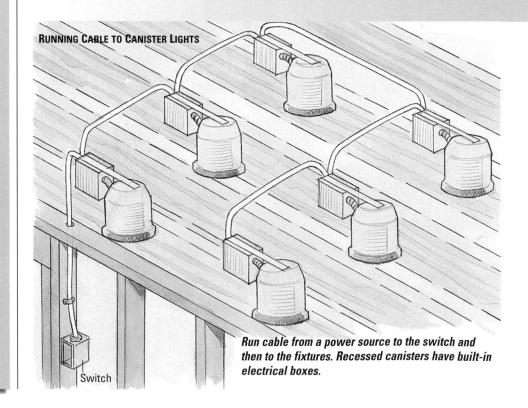

RUNNING CABLE TO CANISTER LIGHTS

Switch

Run cable from a power source to the switch and then to the fixtures. Recessed canisters have built-in electrical boxes.

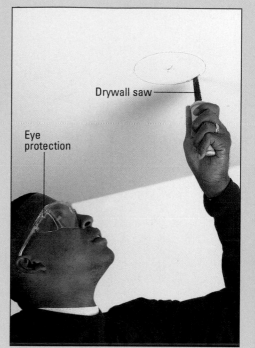

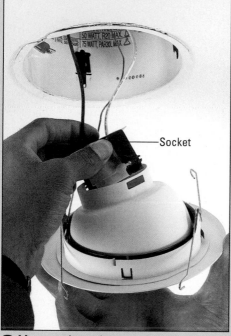

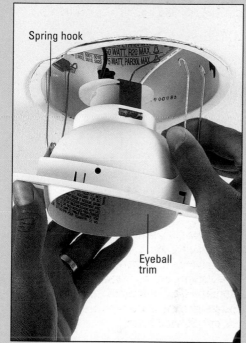

2 Cut the hole with a drywall saw—either as you're installing the ceiling drywall or after it's up. In either case, you must measure and mark the finished surface before you cut it. Cut precisely—the canister trim is narrow and leaves little room for error.

3 Many canisters have sockets that attach to the trim with two spring clips. Slip one clip into the notch provided and rock the socket so the clip engages.

4 If the trim has two spring hooks, squeeze and guide their ends into the slots provided, then push up the trim until it snaps into place. Twist an eyeball trim to face in the desired direction and push it up into the housing.

WHAT IF...
The canister has a spring hook?

To mount trim that uses coil springs (shown), hold the trim in place up against the ceiling. Insert a pencil tip into the looped end of each spring and guide it up into the hole provided.

Trim options

Baffle trim (either white or black) diffuses the light, while reflector trim increases the brightness of a bulb. With open trim the flood bulb protrudes slightly downward. For above a tub or shower, choose a watertight lens. An eyeball (or fish-eye) trim rotates to point where you want it; a wallwasher highlights the texture of a brick or stone wall.

Baffle trim

Reflector trim

Open trim

Flush watertight lens

Wallwasher trim

Eyeball trim

Extended watertight lens

WALL-MOUNTED LIGHTING

Wall sconces can provide indirect or soft lighting that's ideal for just about any room. They are an especially good choice for bathrooms, placed just above eye level.

Use a standard ceiling box and wire just as you would a ceiling light. Most sconces mount with a center stud so you can adjust the fixture for level even if the box is not level. To control sconces from two locations, use three-way switches.

A strip of lights over a bathroom mirror or medicine chest calls for a similar installation method. Such fixtures use several low-wattage bulbs to reduce glare while providing plenty of light.

Although it's easier to install new-work boxes on the studs before drywalling, you can use remodel boxes after the drywall is up as shown here. This is especially helpful if you're not absolutely sure of their location when you frame the walls.

PRESTART CHECKLIST

☐ **TIME**
About three hours to run cable and install a switch and two sconces

☐ **TOOLS**
Voltage tester, drill, saw, hammer, fish tape, screwdriver, wire stripper, long-nose pliers, lineman's pliers

☐ **SKILLS**
Stripping, splicing, and connecting wires to terminals; installing boxes; running cable through walls and ceilings

☐ **PREP**
Find power source and make sure the new lights will not overload the circuit; spread a drop cloth on the floor below

☐ **MATERIALS**
Sconce(s), ceiling boxes, switch box with clamps, cable, switch, wire nuts, electrician's tape

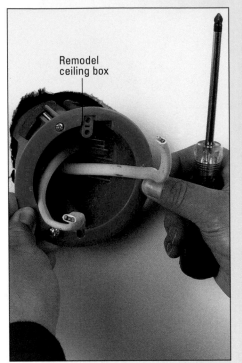

Remodel ceiling box

1 **Shut off power to the circuit.** Cut holes for the sconce boxes and the switch. Run cable from the power source to the switch, then to the sconces.

Center stud

Strap

2 Clamp cable to a wall box and install the box. Most sconces come with all the necessary hardware—usually a strap with a center stud. If the strap is provided, use it; it helps carry away heat from the fixture.

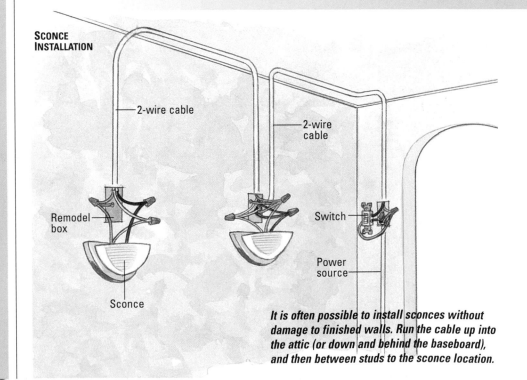

SCONCE INSTALLATION

2-wire cable

2-wire cable

Remodel box

Switch

Power source

Sconce

It is often possible to install sconces without damage to finished walls. Run the cable up into the attic (or down and behind the baseboard), and then between studs to the sconce location.

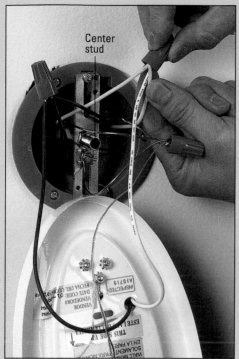

3 To wire a sconce, connect the grounds. Splice the white fixture lead to the white wire(s), and the black lead to the black wire(s).

4 Slip the sconce over the center stud and start to tighten the nut. Stand back and check that the base is plumb, and then tighten the base.

5 Install the lightbulb, making sure it does not exceed the manufacturer's recommended wattage. Clip the lens into place. Wire the switch.

Lights mounted on a mirror

To install a bathroom strip light, center the box over the mirror or medicine chest. Attach the fixture over the box, wire the fixture, and attach the cover.

To install a light fixture directly on a mirror, have a glass supplier cut three holes to match the fixture—a large hole for the electrical box and two smaller holes for mounting screws. Wire the fixture. Apply a thin bead of clear silicone caulk to its back to act as an adhesive. Attach with mounting screws, but don't overtighten them— you might break the mirror.

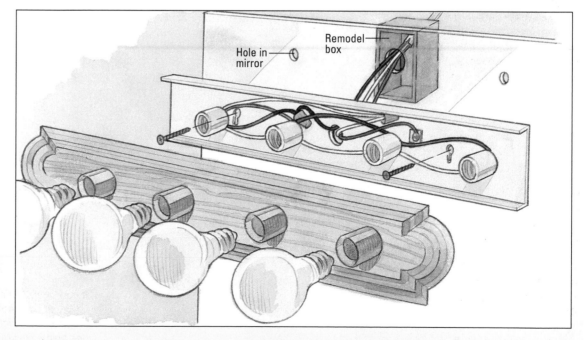

INSTALLING FLUSH-MOUNTED LIGHTS

Installing a flush-mounted ceiling fixture is an easy job. New fixtures come with all the hardware needed to install them.

When buying a fixture, make sure it is designed to provide the amount of light you want. Don't install bulbs whose wattage exceeds recommendations—it will overheat the fixture.

If possible, ground the new fixture. If it is being installed in a metal box, connect the fixture ground lead to the box and to the house ground wire. Local codes may be more specific than national electrical codes. Check with your building department before starting the work.

Like other lighting, it's easier to install new-work boxes on the studs before drywalling, but you can use the old boxes if installing replacements as shown. You can also install remodel boxes after the drywall is up.

PRESTART CHECKLIST

☐ **TIME**
About half an hour to install a fixture

☐ **TOOLS**
Screwdriver, wire stripper, side cutters, voltage tester, ladder

☐ **SKILLS**
Stripping wire, splicing stranded wire to solid wire

☐ **PREP**
In a finished room, spread a drop cloth on the floor below; set up a stable, nonconductive ladder

☐ **MATERIALS**
Replacement fixture, wire nuts (the ones that come with the fixture may be too small), electrician's tape

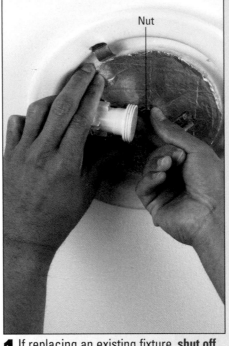

1 If replacing an existing fixture, **shut off power to the circuit.** Open the fixture. Remove the nut or screws holding the fixture to the box and pull the fixture down. Remove the wire nuts and **check for power in the box.** Pull the leads off the house wires and remove the fixture.

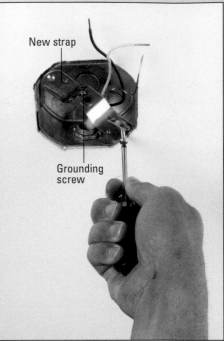

2 If replacing a fixture and the existing hardware will not fit the new fixture, or if it doesn't have a grounding screw, remove it and attach a new strap to the box. If adding a new fixture, run cable and install a ceiling box. Install the mounting strap that came with the fixture.

STANLEY PRO TIP: **Attach a fixture to an older box**

An older "pancake" box like this may have a ⅜-inch pipe running through the middle. To install a center-mount or pendent fixture, use a hickey, which has two sets of threads, one for the pipe attached to the pancake box and the other for a center stud. A hickey is helpful for wiring chandeliers because it has an opening through which a cord can run.

If the pipe protrudes too far, purchase a mounting strap with a hole large enough to accommodate the pipe. Or attach the strap off center by drilling pilot holes in the box and driving sheet metal screws through the slots in the strap and into the box. However, make sure the fixture's canopy is large enough to cover the box.

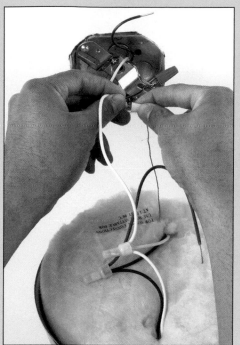

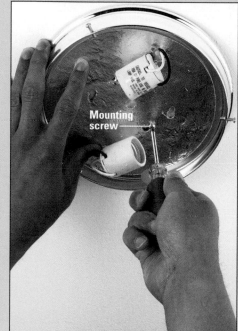

3 If the fixture is heavy, support it with a coat hanger wire while you work. Connect the ground wire. Splice white lead to white wire and black to black. Wrap the wire nuts with electrician's tape. The insulation may be difficult to work around, but don't remove it; it's a safety feature.

4 Fold the wires up into the box. Start one mounting screw, then the other, then tighten them. If the fixture has keyhole-shape screw holes, attach the screws to the box; slip the fixture over the large holes. Rotate the canopy so the screws fit into the smaller slots, then tighten the screws.

5 The setscrews that hold the globe may already be in the base or may have to be installed. Push the globe to raise the lip above all the setscrews, then hand-tighten all the setscrews evenly.

WHAT IF...
The new fixture's canopy doesn't cover the old hole?

If the new canopy is not large enough to cover up holes or unpainted portions of the ceiling—or simply to add a decorative touch—purchase a medallion. Hold it against the ceiling while you wire the fixture. Before tightening the canopy, see that the medallion is centered.

MOUNTING SCREWS
Installing a center-mounted fixture

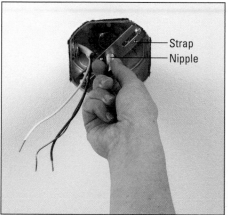

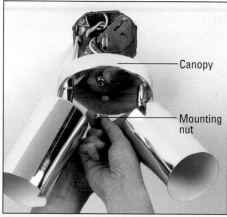

1 Some fixtures mount with a nipple (short threaded pipe) and a nut in the center rather than two screws. Install a strap and screw in a nipple. If the nipple that comes with the fixture is too short or too long, purchase another one.

2 After wiring the fixture, slide the canopy up so the nipple pokes down through the center hole. Screw on and tighten the mounting nut.

INSTALLING TRACK LIGHTS

Track lighting offers plenty of options for style, layout, and design. You can install the track in a straight line, or form a T, L, or H shape. Choose from among a variety of lamp styles. Place them anywhere on the track and point them in any direction. You can even use two or more types of lights, some for general illumination and others to highlight small areas, such as an architectural accent in your bathroom design.

At some point, the track must cross over a light fixture box to grab power via a mounting plate. Sketch your planned installation and show the drawing to a salesperson, who can help assemble all the parts required: track, mounting plate, lamps, and other fittings. Chances are a kit will supply everything needed.

PRESTART CHECKLIST

☐ **TIME**
About four hours to remove an old fixture and install about 8 feet of track with a turn or two, as well as several lamps

☐ **TOOLS**
Screwdriver, tape measure, wire stripper, drill, side cutters, voltage tester, lineman's pliers, stud finder, nonconducting ladder, hacksaw, metal cutting blade

☐ **SKILLS**
Measuring accurately, driving screws into joists, stripping wire, splicing stranded wire to solid wire

☐ **PREP**
Spread a drop cloth on the floor and set up one or two ladders; a helper will come in handy when installing long pieces of track

☐ **MATERIALS**
Parts for the track system (see illustration), plastic anchors, screws, wire nuts, electrician's tape

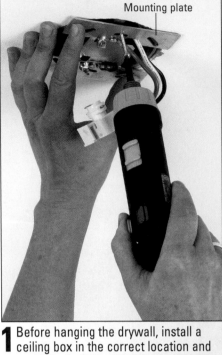

Mounting plate

1 Before hanging the drywall, install a ceiling box in the correct location and run cable to it. Splice the new leads to the house wires, color to color. Fold the wires up into the box. Screw the mounting plate snugly to the box.

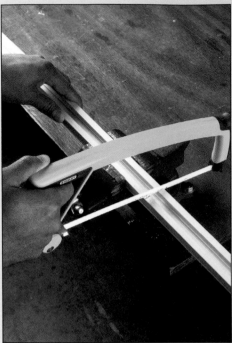

2 If necessary cut pieces of track to length. To cut a track, hold it firmly in place. If you use a vise, take care not to bend the metal. Cut with a hacksaw that has a metal-cutting blade. Support the waste side of the piece when nearing the end of a cut so it does not fall and bend the track.

TRACK LIGHTING SYSTEM

The mounting plate live-end connector supplies power to the track, which carries power to the lamps via two strips of wire.

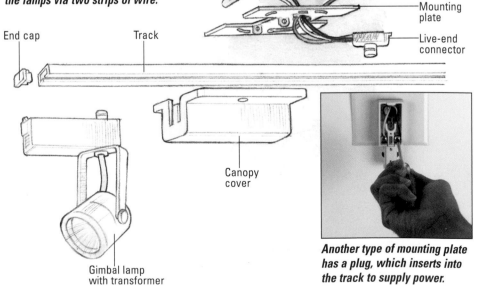

Box

Mounting plate

Live-end connector

End cap

Track

Canopy cover

Gimbal lamp with transformer

Another type of mounting plate has a plug, which inserts into the track to supply power.

3 With a helper holding one end of the track, push the track up against the mounting plate. Secure it by tightening the setscrews.

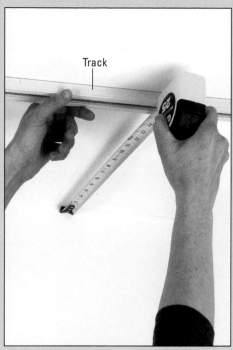

Track

4 Again with a helper holding one end of the track, measure at two points along the track so it is parallel to the nearest wall. If the track configuration includes any 90-degree angles, use a framing square to mark a guideline.

5 Locate joists with a stud finder. Drive a screw into every joist the track crosses. If the track runs parallel to the joists, drill holes every 16 inches, tap in plastic anchors, and drive screws into the anchors.

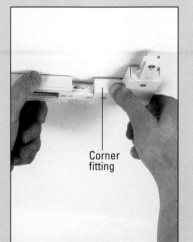

Corner fitting

6 If the track has to turn a corner, slide a fitting onto the track piece just installed. Slide the next piece onto the connector, measure to see that it is parallel to the nearest wall, and anchor it to the ceiling.

Live-end connector

7 Once all the pieces are installed, place end caps on all the track ends. Push the live-end connector plug into the track; twist it to make contact with both strips of metal in the track. Attach the canopy cover.

8 Insert the plug of a lamp into the track and twist to tighten. To move a lamp along the track, loosen it first—do not force it while it is still attached.

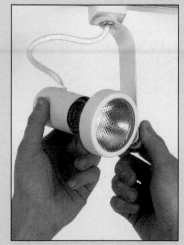

9 Restore power and test. If a lamp does not work, remove it and twist it back on again. Once it works, adjust the lamp to direct the light where needed.

INSTALLING ELECTRIC HEATERS

Even if your home is not heated by electricity, adding an electric baseboard or wall heater can be a cost-effective way to bring heat to a cold room.

When planning, assume 10 watts of heater capacity per square foot of room area. In other words, a 10×10-foot room will need two 500-watt baseboard heaters. Check your local codes for circuit requirements; some municipalities require a dedicated circuit protected by a 20-amp double breaker. In some cases heaters can be added to existing 120-volt circuits. Confirm that the circuit voltage matches that of the unit—120-volt circuit for a 120-volt unit, 240-volt circuit for a 240-volt unit.

Place heaters on outside walls and below windows. Check manufacturer's specs for locating furniture and drapes. Never locate a heater beneath a receptacle. In general baseboard units are best for enhancing whole-room heat; blower-heaters are best for intense heat of short duration.

PRESTART CHECKLIST

☐ **TIME**
About three hours to run cable, install a baseboard heater and thermostat; about two and one-half hours to run cable and install a blower-heater

☐ **TOOLS**
Voltage tester, drill, ½-inch bit, drywall saw, fish tape, screwdriver, wire stripper, long-nose pliers, lineman's pliers, studfinder

☐ **SKILLS**
Cutting into walls; stripping, splicing, and connecting wires to terminals; installing boxes; running cable into boxes

☐ **MATERIALS**
Heater, box for thermostat, 12/2 cable, electrician's tape, wire nuts, drywall screws

12/2 cable from power source

12/2 cable to heater

1 Either install a new-work box on a stud before hanging the drywall or cut an opening for a large-capacity remodel box. Run 12/2 cable to the thermostat location, then from the opening to the heater location. **Do not connect the cable to its power source.** Strip cables (page 104) and clamp them to the box. Install the box.

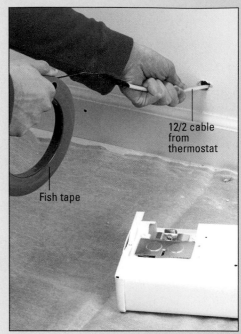

12/2 cable from thermostat

Fish tape

2 No junction box is required for the cable running to the heater because the box is built into the unit. Strip the incoming wires (page 112). (You can also run the feeder line to the heater and then to the thermostat. Check the manufacturer's instructions.)

ASSEMBLING AND WIRING ELECTRIC HEATERS

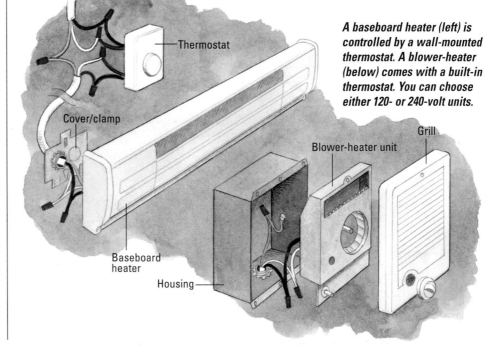

Thermostat

Cover/clamp

Baseboard heater

Housing

Blower-heater unit

Grill

A baseboard heater (left) is controlled by a wall-mounted thermostat. A blower-heater (below) comes with a built-in thermostat. You can choose either 120- or 240-volt units.

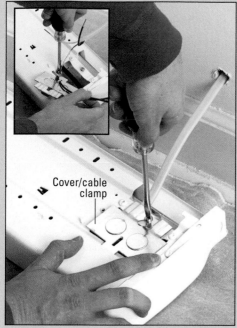

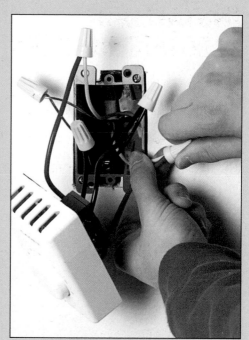

3 Place the heater face down on the floor and remove the cover/cable clamp. Attach the house ground line to the green screw on the heater (inset). Using wire nuts, connect incoming lines to the heater leads. Close and fasten the cover/clamp.

4 Locate and mark wall studs. Push the cable into the wall. Attach the unit with at least two 1½-inch drywall screws. Tighten, then back off a half turn to allow for the expansion and contraction of the metal housing when the unit is turned on and off.

5 Wire the thermostat as shown using wire nuts and electrician's tape. Install the thermostat and snap on its cover. Connect to the power source or new circuit and test the unit.

WHAT IF…
You're installing a blower-heater?

A blower-heater unit fits between wall studs and is somewhat easier to wire because it has a self-contained thermostat. The unit shown runs on 240 volts. Check local codes for requirements.

A blower-heater must be a safe distance from nearby walls and furnishings. When choosing a location for the heater, maintain 12 inches from any adjacent walls. For safe and effective operation, locate the box 12 inches above the floor and keep the area clear 3 feet in front of the box. Check the manufacturer's recommendations before locating the unit.

Before cutting the wall opening, drill a hole and feel around in the wall cavity with a bent wire to check that it is clear of pipes and wires. Use a drywall saw to cut the opening between studs. Run 12/2 cable to the opening.

1 Remove one of the knockouts in the housing. Insert a clamp and pull 10 inches of cable into the box. Clamp the cable and fasten the housing in place with 1-inch (longer if needed) drywall screws. Strip incoming wires.

2 Attach the incoming wires to the heater leads. Fasten the heater unit in the housing, being careful that the wires do not get caught between the motor and the housing. Attach the grill and thermostat knob. Connect to the power source and test the unit.

GLOSSARY

Access panel: A removable panel in a wall or ceiling that permits repair or replacement.

Actual dimensions: The actual size of a tile as measured with a tape or ruler. *See also nominal size.*

Adapter: A plumbing fitting that makes it possible to go from male endings to female endings or vice versa.

Amp: Short for ampere, a measurement of the electrical current flowing through a wire or appliance.

Apron: The bottom piece of window casing that finishes the window frame beneath the sill (stool).

Back blocking: The use of a manufactured or homemade device to draw back the untapered ends of drywall panels to provide clearance for drywall tape and compound. Back blocking helps avoid a bulge at a butt seam.

Backbutter: To apply mortar or adhesive to the rear face of a tile before setting it.

Backerboard: Any of several cement or gypsum-based sheets used as substrate for setting tile. *Also called cement board.*

Banding: Solid wood trim attached to plywood edges to conceal plies.

Baseboard: Trim running along the bottom of a wall to cover gaps between the wall and floor and to protect the bottom of the wall. *See also cap molding.*

Base cap: A piece of molding that covers the top of the traditional baseboard.

Basin wrench: Plumbing tool with a long shaft to reach into small spaces to loosen or tighten hold-down nuts.

Bead: An impact-resistant metal, composite, or vinyl angle that provides mechanical protection at an outside drywall corner.

Bearing wall: A wall that carries a portion of the weight of the building above it.

Bifold door: A door that folds in half as it opens. Often used in pairs as closet doors.

Biscuit joint: A joint that uses wooden wafers glued into slots cut in edges of mating pieces.

Bisque: The clay-and-liquid mixture that forms the body of the tile.

Blocking: Pieces of lumber that are nailed horizontally between wall studs to serve as anchor points for molding or cabinetry.

Blowout: An irregular break, usually at the edge of a drywall panel or along an opening where a portion of the gypsum core detaches from the panel.

Bow: A defect in which a board is warped along its length when viewed along its narrow dimension.

Buffalo box: A type of whole-house shutoff where the valve is in a plastic or concrete box set in the ground.

Bullnose: An edge treatment consisting of a smooth radius.

Bullnose tiles: Flat tile with at least one rounded edge. Used to trim the edges of a tiled installation. *Also called caps.*

Butt joint: A joint where ends of the two adjoining pieces are cut square and the pieces are simply placed against each other.

Butt seam: The junction of two untapered drywall ends or edges. A butt seam requires care to avoid the development of a bulge during the application of drywall tape and compound. Back blocking *(see that entry)* is a technique that can help conceal butt seams.

Bypass doors: Doors that open by sliding past each other—often used for closets.

Cable: Two or more insulated wires wrapped in metal or plastic sheathing.

Cap molding: A molding made to be applied to the top edge of another material as a finishing treatment.

Casing: Trim that surrounds a door or window opening.

Cement-bodied tile: Tile whose bisque is formed of mortar as opposed to clay.

Chair rail: Trim running across a wall approximately midway between the ceiling and the floor.

Check: A crack in a board.

Circuit breaker: A protective device in a service panel that automatically shuts off power to its circuit when it senses a short or circuit overload.

Cleanout: A removable plug in a trap or a drainpipe that allows easier access to blockages inside.

Cleft: Describes the process of forming stone paving pieces by splitting smaller pieces from larger rock.

Closet bend: The elbow-shape fitting beneath a toilet that carries waste to the main drain.

Coffered: A type of ceiling construction consisting of one or more stepped surfaces.

Composite: An engineered plastic material utilized to make inside and outside corners.

Continuity tester: A device that tells whether a circuit is capable of carrying electricity.

Corner bead: A plastic or metal molding that is attached to outside drywall corners to make them easier to finish and to protect them from damage.

Counterbore: A screw hole deep enough to accept a wooden plug after the screw is in place.

Countersink: A drilled hole that fits the shape of a wood screw.

Coupling: A copper, galvanized steel, plastic, or brass fitting used to connect two lengths of pipe in a straight run.

Cripple stud: A short stud. Most typically used above door openings in nonbearing walls and below window openings.

Crook: A defect in a board in which the board is warped along its length when viewed along its wide dimension.

Crosscut: A cut across the grain that reduces material to a desired length.

Dado (groove): A channel cut in wood that runs across the grain. A groove is a channel that runs with the grain.

Deadman: A T-shape brace used to help hold drywall in place against ceiling joists while drywall is fastened in place.

Dielectric fitting: Fitting that joins pipes of dissimilar metals to protect them from a corrosive chemical reaction.

Dimension lumber: Lumber that is 2 to 5 inches in nominal thickness and up to 12 inches in nominal width.

Diverter: A valve on a faucet that changes the flow of water from a faucet spout to a hand sprayer or showerhead.

Dowel: A cylindrical piece of wood, often a joint reinforcement.

Drum trap: Found in older homes, this cylindrical trap is built into the floor and covered with a brass, chrome-plated, or expandable cap.

Dry-fit: Preliminary joining of wood or other materials without glue to check fit.

Drywall clip: A device that secures to the edge of a drywall panel and is screwed through its flange to the framing.

Elbow: A fitting used to change the direction of a water supply line. *Also known as an ell.*

Face frame: A four-piece wooden assembly attached to the front of a cabinet.

Fall: A word used to express the slope of drain lines.

Feathering: The process of tapering the edge of drywall compound so that its thickness gradually diminishes.

Field tiles: Flat tiles with unrounded edges used within the edges of a tiled installation.

Fire stop: A piece of wood nailed across a stud bay to prevent the bay from acting as a chimney and conduit for fire.

Fitting: Any connector (except a valve) that joins pipes.

Floating joint: A drywall junction that is fastened so that the framing can move independently of the panel. The technique helps prevent cracked joints.

Flow restrictor: A device found in some showerheads to restrict the flow of water and thus reduce water use.

Flush: Having the same surface or plane as an adjoining surface.

Flux: A stiff jelly brushed or smeared on the surfaces of copper and brass pipes and fittings before joining them.

Furring strips: Strips of wood attached to a surface as spacers/anchor points for an additional wall surface. Often made from 1×2s or 1×3s.

Green bisque: Clay that has not been fired (not a reference to its color).

Greenboard: A moisture-resistant drywall product made for wet installations, such as baths and showers. Greenboard is not waterproof.

Hammer arrester: A shock-absorbing device that provides a cushion of air to prevent water hammer—sudden surges in water pressure that sometimes result in noisy pipes.

Header: The part of a house's frame that spans a door or window opening. Often made from two pieces of 2× lumber with a spacer of ½-inch plywood. Also, any piece of wood (such as trim) which spans the top of an opening.

I.D.: The abbreviation for inside diameter. All plumbing pipes are sized according to their inside diameter. *See also* O.D.

Jamb: The wooden frame that lines a door or window opening.

J-bead: A molding made to cover the edge of a drywall sheet so the raw edge does not show in the finished product.

Jig: A device that holds a workpiece or tool in a certain way to efficiently and accurately saw or shape wood.

Kerf: The slot left by a saw blade as it cuts through material.

Knife: Drywall knife—used for applying and smoothing drywall.

Knockdown: A finishing technique in which a tool such as a drywall knife, trowel, or squeegee is lightly dragged across an application of texturing material to flatten sharp peaks.

Latex-modified thinset: Thinset mortar mixed with latex additive to increase its flexibility, resistance to water, and adhesion.

GLOSSARY (continued)

L-bead: A metal or plastic drywall molding utilized to neatly terminate an edge.

Middle-of-run: A receptacle located between the service panel and another receptacle.

Mil: A measurement of thickness equal to one one-thousandth of an inch.

Miter: An angle, often 45 degrees, cut across the grain on a piece of wood.

Molding: Shaped wood used as trim.

Mortar: Any mixture of masonry cement, sand, water, and other additives. Also describes the action of applying mortar to surfaces or joints.

Mortise: An opening cut in a piece of wood to accept a mating piece of wood (tenon).

Mud: Trade jargon for cement-based mortars.

Nail pops: Places in finished drywall where a nail has begun to back out of the stud (or was never completely driven home). Nail pops show up as a small circular lump on the wall surface.

Nipple: A 12-inch or shorter pipe with threads on both ends that is used to join fittings.

No-hub fitting: A neoprene gasket with a stainless-steel band that tightens to join PVC drainpipe to ABS or cast-iron pipe.

Nominal size: The designated dimension of a pipe or fitting or piece of lumber. It varies slightly from the actual size.

Nonloadbearing wall: Also called nonbearing. *See partition wall.*

O.D.: The abbreviation for outside diameter. *See also I.D.*

Open time: The interval between application of adhesive and when it can no longer be worked. *Also called working time.*

Organic mastic: One of several petroleum or latex-based adhesives for setting tiles. Exhibits less strength, flexibility, and resistance to water than thinset adhesives.

Packing: A plastic or metallic cordlike material used chiefly around faucet stems. When compressed it results in a watertight seal.

Partition wall: A wall whose only purpose is to divide a space—it does not contribute to supporting the weight of the building.

Pigtail: A short length of wire spliced with two or more wires in a box and connected to a terminal so that two or more wires will not be attached to a terminal.

Plate: A horizontal piece of lumber to which the wall studs are attached. The bottom plate is anchored to the floor. The top plate is usually a double thickness to tie walls together and help carry the load from above.

Plumb: A surface that lies on a true vertical plane.

Plunge cut: Starting a saw in wood away from an edge.

Pocket-hole: A joining technique that employs screws driven into holes drilled at an angle.

Polymer-modified: A substance like grout or mortar to which an acrylic or latex solution has been added to increase its strength and workability.

Popcorn: The informal name of a ceiling texture that contains a soft material such as vermiculite to give the installation increased volume at a low weight. *Also called cottage cheese.*

Powder-actuated fastener: A hardened nail that's shot into a dense material such as concrete or metal by the explosive force of a cartridge. The cartridges (called boosters) are available in a variety of strengths to meet the requirements of various target materials.

Rabbet: A channel sawed or formed on the edge of a board or panel.

Radius trim: A trim tile whose edge turns down to form a smooth, glazed border.

Rail: One of the two horizontal pieces in a face frame.

Reducer: A fitting with different size openings at either end used to go from a larger to a smaller pipe.

Resilient channel: A metal strip that's attached to framing and to which drywall panels are secured. Resilient channels are sometimes utilized for sound control purposes or as furring strips. *See also furring strips.*

Revent: A pipe that connects a fixture drainpipe to a main or secondary vent stack.

Rip-cut: To reduce a wide board by sawing with the grain; a cut along the long dimension of a sheet or panel.

Riser: A pipe supplying water to a location or a supply tube running from a pipe to a sink or toilet.

Rough-in: The early stages of a plumbing project during which supply and drain-waste-vent lines are run to their destinations.

Rough opening: The opening in the framing made to accommodate a door or window.

Rout: Shaping or cutting wood with a router and bit.

Run: Any length of pipe or pipes and fittings going in a straight line.

Runner: The C-shaped sheet metal track that serves as the top and bottom plate in metal stud construction.

Saddle-T valve: A fitting used to tap into a water line without having to cut the line apart.

Sanded grout: Grout containing sand, which increases the strength and decreases the contraction of the joint.

Sanitary fitting: Any of several connectors used to join drain-waste-vent lines. Their design helps direct waste downward.

Sanitary sewer: Underground drainage network that carries liquid and solid wastes to a treatment plant.

Scribe: The process of making an item, such as shelf or countertop, conform to the irregularities of another surface—such as a wall—in order to achieve a fit without gaps.

Self-rimming sink: A common type of kitchen or bathroom sink that includes a formed lip that rests on the countertop, holding the sink in place.

Semivitreous tile: Tile of moderate density that exhibits only a partial resistance to water and other liquids.

Septic tank: A reservoir that collects and separates liquid and solid wastes, then digests the organic material and passes the liquid waste onto a drainage field.

Service entrance: The point where power from the utility enters the house.

Service panel: A large electrical box containing either fuses or circuit breakers.

Skim coating: The process of covering the entire surface of a drywall installation with a thin layer of joint compound.

Slake: To allow a masonry mixture additional time after initial mixing. Allows the liquid to thoroughly penetrate the solids.

Soffit: An enclosed architectural feature, usually at the junction of a wall and ceiling. Sometimes called a bulkhead.

Soil stack: The main vertical drainpipe that carries waste toward the sewer drain.

Square: Surfaces exactly perpendicular or at 90 degrees to another. Also describes a hand tool used to determine square.

Standpipe: A special pipe that connects a washing machine drain hose to the drain system.

Stile: One of the two vertical pieces in a face frame.

Straightedge: A metal or wood implement clamped to the workpiece to ensure a straight cut.

Stubout: A brass drop-ear elbow that has one threaded opening and two holes that can be screwed tightly against a wall. Some can be sweated; some have threaded ends.

Stud bay: The space between two studs installed in a wall.

Subfloor: A layer of wood sheet material, generally plywood, used to provide a stable foundation for other flooring materials.

Substrate: Any of several layers, including the subfloor, beneath a tile surface.

Tailpiece: That part of a fixture drain that runs from the drain outlet to the trap.

Tapered edge: The long edges of drywall sheets usually have their thickness gradually reduced in order to permit the embedding of drywall tape without developing a bulge.

T: A T-shape fitting used to tap into a length of pipe at a 90-degree angle to begin a branch line.

Toe-kick: The wood part that is recessed beneath a cabinet base.

Toenailing: Driving a nail at an angle through one framing member so it can penetrate a second framing surface.

Trap: Part of a fixture drain required by code that creates a water seal to prevent sewer gases from penetrating a home's interior.

Trim-head screw: A design of screw with an extremely small head, making it a useful fastener for attaching moldings while producing a minimal hole to be filled.

Twist: A defect in a board in which the board is warped along its length similar to an airplane propeller.

Union: A fitting used in runs of threaded pipe to facilitate disconnecting the line (without having to cut it).

V-cap: V-shape trim, often with a rounded upper corner, used to edge countertops.

Veneer: Thin sheets or strips of solid wood.

Vent: The vertical or sloping horizontal portion of a drain line that permits sewer gases to rise out of the house. Every fixture in a house must be vented.

Vent stack: The upper portion of a vertical drain line through which gases pass to the outside.

Vitreous tile: An extremely dense ceramic tile with a high resistance to water absorption.

Wet wall: A strategically placed cavity (usually a 2×6 wall) in which the main drain/vent stack and a cluster of supply and drain-waste-vent lines are housed.

Y: A Y-shape drainage fitting that serves as the starting point for a branch drain supplying one or more fixtures.

INDEX

METRIC CONVERSIONS

U.S. Units to Metric Equivalents			Metric Units to U.S. Equivalents		
To convert from	Multiply by	To get	To convert from	Multiply by	To get
Inches	25.4	Millimeters	Millimeters	0.0394	Inches
Inches	2.54	Centimeters	Centimeters	0.3937	Inches
Feet	30.48	Centimeters	Centimeters	0.0328	Feet
Feet	0.3048	Meters	Meters	3.2808	Feet
Yards	0.9144	Meters	Meters	1.0936	Yards
Square inches	6.4516	Square centimeters	Square centimeters	0.1550	Square inches
Square feet	0.0929	Square meters	Square meters	10.764	Square feet
Square yards	0.8361	Square meters	Square meters	1.1960	Square yards
Acres	0.4047	Hectares	Hectares	2.4711	Acres
Cubic inches	16.387	Cubic centimeters	Cubic centimeters	0.0610	Cubic inches
Cubic feet	0.0283	Cubic meters	Cubic meters	35.315	Cubic feet
Cubic feet	28.316	Liters	Liters	0.0353	Cubic feet
Cubic yards	0.7646	Cubic meters	Cubic meters	1.308	Cubic yards
Cubic yards	764.55	Liters	Liters	0.0013	Cubic yards

To convert from degrees Fahrenheit (F) to degrees Celsius (C), first subtract 32, then multiply by $\frac{5}{9}$.

To convert from degrees Celsius to degrees Fahrenheit, multiply by $\frac{9}{5}$, then add 32.

KNOWLEDGE IS
THE BEST TOOL

STANLEY COMPLETE
DRYWALL

STANLEY COMPLETE
Trimwork
& Carpentry

STANLEY COMPLETE
Built-Ins,
Shelves & Bookcases

STANLEY COMPLETE
PLUMBING

STANLEY COMPLETE
WIRING

CONSTRUCT

REJUVENATE

PLAN & REPAIR

ENHANCE

MAINTAIN